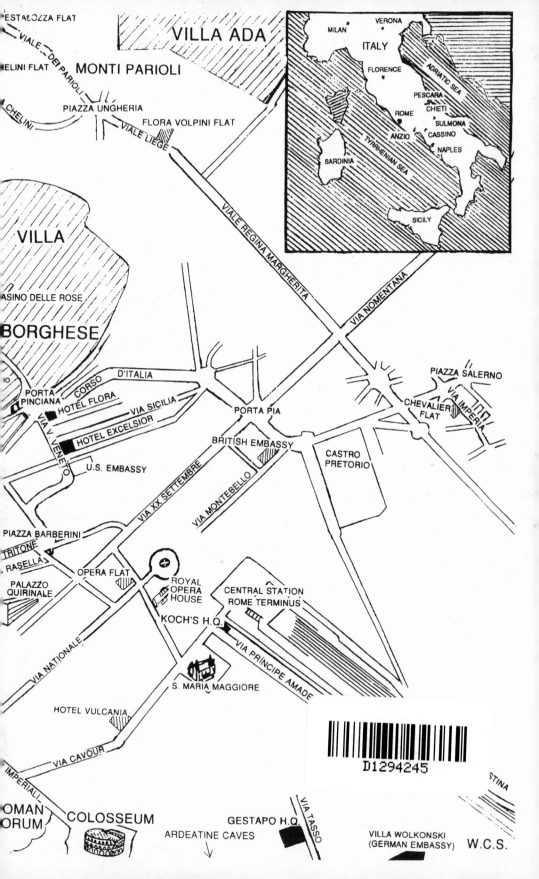

A VATICAN LIFELINE

Che non a salito i tre scalini da Regina Coeli non e un Romano.

He who has not climbed the three steps into Regina Coeli prison is not a Roman.

Old Maxim

To Henry - (good friend). Auguri! Ciao! Bill Simpson

A VATICAN LIFELINE

Allied Fugitives, aided by the
Italian Resistance, foil the Gestapo
in Nazi-Occupied Rome, 1944

by

William C Simpson

SARPEDON
New York

DEDICATION

To those Italian men and women who, beyond rational explanation, rose during the Nazi Occupation from submission to heroism without leaving home.

Published in the United States in 1996 by
SARPEDON

First published in Great Britain in 1996 by
LEO COOPER
an imprint of Pen & Sword Books Ltd

Library of Congress Catalog Card Number: 95-71926

ISBN: 1-885119-22-4

Manufactured in Great Britain

10 9 8 7 6 5 4 3 2 1

CONTENTS

PREFACE

To prepare for incidents bordering on the ridiculous but nevertheless true, the reader is entitled to the following background.

Upon returning from Italy to Britain and leaving the Army in the summer of 1946, I was retraining with my pre-war employer, Royal Insurance Company in Liverpool, prior to a scheduled posting to New York, when on the Mersey ferry I ran into a typist who, in A.T.S. uniform, had worked with me in Rome.

Still weighed down by the events from the moment of escape in Nazi-occupied Abruzzi through the underground life in Gestapo-controlled Rome and two intense but exhilarating years immersed in the 'follow-through' Allied Screening Commission, I needed to unburden in order to focus on the future.

In frequent evening sessions with my ex-secretary and her notebooks, I poured it out. Somehow she completed the typed volume before I boarded the *Queen Elizabeth* in March, 1947. It was not a literary event, but the result was an exhaustive record of happenings, names, places, times and clearly-recalled dialogue, starting from the Italian surrender to the Allies on 8 September 1943.

In New York the information lay dormant for years. In 1993, after gentle prodding from my wife and my son, I dropped all and wrote.

Two long British Intelligence reports (WO204/1012 and WO208/3396) entitled 'The Activities of the British Organization in Rome for Assisting Allied Escaped Prisoners of War' which, thanks to the 'Thirty Year Rule' on public security, have now been downgraded from 'Top Secret', provide abundant, if cold, authentication for the veracity of this book. Those reports, compiled from interrogation by the appropriate Intelligence Branch in Allied Forces Headquarters in Italy, are now available in the Public Record Office at Kew and, with their ample statistics, constitute a massive footnote for the scholar.

This story incorporates only essential statistics. My intent rather is to draw the reader into the taut atmosphere of this moment-to-moment underground existence. While the exploits of a somewhat cavalier group of British and American officers and their audacious Italian accomplices may have been uniquely colourful with the backdrop of Rome itself and the Vatican, the reader by projection can begin to comprehend the odyssey of 75,000 Allied prisoners let loose in Italy, and wonder at the wave of humanity which greeted them.

By virtue of adherence to fact, many emerging characters do not continue throughout, particularly as the scene moves abruptly from Abruzzi to Rome.

I acknowledge the generous co-operation of:

Staff of the Public Record Office, Kew, near London.

Tomaso Bracci and Tullio Zucaro, archivists of *Il Tempo*, Rome.

Artist Gordon Horner of Horam, E. Sussex for kind permission to reprint sketches from his book, *For You The War Is Over*. London, 1948.

Colonel Samuel I. Derry, DSO, MC, for kind permission to reproduce two photographs from his book, *Rome Escape Line*, London, 1961, and New York, 1961.

A Crown copyright excerpt is reproduced by kind permission of Her Majesty's Stationery Office.

I am greatly indebted to Mrs Dorothy Marcinek of Bayville, N.Y., for her superb secretarial performance in word-processing the manuscript and with unfailing good humour performing myriad related tasks.

Special thanks to my wife, Sally, for her encouragement, tolerance of domestic adjustments, and editorial hints.

Apologies to my chocolate Lab 'Barney' for shortened walks.

PROLOGUE

In July, 1943, Allied armour overran Sicily, fresh from defeating the German Afrika Korps in Tunisia. In Rome dissident Italian Government ministers prodded King Vittorio Emanuele III to take a bold step. On 27 July the King removed the Fascist *Duce* Benito Mussolini from office and abducted him to Abruzzi. To head the Italian Government, the King appointed Marshal Pietro Badoglio, the conqueror of Ethiopia in 1936.

On 8 September, 1943, as British invading forces gained footholds on the southern tip of the Italian mainland and American forces prepared to land at Salerno, Marshal Badoglio and the Italian King declared an unconditional surrender of their country to the Allies and fled south to Allied territory.

In the ensuing military vacuum Italian military depots and installations closed down. Hundreds of thousands of conscripted Italian soldiers simply quit and went home. Among them were units assigned to guard duty at seventy Prisoner of War camps containing 75,000 Allied officers and men. Of these the majority, from British Commonwealth countries, had been captured by the German Afrika Korps over two years of desert warfare from Egypt to Morocco. 1500 Americans were mostly US Army Air Force personnel – downed pilots and their crews.

Since Nazi Germany maintained no garrison in the country of its Axis partner, Fascist Italy, the citizens of Rome and of other towns in Central Italy anticipated nothing worse than a brief period of nebulous German influence before the triumphant arrival of Allied armies which were expected to advance unopposed right up the leg of Italy – in a matter of weeks at the most.

With good reason, a similar optimism permeated the ranks of every POW camp. By secret methods a coded order from the British War

Office had successfully reached the senior British officer of each camp: in the event of an Italian capitulation all POWs should 'stay put' within the camp to await the early arrival of Allied ground forces.

In reality, an incensed German Führer, despite preoccupation with threatening military reverses in Russia, began to pour two German armies into southern Italy within days of the Armistice. Their divisions formed a defence line in the mountains east and west of Cassino which was to withstand the might of Allied attacks through the entire winter of 1943/44. With equal speed Nazi *Schutzstaffel* or SS battalions occupied Rome and took control of its state government apparatus. Soon they blanketed the city with an ominous panoply of security.

Optimism across central Italy faded. In the capital city Romans submitted to a despairing ordeal of German police control, of Gestapo surveillance, raids and brutality.

Sulmona

ARMISTICE!
Drawn by Gordon Horner at P.G. 21-Chieti.
From *For You the War Is Over*
By Gordon Horner, Falcon Press, London, 1948.
Reprinted with the kind permission of the author.

1

GO ON, JUMP!

Under the high Italian sun only the metal spars rising from the vertical sides of the old truck interrupted the passing spectacle of the Abruzzi countryside. From the colourful farmland of the rolling hills around the Prisoner of War Officers' Camp at Chieti this truck, one of a convoy of worn-out Italian army transports driven and heavily guarded by German SS parachutists, had followed an ascending road heading south-west, first along the valley of the Pescara River before rising more sharply around mountainous bends.

To the north-west stood the majestic mass of the Gran Sasso. From inside the prison camp, which had been our home for 14 months since July, 1942, the unfailing presence of that distant peak, whether glistening in sunlight or colliding with stormclouds, had provided spiritual uplift, raising our depressed thoughts above and beyond the confines of the 12-foot-high camp walls.

Since yesterday the same convoy had made three round trips to evacuate the bulk of the 1300 British and American officers from Chieti. The destination was Sulmona, to the south. In addition to being an important railhead, near Sulmona stood an empty prison camp which had held 2000 British and Commonwealth POWs until the Italian Government had surrendered on 8 September, 1943, when the Italian guards had fled and the prisoners had walked out.

By contrast, our officers' camp at Chieti, following the alleged receipt of secret orders from the War Office, had 'stayed put', to await the arrival of advancing Allied forces. After initial excitement over the news that Marshal Badoglio, representing the Italian King and Government, had declared an Armistice with the Allies, an uneasy ten days of patrolling ourselves inside the camp had ended in disaster. Under cover of darkness companies of the German 1st SS Parachute Regiment, bivouacked in nearby Aquila following their daring retrieval from Italian partisans of the deposed *Duce*, Benito Mussolini, pounced on the camp. At daylight consternation hit a peak when it became clear that, by posting a wide ring of machine guns around the camp, our new captors had rendered useless for mass escape two tunnels which burrowing squads of 'moles' had laboriously completed just before the Armistice.

In a hastily arranged lottery, fifty tunnel-diggers won the chance to lie end-to-end in the tunnels with their homemade ventilation fans to await the final departure of the Germans.

The camp's Escape Committee, arbiter of all escape plans, passed the word that all rules were suspended. It was every man for himself.

Just the prospect of being on the move outside these walls was exhilarating. Less exciting was the realization that this was the start of a long trek to Germany. A disagreeable thought, particularly when Allied forces, after defeating General Rommel in Tunisia, had raced through Sicily and gained a foothold on the Italian mainland. On 3 September the British 8th Army had landed on the Toe of Italy and, six days later, the US Fifth Army had begun a more precarious landing at Salerno. Faced with no significant German opposition, the British in the east and the Americans in the west should, we figured, advance north rapidly. They could be here in Abruzzi in a couple of weeks.

Our contingent of 150 officers was the last to be moved, along with some forty non-commissioned men who formed the work squad of the Camp. Just before the Germans called us on parade with our rag-tag belongings, I had switched identities and badges of rank with an understanding American GI. He joined the officers' line-up. I fell in with the 'non-coms', whose truckload might be less closely guarded en route.

Now, as our rickety truck reached a high mountain pass near Popoli, the unfolding panorama of the Apennines to the west was of very secondary interest to me.

My simple plan had little chance, but the forty men in the truck were co-operating. Four times already in response to my signal, they had risen slowly from among assorted frayed kits and gripped the arching overhead spars as the truck swayed on its springs. The German guard who sat in the rear had not seemed to notice that these men blocked his view of my near-side of the truck.

In the enclosed front cab, a German corporal rode with a German driver. The cab had a rear window; with each signal two soldiers eased over to block it. More of a problem was an external driving mirror which reflected the vibrating face of the German corporal. To remedy this, a heavy-set Cockney who was on the side-wall between me and the cab, tested while clutching the vertical spars how far he could extend his ample bulk backwards over the edge of the truck. It didn't help much.

The Cockney agreed that we needed a sharp left-hand corner to divert the German corporal's attention and a high wall or hedge to dive over in the seconds before the goggled German rearguards in their motorcycle-sidecar combination hit the corner. Twice when our truck, the last in the convoy, had sputtered during the hard grind uphill, I had swung my legs over the side, only to pull them back fast when the motorcycle-sidecar had roared into view.

As we began a descent from the high point our truck picked up speed. Soon the hairpin curves lessened, until ahead lay a long straight ribbon of road shining in the sun as it headed due south. Through a faint haze a broad cultivated valley and a narrow winding river faded into a large fortress-like town. Our truck careered along now, as it tried to catch up with the convoy.

The Cockney jabbed my ribs and pointed forward. Each of the nine trucks ahead had disappeared to the left off the main road. The last one, slowed almost to a stop, had turned in sharply; now only its top spars and some heads showed above a tall hedge as it moved off, it seemed, through open fields.

Our truck began to slow down. The German guard in the rear seemed drowsy. I gave the men one last signal. They moved into position. A home-made haversack filled with tinned rations saved from Red Cross food parcels and a metal water-bottle lay at the feet of the soldier behind me. If I suddenly disappeared he would throw them right after me.

The driver braked hard. The Cockney, ready on the side-wall, watched me. As we turned off the main road I gave him a nod. Quickly he leaned his rear-end out and braced himself. Grabbing an overhead spar, I hopped up on the side-wall, wedged my left foot on the Cockney's thigh and crouched. On this side ran a tall hedge. My heart thumped.

Gears grated. The truck began to accelerate. I froze. This was suicide! The Cockney, straining to hold his left thigh firm, saw me falter. 'Go on, jump!' he yelled. I lunged outward, headfirst over the hedge.

Thought of the guard's machine pistol numbed my impact with the ground. Still rolling, I remembered the motor-cycle rearguards. Under the hedge ran a shallow ditch. I slithered in face down. The motorcycle combination screeched around the corner and roared past within feet. The noise faded. I flexed an arm, a leg; they moved. Scrambling up, I shook earth and straw from my British battledress top and light desert khaki-drill slacks. In this small field hay had just been cut. A lop-sided haystack looked about to topple.

'Haversack,' I mumbled, half-dazed. Up and down the length of the hedge, the field produced no sign of the brown bag. I squeezed through onto the deserted road. Nothing there either.

By now the truck must have reached the camp. Finding one prisoner missing, my imagination raced on, a swarm of furious, well-armed German parachutists would come searching.

Surely the little fellow on the truck could not have forgotten to throw the haversack and the water-bottle. My neck was wet, my tongue parched. Without these essentials it would be impossible to go far, certainly not eight, maybe twelve, days over uncharted mountain paths, guided only by the rough topographical tracing on silk, concealed inside the lining of my battledress. The tins of meat, chocolate and powdered milk would have lasted that long.

To lose the haversack, whose contents represented months of disciplined self-denial, was to lose the means to survive. For a moment I felt lonely and defeated, then quickly focused on what had happened.

I was free! Captivity had moved on in the truck ... captivity which had begun back in Tobruk in Libya on that fateful 20 June in 1942 when General Rommel's German Afrika Korps drove a wedge through the thirty-mile long perimeter of our besieged garrison, almost destroying the 9th Indian Infantry Brigade. In the chaos that followed, to the shocked disbelief of the 2nd South African Division and dozens of British infantry battalions not committed to action in their sectors, Rommel obtained a complete surrender within 24 hours from the bewildered South African Commander of Tobruk, Major General H.B. Klopper. The ignominy of this defeat had cut deeply into the 32,000 defenders, as they were corralled into our first prison enclosure, an immense sun-baked assembly area on an escarpment of Tobruk high above the harbour.

For the previous seven months our own 277th Battery of the 68th (City of Nottingham) Heavy Anti-Aircraft Regiment, RA, TA, had helped to defend this harbour against day and night air bombardment. A territorial unit formed in 1938, following the Munich meeting of Adolf Hitler and Britain's Neville Chamberlain, under the same exigencies as my original unit, the 231st Battery/74th (City of Glasgow) Heavy AA Regiment, RA, TA, I had been posted to it upon being commissioned from the Middle East OCTU in Cairo in May, 1941, aged 22. We knew our Ack-Ack gunnery; we were the best. But Tobruk lacked anti-tank guns. On the day the German armour broke through into Tobruk, our role had switched to anti-tank. This we had not rehearsed.

From all four gun-pits hundreds of tightly-packed sandbags were cast aside until the long-barrelled 3.7 inch guns could depress to elevation zero. When German tanks appeared over the escarpment south of us we dynamited our secret mobile radar set. At close range for an hour, from these fixed gun emplacements west of the harbour, we had engaged an attacking forward squadron of German Panzer Mark IIIs.

In the carnage which ensued, the cool leadership of my senior officer on the gun site, Tim Toppin, was outstanding. Before two of our four guns were blasted into silence, the gun crews with great nerve had disabled five enemy tanks, but the cost in casualties had been heavy. By contrast, the bulk of the garrison's forces, of which the entire 2nd South African Division (Union Defence Force) was the core, found themselves prisoners without having fired a shot.

In a black mood of depression, this huge mass, officers first, was gradually convoyed under German guard westward along the coast of Cyrenaica to Barce, where the Germans handed us over to the Italians. Thence, by way of Benghazi, Italian planes to Lecci on the heel of Italy, and a brief stay in a transit prison camp at Bari, 1300 officers had finally arrived inside the high walls of a permanent prison camp, *Campo di Concentramento* P.G. 21 at Chieti, safely isolated near the Adriatic coast of Central Italy.

Built originally as a Fascist internment camp for political prisoners, P.G. 21 was solidly constructed; escape had been difficult. Suspicious and nervous, the Italians guarded the camp heavily. Through the Escape Committee endless plans were devised and ingenious preparations made. Some escape attempts had proved successful, only to result in recapture within hours or days outside. Italian civilians had been both hostile and afraid.

Now the moment had come. Why worry about the haversack? I was out, and in one piece. Perhaps the peasants were friendlier now and would help. While this British battledress top would speak for itself, I could try out the Italian I had studied in Camp.

A white cottage stood on the far side of the main road. I ran to the end of the field, sprinted across to the door and knocked. A middle-aged woman answered. She looked scared. '*Prigioniero Inglese ... acqua*,' I stammered, but she only shook her head vigorously and waved her arms for me to go. When I asked her where, she calmed down enough to point to a rust-coloured farmhouse half a mile back from the main road.

Half-crouching, I ran along a low ditch bordering fields of young vines. Close to the red house, I halted, panting. On a low stone wall sat an elderly farmer, a youth and a stout peasant woman. I came out of the vines and walked up. Before I could say '*prigioniero Inglese*', the youth came forward smiling. The heavy old lady hurried inside and returned with water. Taking me by the arm, the youth led me down to a hay shed behind the house and left.

Soon the youth returned carrying overalls and a peaked cap. He signalled me to change into these. After a moment's reflection as to the wisdom of this, I cast off my uniform and within a few minutes took on the appearance of an odd-looking Italian railway-man. The small hat perched unsteadily on my long head, poor concealment for reddish-brown hair. The old lady shuffled down carrying bread, cheese and a pitcher of water. At this exhibition of friendliness, I calmed down.

Bales of straw filled the small shed. When the boy indicated I would sleep here, I heaved the bales to form a hiding place between the straw and the wall. The entire German Army, I still felt, would stop the war to search for me.

Outside, chickens fluttered around my feet as I tried to work out where I was. Sulmona lay a mile to the south. On the far side of a deep valley, straight across, stood the bombed ruins of a railway terminal. To the east, where Sulmona Camp with the unlikely name of *Fonte d'Amore*, 'Fountain of Love', was located, rose the high bulk of Monte Morrone. Farther off to the south lay the higher and grander Monte Maiella. The entire vicinity of Sulmona was a basin surrounded by mountains.

From the silk tracing of the map of Italy which I had removed from the lining of my battledress before the youth disappeared with my British uniform I figured out where Sulmona was. We had come 50 miles south from Chieti today. For the next 50 miles south lay nothing but mountains. Due east, beyond Monte Morrone, the Adriatic coast was a good 40 miles off. Rome, one of the few cities marked on my cloth map, was 100 miles west.

Two large related families lived here. The fathers of the house, when they returned from work, explained they were railway engine-drivers. The elder told me how a week earlier he had sabotaged an important train at Chieti by running his locomotive straight into a line of stationary wagons and jumping clear. They were undoubtedly anti-German and, now that the Armistice had been declared, were impatient for the arrival of Allied troops.

Following a big meal of pasta and vegetables in the kitchen, a whispered conference between my hosts and another slightly younger peasant woman was interrupted by surreptitious glances in my direction by the womenfolk and stifled nervous giggles from two of the girls. As a result, instead of sleeping in the hay shed, I was escorted by this woman and the youth down a winding path to the former's house two hundred yards away.

The far end of it was shattered by bomb-blasts; this end, into which I followed the woman, was still relatively intact. Lighting a candle, she led me up a creaking staircase into a large room. The flickering light revealed a narrow bed by the wall. In minutes I was asleep.

The morning was bright when she woke me with warm ersatz coffee, the substitute made from acorns. I was plucking ripe figs from a tree outside when hurried footsteps announced the older girl from the big red house.

'*C'e arrivato un'altro Inglese*,' she exclaimed.

Another Englishman? In a large cellar a somewhat uncertain Captain Dennis Rendell, of the 2nd British Parachute Regiment, broke into a broad smile.

'Good to see you, Dennis. When did you arrive?'

'An hour ago, after floundering around in that river bed all night. I must have been walking in circles.'

At the Sulmona Camp, he said, many were frantic to escape because the Germans planned to evacuate them as soon as they had a train. His own escape had been simple but testing. Just at dark, attracted to an unattended German truck near the main entrance, he had suspended himself under the cab. Two German guards drove the truck a short distance outside but, when they switched off the motor, stayed to talk. He had been about to let go when they finally left. When daylight came, unprepared to start the trek south, he had sought shelter here.

Lacking access to war news, we presumed our troops' progress was unobstructed and rapid. Therefore, since these Italians seemed willing to hide and feed us, at least for the time being, it was logical to stay put and await developments.

Unknown to us was the massive German reaction to the Allied landings and Italy's surrender. Two German armies, rushing down into Italy, were establishing formidable defences in depth across the rugged mountainous terrain seventy miles south of us.

At the red farm the families invited us to supper in the kitchen. Dennis was now also attired in railwayman's overalls. Thanks to months of erratic study at Chieti, I was already finding my Italian tongue. Haltingly I could communicate, and in turn catch the drift of their slurred Abruzzi dialect.

The next morning a steady traffic of trucks, each packed with prisoners on their journey north to Germany, passed along the main road from the Sulmona Camp and, after skirting the town out of sight, appeared again on the long straight hill leading down to the battered railway station. From our vantage point overlooking the valley, Dennis and I watched these convoys shuttle back and forth all day. Without saying a word, we were inwardly feeling thankful that, even if our own future at this point was a large question mark, at least we were immeasurably better off than those hundreds of our fellows being offloaded less than a mile away at the station under heavy German guard, and herded into box-cars and coaches. After the optimism of three weeks ago, I imagined their despondency now as the locks clicked shut behind them.

At dusk, when a large group still stood marshalled alongside the wagons, the crack of rifle fire echoed across the valley. Standing beside me, Dennis could not know that the shots had just killed his close friend and genial fellow officer from the 2nd Parachute Regiment, Captain 'Jock' Short, in a last bold dive for freedom.

The train pulled out and disappeared into the night.

2

VICO BREVE

The slim, slightly bent gentleman who arrived at the red house clearly enjoyed the respect of our railway friends. Upon hearing that two British officers were here, Mario Scocco, Sulmona's dentist, had walked out from the town to check on our needs. Explaining that he wanted to bring us new civilian clothes, he took our approximate measurements and left. The following evening he returned, accompanied by a short, sharp-featured young man carrying in a suitcase two new tweed suits, shirts, ties, toothbrushes, soap and safety razors.

'Warm work,' exclaimed the smiling young man in English. 'We dragged this from the town.'

He looked familiar. 'Weren't you once at Chieti?'

'Yes. I'm Joe Pollak. Worked in the hospital.'

Joe was a Czechoslovakian Jew who, after fleeing from Prague in 1939 while a medical student, had made his way to Palestine and there joined the Palestinian Pioneer forces attached to the British Army. Taken prisoner in the German invasion of Greece in 1941, he had escaped, been recaptured by the Italians and brought to Italy. In the Chieti Camp, his antics had attracted the suspicion of the Italian staff. With some Cypriots he had been moved to Sulmona. In addition to German, Hebrew, French, Greek and English, he now spoke fluent Italian. Joe reassured us on Mario Scocco.

'He hasn't pulled many teeth since the Armistice. He's been busy organizing help for all the prisoners free in the area and running most of the old Fascists out of town.' Heading the local Resistance group, Scocco apparently had many reliable friends working for him in the town.

In an adjoining room Dennis and I hastily changed. The suits fitted reasonably well. Returning to the kitchen in grey herringbone tweeds, we questioned Joe further.

'Are there many of our lads around?'

'Hundreds! They're living in the fields, up in the hills and a few with families nearer the town. The camp at Sulmona was thrown open. We walked out.' In the absence of news, everybody was lying low waiting for our troops to arrive. Scocco pulled Joe Pollak aside.

'Mario,' Joe said to us, 'says he can put you up in a house in the town. Much better than staying here. D'you want to go?'

'Yes.'

'I'll be here this time tomorrow.'

At dusk the next evening, after handing notes of thanks to our hosts, we set out with Joe. He led us along the edge of a broad square. On the far side stood a brightly lit fairground, with merry-go-rounds and a score of side-shows and shooting galleries. No black-out regulations here. In the light of the shooting ranges moved the blue-grey uniforms of German soldiers. Clusters of irregular two-storey dwellings lined short unevenly cobbled streets, down which Joe walked ahead of us. At each corner he glanced back. Following him up a flight of stairs, we blinked as we entered a brightly lit room crowded with men, laughing and talking.

Mario Scocco came forward. The chatter died as all faces turned toward us. 'John Furman!' I burst out, recognizing a beaming face from Chieti. Next to him stood the one American who had shared our bungalow at Chieti, US Army Air Force Captain Elbert L. Dukate. A small dapper individual with well-groomed wavy red hair introduced himself in excellent English. Henri Payonne, a Free French officer who had been a schoolteacher in New Caledonia before the war, was one of the few survivors from the gallant defence of Bir Hakeim. Two weeks ago he had walked out of the Sulmona Camp.

'I'm living here,' he said. 'That's my *padrone*, my landlord, over there, Roberto Cicerone, quite a character.' He pointed to a small, thick-set man with unruly grey hair.

'Roberto speaks broken English with a strong Pittsburgh flavour,' the Frenchman went on. 'All the locals call him *Pazzone* – madman. But he's Scocco's right-hand man. Keeps a good barrel of wine.'

'Bill, just been to your Glasgow tailor?' John Furman smiled at the contrast between his clothing and mine. This was the brisk, precise London voice which had made John pre-eminent in debate and on stage at Chieti. A Medium Artillery officer, he had been taken prisoner in Libya.

At the Sulmona Camp gate a German guard, observing John's dress of shirt, shorts and sandals, had permitted him to join a fatigue party of British soldiers working a hundred yards outside with only one sentry. At the right moment he had dived into bushes and taken off. One soldier from my truck, he knew, had arrived at Sulmona very upset, carrying a satchel of food belonging to me. In the excitement, he had forgotten to throw it.

Dukate joined us. A jovial fellow from Biloxi, Mississippi, he was of French stock. A large head with ample black wavy hair made him appear shorter than his well-built five foot eight. A radio announcer on the Columbia Broadcasting network before learning to pilot American bombers, Duke, through speech-training, had neutralized his native Mississippi drawl.

In the fever to escape from Sulmona Camp, Duke and others had reconnoitred the entire perimeter, seeking blind spots in the jagged wall of wire, through which after dark they might attempt to crawl.

'Remember big Joe Frelinghuysen?' Duke asked. I nodded. 'He found a likely spot at the top end of the Camp. But wait for dark? No. He starts crawling under the wire and, by God, he gets through. He's walking off – nobody in sight – when a Kraut rushes out of a hut with shaving soap on his face and pulls a gun on him. I saw him when they brought him back. That wire had clawed him all over.'

After dark, at an anticipated blind spot, two British prisoners wriggled cautiously forward on the ground under the wire. At regular intervals around the perimeter bright arc-lamps on high posts illuminated the wire wall, but at this section an ingenious Royal Engineer officer had worked carefully on the torn-up power lead to the nearest lamp. To cut the light out completely would have drawn attention. Instead, this lamp now shone dimly, as dimly as the sapper dared adjust it. Nearby in the shadow of a hut crouched a small group including Dukate and Frelinghuysen, listening. As the two Englishmen crawled on, only the sound of wire tweaking on wire signalled their progress. Finally the wires were silent. The two had made it. Quickly, Frelinghuysen, another, then Dukate, began the same slow-motion crawl under the wire. In ten minutes they were clear and staggering off across fields in the dark. A later starter was spotted, shot and killed.

Scocco signalled to Dennis and me to leave with him. In a narrow cobbled lane, a door opened. We followed Scocco inside. A narrow dark hall led into an irregularly shaped room. A single electric bulb hanging from a high ceiling cast a dim light on two people who stood by a fire and an old black range. Scocco introduced us to our new host and hostess and left.

Our hosts were a strange-looking pair. Angelo Carugno and his wife Anna were in their middle fifties. Angelo was short, with drooping shoulders and a thin frame seemingly held together by a drab suit. Behind metal-rimmed spectacles and under an old woollen cap, he was smiling at us.

Anna was taller than Angelo, and large. Her pale puffy face hinted at sadness. However, as she smiled faintly, shyly, bright brown eyes gave her a warm, kindly look. They motioned us to sit down on two upright wooden chairs beside a bare table set against the wall. Obviously they spoke no English, and I was trying to think of something to say in Italian.

Above our heads was the bottom side of a wooden staircase, built out from the wall and leading to the floor above. Recessed in the wall under the stair was a sink. Since it had no water taps, a huge copper vessel alongside presumably contained the house's water supply. This Anna carried back on her head each day, filled from the town spring. At the far end of the room was a second doorway.

Clearly nervous over our arrival, Angelo and Anna were trying to cover their agitation. No doubt they were imagining what could happen to them if the Germans who filled the town caught them with two British escaped prisoners in their home.

Anna produced ersatz coffee. They had not seen real coffee in years. Only the pair of them lived here. They had two sons, one in the neighbouring hills with a group of partisans, the other a prisoner-of-war in England. It was this latter fact that had persuaded them to shelter us. Scocco had talked many into opening their homes in this poor quarter of Sulmona.

We followed them upstairs. The door at the top led straight into a long narrow room with a single bed. A communicating door opened into a larger, square-shaped room containing a double bed. The old pair graciously gestured that the larger room would be ours. Where were they going to sleep, I asked. They would make up another bed downstairs for themselves. We protested. After a little fuss, they agreed to occupy their own room with the double bed. Dennis and I, we insisted, could manage perfectly well in the single bed. Dennis scratched his head.

'I know,' I muttered, with a shrug, 'it won't be funny, but we can sleep head to foot, somehow.'

A trapdoor in the ceiling led up to a loft. A ladder was in place against the wall. This we would drag up after us, they indicated, if we had to hide up there in an emergency. Downstairs the two doors exited on to different lanes. Beside the door we had entered on arrival, they pointed out, was a toilet. It had no cistern; just a seat of sorts with a hole under-neath which shot down straight into the main sewer under the street.

To the accompaniment of repeated '*buona notte*' and '*buon reposo*', we all retired. With careful manoeuvring, Dennis and I succeeded in fitting into the single bed, but not before I had struck his ear with my heel. Still wearing his old cap, Angelo came out of his bedroom. I had opened the only window. He hastened to shut it, explaining with much chest-slapping that the heavy humidity of Sulmona, situated as it was at the base of the mountains, was dangerous at night. '*Pulmone, i pulmone*', he kept repeating, as he returned to his room and closed their door. 'Hell,' moaned Dennis, 'we've got to have air, damp or not!' The window was quietly reopened.

Breakfast of ersatz coffee in a bowl of warm milk, and bread, Angelo brought upstairs. Except for washing below in the morning, he empha-sized, we must remain upstairs, and the window shutters had to be drawn.

Cooped up in this small bedroom over the next four days, our boredom was broken only by visits from Joe Pollak, Henri Payonne the Frenchman, and one or two curious neighbours who were also hiding escaped prisoners.

We were hungry. For lunch Anna brought up vegetable soup and bread. Around 6 pm Angelo, when he returned from his carpenter's shop nearby, appeared upstairs with potatoes and stewed peppers. Actu-ally, they were sharing with us the little they had, and we showed our gratitude. We were restless. This confinement could not last long.

Scocco and *Pazzone* called to give us the local news. More ex-prison-ers, who had earlier taken refuge in the hills, were encroaching on Sulmona in search of help. Since German surveillance was increasing, as was the staff at the local German Headquarters, Scocco, who was too well known, and *Pazzone* were finding it difficult to continue their work.

From their temporary home around the corner, the Carabbia family permitted Duke to visit us one afternoon. The story of his last mission as pilot of a Liberator, on the first dramatic US bombing raid on the strate-gically vital oil refineries at Ploesti in Roumania, captivated us. German anti-aircraft artillery fire over the target had been fierce; many of the American bombers had been lost. Having limped back over the moun-tains with only one engine left out of four, he was finally forced down in the sea near Sicily and later picked up by an Italian sea rescue plane.

To escort Duke back, two pretty young girls arrived upstairs in our room. Lolla Carabbia, about twenty-one, was shy but friendly. Her cotton dress was plain, but could not conceal an attractive figure. Her younger sister, almost as cute, was a rogue. The cloistered existence of a prison camp and the equally void social life of the Libyan Desert before that, had lasted too long, I reflected. In Dennis's eye too, I noted a fresh look.

'Where did you find these beauties, Duke?' Dennis asked, still smiling at the girls.

'They're the daughters of the family I'm with,' Duke replied.

'You mean they're actually living in the same house?' I asked. Duke grinned as the two lovely young escorts pulled him downstairs.

The presence in her household of two British officers, Hill and Roberts, also from Chieti, was the reason for the visit the next day of an attractive young lady from another part of Sulmona. With her came a girl, about twenty-two, whose contrastingly plain features were unusually pale. More startling, however, she was missing an arm. When the pretty one told us that an Allied bombing raid had caused the loss of her friend's arm, we felt not a little embarrassed and, with our limited eloquence, conveyed our genuine sympathy. In the circumstances it was surprising she could smile and appear friendly.

Now Angelo and Anna overcame their fears. We had the freedom of the house, with meals down in the kitchen. It was none too soon. What was really happening to the Allied advance? We couldn't just sit here.

Two days later Anna let Dennis accompany Joe Pollak to visit two British Brigadiers, Boucher and Anderson, whom Joe had contacted in the country. The Brigadiers, themselves ex-prisoners, were about to try the journey to our lines.

'They know no more than we do,' Dennis said on returning. Rumour had it that important elements of the British 8th Army had been switched to the US 5th Army Zone on the west side of the Italian peninsula, where German reaction to the Salerno landing was severe.

Joe Pollak was excited. He was in touch with Major Cochrane who had been Senior British Officer in Sulmona Camp.

'He's found an Italian guide for the mountains. I'm leaving with him tonight, to try to get through.' Doctor Scocco had given Joe money and food, and he was already clad for the trip.

3

GREAT HOSPITAL ESCAPE

Working against time, Mario Scocco and his collaborators were planning. In the local civil hospital, a two-storey building at the north end of the town, one ward contained ten British officer POWs who, declared by the Germans too ill to travel, had been left behind when the 1300 were removed recently by train. Any day these prisoners, most of whom were now fit, would be transported north. The German Commandant of Sulmona administered the hospital and German sentries guarded the exits day and night. But Scocco was determined.

For days, with the tacit cooperation of Italian nurses and the one Italian doctor, a group of trusted local girls, including the two Carabbias, smuggled civilian clothes past the German sentries into the hospital. Inside, while appearing to ask after the health of these Britishers by their bedsides, they surreptitiously slipped these garments under their sheets. Ten pairs of rubber-soled shoes also entered the ward.

The moment came when Scocco was tipped off that the Germans would move those fit to travel the next morning. The team worked fast. To complete the outfitting of all ten prisoners, Scocco dispatched his girls on repeat visits to the hospital all day. Each time they smiled more coquettishly at the unsuspecting German sentries, to distract attention from their unusually full skirts. Zero hour was 9 pm. By then the German Medical Officer would have finished his evening round of the ward. Outside it would be dark, leaving half an hour before the recently imposed curfew – scarcely enough time, but darkness was essential.

The ward holding the British officers was one floor up. A large end window overlooked the gable. Only twenty yards around each corner of the building, German sentries guarded the front and rear entrances to the hospital. Exactly at 9 pm the window opened gently. Over the sill appeared the end of a long rope of knotted sheets which quickly descended the twenty-five feet to the ground. Close by in the dark angles of doorways and buildings *Pazzone* and eight other stalwarts, all briefed on sequence and timing, braced themselves. When a dark figure emerged from the high window and swiftly shinned down the rope an Italian appeared silently from the shadows and grabbed him as he touched the ground. Stealthily the guide hustled the prisoner off down a nearby alley. Another figure appeared on the rope, then another, and another. On reaching the ground, each vanished quickly with his rescuer. Only one 'patient' elected not to escape. Of the nine who descended the rope all but one were safely tucked away in pre-arranged homes before the 9.30 pm curfew.

When the excited guide ushered Captain Gilbert Smith, 4th Royal Tank Regiment, into his appointed house, the family panicked and would not accept him. With time running out, the frantic guide tried another family nearby. They too refused. At a loss, the guide sent a friend speeding to Scocco's temporary 'Operations' room. Scocco, in the process of receiving reports from all his men of 'mission accomplished', raced around just at curfew time to intervene himself. Right away he understood why the allotted family, who had children, refused Smith. It was hard in fact to believe Smith had dared escape. He was suffering from severe eczema and his head and hands were swathed in hospital bandages. Moreover, those on his hands were torn and ragged from his painful descent of the rope. He was extremely weak when Scocco, guiding him along the shadows of back lanes, finally persuaded a family at the top of our own short Vico Breve to take him in and succour him.

At about the time that the weary but inwardly gratified dentist crept home in the dark to his anxious wife and little daughter, a flustered German Commandant exploded at the startling news of this Italian trickery and ordered an immediate house-to-house search of the entire town. Just as quickly, however, he must have realized that to uncover tonight's escapers somewhere in this sprawling town, whose devious citizens he did not understand, would be well-nigh impossible. So he decided to do nothing for the time being.

But Sulmona had challenged him. Scocco, his confederates and the scores of escapers had better look out; from tonight they were targets.

Impatiently we extracted the details from Dr Scocco the next morning. To my surprise, among the eight who had escaped was Lieutenant Jack 'Pop' Hunter. This irrepressible Ulsterman from Fermanagh and I had been together from Officer Cadet Training Unit in Cairo in 1941, zig-zagging across the Western and Libyan Deserts with the 277th Heavy AA Battery, through sandstorms for one wild leave in Alexandria a month before returning to Tobruk to be captured, and latterly pacing endlessly around PG 21 at Chieti. By now I had supposed he was entering Germany. Scocco agreed to take me to him. The mile-long walk, my first leg-stretch, led around the outside of the massive old town wall. After ten days cooped up in Carugno's, the sun and brisk fresh air were a release.

As we entered the living-room of a cottage, 'Pop', standing in a baggy tweed suit, let forth his old high-pitched laugh, revealing two front rabbit teeth which, along with his prematurely bald head, were his distinguishing features.

'Gil Smith's eczema is so bad – all over him – that the Germans wouldn't have moved him anyway, but he insisted on coming. He must have been in dreadful pain coming down the sheets.'

'Pop' screwed up his face. 'It took me all my time, and I'm all right. I'll admit I was leery about the whole business ... just didn't believe these crazy Italians knew what they were doing. But they certainly pulled it off.'

'Scocco's the local leader,' I explained. 'Brave chap, and clever. All his pals are poor, but smart.' 'Pop' signalled his appreciation to Scocco, who brushed it aside.

At that point, surprisingly, John Furman walked in. 'I'm two houses down the road with a widow Maria and her children. Saw you pass by.' John was cheery. An old suit and shoes had replaced his shorts and sandals, but his reddish hair and moustache did not enhance his chance of passing as an Italian.

After dark, back at Vico Breve, I slipped the hundred yards up to Gil Smith's home. While his hands, arms and face were freshly bandaged, he looked far from well, lying in a large recessed kitchen bed. He discounted his misery of the night before.

'They took me all over the bloody town,' he mumbled, forcing a smile on the exposed part of his face. 'All these wops have too many babies. That's why they didn't want me. Don't blame them. They waved their hands...' – he tried to raise his straight bandaged arms – 'Scared the *bambini* might catch this.'

'Anything I can do, Gil?'

'No, old Maria here is doing fine. And this fellow Scocco – good chap – has laid on a nurse to change these dressings every day. I'll be all right.'

'Old Maria', standing alongside making a silly face at Gil, was hard to look at without flinching. Deep lines and wrinkles covered her impossibly ugly old wizened face, and her eyebrows shot up at a steep angle above piercing black eyes. A large wart on her forehead had a twin further down on her left cheek. Below a long thin nose, her pursed mouth sank into her gums and a small clump of hairs sprouted from a narrow chin which jutted to a point.

Now, as I rose, she laughed again, in a chilling '*hgi, hgi, hgi*' falsetto, revealing her two remaining teeth. But this witch-like appearance concealed an angel. She nursed Gil like a son. He had the best bed and, with Doctor Scocco's help, the most nourishing food available. In two weeks, miraculously, he was cured.

4

RASTRELLAMENTI

To the German Army Command, labouring by mid-October on the gigantic task of fortifying their deep line in the mountains to the south, Sulmona became more than a communications centre. Its population of some 5000 represented a fertile source of immediate manpower. Posters throughout the town called on all men of military age to report for labour. When these met with no response, the local German Commandant swung his augmented garrison into action.

'*I Tedeschi, vengano chiapan*'!' the warning cry in shrill dialect echoed through the streets each day as a Company of Germans fell upon some part of the town, grabbed men on the street and from houses and bundled them off in trucks directly to forced-labour encampments 17 miles south. Few in the early raids had time to dive for cover.

Now the womenfolk in our little congested quarter, Burgo Pacentrale, maintained a constant alert. Not only were young husbands and sons to be protected, but, much more compromising for them, some forty British, American and French escapers were now concealed within this maze of old cramped homes.

Realizing that we moved carefully, our hosts the Carugnos no longer fretted over Dennis and me going out frequently. In any case, with these little houses jammed together on both sides of the short and narrow Vico Breve, the presence of six other escapers in the lane was no longer a secret.

'*I Tedeschi! Rastrellamenti!*' cried panicked voices when one forenoon German troops threw a lightning cordon around Burgo Pacentrale. His arms beating the air, old Angelo hustled us out of the house. On Vico Breve young men bursting from doorways raced to the top and disappeared around the corner. We followed. In the alley off the corner a woman waved us forward to raised heavy timber covers of an opening in the ground. Men were jumping in. We tumbled in after them. With some sixty young men, we stood in a cavernous basement cellar. Through the opening above our heads, others, including the Frenchman Robert Meurant and a still-partly-bandaged Gil Smith, jumped down after us.

'*Qui, qui, vieni! Qui, an'iamo!*' still screamed the women. When fresh yells signalled that the Germans were in sight down Vico Breve, the women slammed the trap door shut and heaved sacks of potatoes across it.

Below, in the dark, nobody breathed. Heavy boots approached and passed overhead. The German soldiers scarcely looked at a small group of elderly women sitting on a pile of sacks. Then the moving of the sacks signified the All-Clear. Not a man under fifty had been found.

Two days later cries of alarm again filled the narrow streets and we all raced for the cellar. Again women sitting on bags of potatoes momentarily broke their idle chatter to look up curiously, half-smiling, as stern-faced German soldiers clambered by looking for doors to enter. This time our confinement lasted two hours.

The next Sunday, however, another *rastrellamento* in the high and more open part of Sulmona hit our ranks. German soldiers jumped off trucks and ran to search cottages lining the streets. Losing her nerve, John Furman's excitable landlady Maria waved him out of her back door. The only visible cover in the yard was a large dog kennel. Into this he wriggled backwards. Five minutes passed.

'*Giovanni! Oh Giovanni!*' he heard Maria wail from the door. Good, the road must be clear, he thought, and crawled out of the kennel – right alongside a pair of boots, leggings and blue-grey trousers. The equally surprised German officer picked him up and escorted him to the waiting truck.

Two houses down, another German was dragging away the grown son of the house. Inside, two women, reacting quickly, pushed a non-plussed 'Pop' Hunter into a recess in his bedroom wall and slid a tall wardrobe across the front. 'Pop' escaped detection.

Less fortunate in the same roundup were two Americans, Glenn Wilson of Detroit, a Flying Officer in the Royal Canadian Air Force, and Captain Herbert Perry, US Army Air Force. Both were from Chieti Camp, where Herb Perry, a musical director to Walt Disney before the war, had played a prominent role in the spectacular theatrical achievements of the Camp.

While wiry 'Pat' Wilson, with his dark hair, brown eyes and thin black moustache, was the only one likely to pass as Italian, nevertheless the squarely-built Herb Perry, whose blond hair sported a crew-cut, and red-haired John Furman were also assumed by their German captors to be Italian. Along with a hundred real Italians picked up in this raid, they were rushed south in guarded trucks to Pescacostanza, a village ten miles behind the forward line of German defences. Here the Germans dumped them into a labour camp containing several hundred others.

Conditions were grim. Food was meagre. Each morning guards assigned working parties to building defence posts and gun emplacements. The Italians in contact with Furman, Wilson and Perry quickly realized their identify, but kept quiet. Soon Furman had a 'go slow' campaign in operation.

From the start all three watched for the chance to escape. Their fellow-workers co-operated by giving them part of their scarce rations. Among the guards, John Furman, using his fluent German, struck up a lucky 'friendship' with two disgruntled Austrians. This produced a pocket compass, cans of meat, and on the ninth day a large-scale German survey map of the entire region.

On the eleventh night, just before the moon rose, three 'slave labourers', helped by the Austrians, crawled through a prearranged gap in the fencing and made off. Though tantalized by their proximity to the Allied forward positions southward, they had concluded that, because of the depth of the German defences and the extensive ground-patrol activity described by the Austrians, their chance of reaching our lines was remote.

Navigator Herb Perry took charge and by compass, the stars and the survey map, plotted their route north. Even with Furman newly handicapped by dysentery, by daylight they arrived exhausted within six miles of Sulmona. The curfew hour found them dining in the same house which Wilson and Perry had unceremoniously left twelve days before.

Early next day the ever-alert Dr Scocco brought Wilson and Furman to a new home opposite ours in Vico Breve. Furman's dysentery was now severe. Somehow neighbours spirited up tins of oatmeal which had once belonged in Red Cross food parcels. These and other scarce items gave him the diet he required.

Joe Pollak came back. Lameness had forced Major Cochrane to halt in desolate Palena on Monte Maiella. Pollak headed on with the elderly Italian guide, but, when within sight of British forward positions on the far south bank of the Sangro River, they were spotted by a German patrol who opened fire. While scrambling back up the mountain, the plucky old guide received a flesh wound, but Joe and he pressed on and eluded their pursuers. Following a respite at Palena, where, just a few days before, a German firing squad had executed two hapless Italian peasants caught sheltering British escapers, they completed their journey to Sulmona on the back of a German truck.

5

LET'S TRY THE VATICAN

Despite the growing shadow of local German control, a bright atmosphere reigned in the living-room of the Imperoli family on the last Sunday in October, when six escapers escorted by local girls arrived by invitation for afternoon tea. Maria Imperoli, who with the other girls had participated in the brilliant hospital escape, served the specially acquired tea with ceremony.

One girl differed from all the others. Tall and slim, Iride Imperoli, the older sister of our young hostess Maria, wore smart, stylish clothes. Sophisticated and extrovert, she appeared very sure of herself. A faint pallor in her lean cheeks emphasized the fine features of her small oval face and the scarlet of her full lips. As she moved around the group, long dark hair and flashing dark brown eyes gave her an air of intrigue.

At dusk the beautiful and less complex Lolla Carabbia agreed to be my escort home. Iride attached herself to Dennis. Even if his Italian was fragmentary, he was dashing, and a *Capitano*. From that day on, Iride often visited Vico Breve.

In the country, when early November brought cold rain, scores of ex-prisoners could no longer exist in their rude *capanne* in the fields. With food running low, the well-meaning peasants could spare them little.

From dawn to dusk the tireless *Pazzone* and his handful of bold friends, hearing of one plight after another, escorted these men into friendly billets in the town. Thanks to informers, Mario Scocco was now strongly suspected by the Germans. With his own personal resources exhausted, and no longer living in his own home, he continued to operate from constantly changing hideouts. Such was the audacity of this activist that, when *Pazzone* relayed to him in hiding that I had developed a throbbing abscessed tooth, he appeared at Vico Breve the same afternoon and led me to his home outside the town boundary. One section of the house was his dental surgery. Within minutes he had me leaning back in his dentist's chair and with little more paregoric than a smiling preamble of reassurance he extracted my upper front tooth. In the growing dusk he escorted me back to the Carugnos' house.

With sources of food and clothes drying up, we had to get organized. To maintain this steadily growing force of escapers hidden in the town, with frequent German *rastrellamenti* threatening not only their freedom but the very lives of their willing, if fearful, Italian hosts, was too big a task for *Pazzone*'s friends to handle alone. Moreover, John Furman's realistic opinion about the impregnability of the German mountain defence barrier dimmed hopes of early liberation. Yet, rather than admit that the Allied advance was stalemated, we clung to a belief that, to out-flank the German defences, the British 8th Army would somehow stage amphibious landings on the Adriatic coast north of us.

As responsibility gravitated somehow to Dennis and me, so the Carugno home became the centre of operations. Already, with my Italian improving, I went out each day with *Pazzone* or another to contact the newly reported arrivals. Besides Duke, Wilson, Payonne, Pollak, a vastly improved Gil Smith and a weakened John Furman, our upstairs room saw a steady traffic from the neighbouring *padrone* who were hiding others. But material help was vital. We needed money, and we needed clothes.

Through one young man, Pietrorazio, who was feeding two American airmen, Captain F.B. Hawkins and Captain R.J. Gardiner, we obtained access to an abundant store of Italian military uniforms, heavy under-clothing and blankets, which a sympathetic Italian Major Balassone kept hidden in his *magazino*. On our signatures as British officers, he would release these. Frequent calls thereafter at the *magazino*, where the Major carried on a lucrative business in rawhides, purchased from the local slaughterhouse now operated by the German Army, produced these valuable items from the cellar beneath the blood-wet stone floor. As German soldiers entered with fresh loads of skins, we slipped out of sight into the rear office. When they left, Pietrorazio shouldered the bulky supplies of clothing back to Vico Breve for distribution later by *Pazzone* and his friends.

But this was no answer. The local farmers could not work their fields freely, and any food supplies they did market were soon requisitioned by alert German quartermasters. In a month black-market prices had soared beyond anyone's capacity to buy. With transport by road or rail virtually impossible for civilians, nothing entered Sulmona. On a meagre diet of thin bean soup, occasional *gnocchi* when Angelo could buy a little flour, and stewed *pepperone* contributed from the field worker next door, Dennis and I were relatively lucky.

Twice Joe Pollak had suggested that we should move to Rome, 100 miles north-west, but, since Sulmona lay closer to the Front here, this option did not appeal.

Joined in our room by Gil Smith, Dukate and Pollak, we speculated on ways to have a message delivered to the British or American diplomats within the neutral Vatican State. Maybe they could send money – but how?

'Oh, simple,' said Duke, 'they'd mail us a money order care of the German Commandant, and we'd cash it at the bank.'

Yet Duke's quip posed an idea. I hadn't thought of the local bank. I had passed it, the *Banco di Napoli*.

Footsteps on the stairs announced Iride and her sister Maria. The discussion switched back to the Vatican. Joe translated the gist of our conversation to Iride.

'*Vado io a Roma!*' she announced firmly.

'But how would you get there?' asked Duke.

Iride spoke quickly to Joe.

'She knows Rome well,' relayed Joe. 'She travelled there and back recently on German trucks. She'll do it again. Then go to St Peter's to confessional, with your letters. Ask the priest to put her in touch with a British representative inside. If he's the right priest, he'll do it. If not, she'll try another one. At least a priest will deliver her letters, and she could come back later for replies.'

Noting our reaction, Iride was beaming. Dennis gave her an admiring hug.

'Let's try it anyway,' said Gil Smith.

Four of us signed a letter to the British Minister explaining our position. If the situation deteriorated, should we come to Rome? If not, what? Could he send money? To the American Representative Duke wrote a similar letter.

The next morning, with the letters tucked safely away on her body, Iride left on her mission.

Henri Payonne brought word that a young shepherd who knew the mountains was prepared to attempt the journey to our lines with a party of escapers. Henri, Dennis and I discussed it. Our Italian friends had doubts about the guide. We decided to await news from Rome.

Five days later a triumphant Iride was back. She handed Dennis a small sheet of paper bearing microscopic writing in English, signed by nobody and addressed to nobody. Crossing the lines had become most hazardous and we should not come to Rome except as a last resort. The sum of three thousand lire was enclosed for the four signatories of the letter, and more would be sent if desired, upon receipt of names, regimental numbers and ranks of the other escapers mentioned. Moreover, if we sent the addresses of next-of-kin, efforts would be made to relay messages.

For Dukate Iride had also brought cash, a fine worsted suit and a letter from an anonymous American. She had travelled both ways on German trucks and her little plan at St Peter's had worked perfectly. Whilst there, she had also met a French official who had given her an address in Rome where, should we have to come in an emergency, we could call for help. After memorizing '62 *Via Sicilia*' we burned her note.

All were in good spirits this morning, particularly Duke who was clowning around in his new smart suit. Even old Angelo and Anna downstairs looked happier. In recent weeks, without losing any of their normal humility, they were, I thought, secretly enjoying the touch of prestige which sprang from their house becoming the unofficial headquarters for our activity.

For three days the Carugnos scarcely saw Dennis and me as, with the co-ordinated help of *Pazzone* and Joe Pollak, we called on all the known escapers in the area, including outlying farms, to obtain their personal particulars and those of their next-of-kin and pass out more clothing. As his guide, Dennis had Iride. Back at Vico Breve, we collated data on eighty escapers, British, American and South African.

Lists of these, together with further letters and notes of things to buy, lay snugly under Iride's clothes when she left again for Rome. With her went her sister Maria to assist in carrying the goods back. In five days, after hitching back on four different German trucks, all the time loaded with parcels of shirts, socks, cigarettes and more anonymous letters, they received a warm reception at Vico Breve. They handed over 15,000 lire in cash.

This evening Iride basked in our compliments. Although the local people here visibly lacked respect for her, she was certainly performing magnificently for us and we were content to judge her on that.

Disappearing again for the daylight hours, Dennis and I distributed cash among the *padrone* of our recorded escapers. Though only a few hundred lire each, it reassured these confused people, now at a low point and understandably reluctant to house their compromising foreign guests any longer.

For accountability, Dennis and I took receipts from the escapers and kept a book record.

Inevitably, rumours circulated that fabulous sums had arrived from Rome, and that some families were receiving unjustified cash, but we soon quieted the mild flutter and momentary jealousies.

For those of us now circulating openly in the town, the principal risk lay in a possible challenge of identity by Germans or local collaborators. Through the town photographer and a friend of Ballasone, a civic employee who filched blank Italian identity cards and 'borrowed' the official Sulmona Commune stamp, I, Guglielmo de Cesare, and seven others soon carried genuine-looking documents.

Enthused by our gratitude for these, the team willingly undertook to carry the forgery business further. Within two weeks, similar identity cards, complete with photographs and official stamps, established the 'citizenship' of fifty escapers living within the town boundary.

* * *

The local branch of the Bank of Naples intrigued me as a source of cash. Following inquiries which suggested that the manager was now pro-Allied, Joe Pollak and I had walked into the sizeable bank office one morning, only to be confronted by several German officers. Observing the manager in conversation with one of them, we withdrew discreetly.

As another approach, Joe had met one of the young bank clerks who was sympathetic. I had already been to this young man's home with Joe and met his pleasant family. Tonight I returned again to learn of any progress. Reaching their house in the northern end of the town, I knocked and entered the open front door.

'*Buona sera, tutti*,' I called, but in the living-room I stopped short. Two young sisters on the settee froze when they saw me. Standing by the table with their backs to me were the young banker and a German officer, looking down at a chart. For the moment, coming from the darkness outside, the light in here had dazzled me.

As the young banker turned his head quickly, a look of consternation shot across his face. Quickly grasping the officer's arm as he too began to turn, the young man hastily re-engaged his attention on the map on the table.

Moving forward, smiling and winking toward the two young girls, I rustled their hair. They were too scared to speak. With my back to the German, I moved to the door and left.

Relieved, I started the half-mile walk around the outside of the high town wall, toward Burgo Pacentrale. Halfway, out of the pitch dark two young German soldiers stopped me. Curbing an urge to run for it, I waited for them to speak.

'*Dove il casino?*' the taller one asked in Italian. A large villa with a name like that, I remembered, lay about two kilometres out in the country, along a rough track which happened to lead off the main road just where they had stopped me. Scratching my head, I played for time to frame my reply in Italian. Close up now, they stared at me.

'*Casino? Ah, si, si, due chilometri, questa strada,*' I stammered, pointing in the direction of the bleak track leading away from the town.

'*Due chilometri? No, no. Nein!*' The German did not agree.

'*Si, si,*' I insisted, '*forse no due chilometri, ma certo questa strada*' (If not two kilometres, certainly this is the road), I found myself saying, continuing to point.

'*Ja? Va bene. Grazie,*' the same German said, as they both went stumbling in the dark down a steep slope to this path which led past a farm and out through fields.

Still tense, I walked fast home to Vico Breve. When I related the incident to the Carugnos and to Iride, they started to laugh. The distinguished villa to which I had directed the German soldiers was named 'Casina' something. The Casino – built into the massive town wall only yards from where they had stopped me – was quite different. The town brothel had lost two customers.

* * *

Each Sunday evening since money had reached us from Rome, old Angelo, reminding us that '*Oggi é Festa*' (today's a holiday), ran willingly to a nearby wine store whence for a small quantity of our lire he brought back in *fiasci* a large quantity of local barrel wine. Neighbours would stop by with their British, French or American 'guests'.

Thus, at dusk of Sunday, 28 November, before I returned from a field trip, Joe Pollak burst into the Carugnos' kitchen waving a large photograph, still damp, of himself aiming a rifle surrounded by smiling German soldiers.

'It's the shooting gallery,' he explained. 'The target shoots your photo. I got these Germans to watch me! Good, eh?'

Downing their wine, Rendell, Smith and Payonne took off with Joe to the fairground in the square to repeat the gag. They returned in high spirits, all of them in a photo with German soldiers.

News of this, however, angered some of our good Italian friends who were risking their skins. Particularly disturbed was a major benefactor,

William DiCarlo, the prosperous owner of a local confectionery factory, who wielded valuable influence with our helpers. He called at the Carugnos' and politely cautioned us. I assured him such indiscretions would not be repeated, although inwardly I regretted I had missed participating.

Eight new escapers had arrived at an outlying farm. From Balassone's hidden store, *Pazzone* and I carried blankets, Italian army 'long-johns' and a few scarce toothbrushes and razors out across the fields to them. Three of these English soldiers had made a gutsy attempt to reach the British lines through the mountains to the south, only to be recaptured by a German patrol near the River Sangro. Transported back to the *Fonte D'Amore* Camp near Sulmona, they had succeeded in escaping again. They confirmed that making it to our lines was close to impossible now.

On the tramp back with *Pazzone*, this courageous, generous and self-effacing man, I wondered how much longer he and the rest of these astonishingly supportive people could keep up this level of help. Soon weather conditions would be so cold and wet that none of the scores of escapers living in rude huts and makeshift hideouts in the fields could go on that way. It bothered me that I couldn't see a solution.

Back at the Carugnos' in the afternoon, old Anna called from downstairs.

'*Guglielmo! C'e son'Tedeschi qui fuori!*'

Germans outside? I grabbed my jacket, rushed down and, following Anna's pointing, peered through the patterned glass of the rear door. Twenty yards away, moving slowly toward this, the only door on the narrow Church lane, came a German officer and a soldier. Snatching my raincoat and hat, I bolted through the living-room, out the front door and into the house opposite.

Meanwhile, Anna, moving her heavy frame faster probably than at any moment in her life, raced upstairs. She had just finished stuffing away telltale traces when a loud knock sounded on the door below. Coming down again, she opened it to the Germans. Could they come in and look around, the officer asked politely. Anna shrugged her shoulders and bade them enter. They inspected both floors and, with a curt apology for the intrusion, left by the same rear door.

As soon as they were out of sight down the Church lane, Anna came puffing across Vico Breve. Between excited breaths she was relating the incident when Angelo appeared. The word had flashed to his carpenter's shop around the corner.

Soon they calmed down. I suggested that Dennis and I would move out, but Anna would not hear of it.

Inevitably the occurrence upset other *padrone* in the area. Worried housewives plagued poor *Pazzone* to remove their guests. When he came to me with these reports, together we spent a day calling on each of these nervous women, encouraging them to keep going, because surely our Forces would bring relief soon. With a few '*Bravas*' and a pat on the shoulder, they seemed reassured. They liked their boys.

But the snow line on the mountains was daily creeping lower. On a recently acquired radio set, up in the loft at the Carugnos', even the BBC offered no encouragement.

Pazzone arrived looking worried. Local German commanders had ordered the evacuation of the entire village of Pacentro, only three miles away. The whole population of a hundred or so, most of whom had never travelled more than a few miles from the village, would be packed on to German trucks for transportation to camps in Northern Italy.

Pazzone's concern was that with these kindly villagers he had hidden thirty escapers. Singlehanded in the next thirty-six hours, he ferried twenty of them in relays to barns and *capanne* close to Sulmona. The others made off independently. In two days, *Pazzone* parked all twenty with families in the town.

As I left Balassone's hide store after signing for clothes for the Pacentro influx, a little middle-aged woman who was feeding four escapers in a barn outside the town wall insisted I come to her home at the edge of town. When I followed her into a small living room, looking straight at me was an armed German soldier. A moment's tension passed when they both smiled. He was French, she explained, conscripted in Alsace.

Attached to a Mule Company headquartered just south, he had become friendly with the little woman here and still more friendly with her pretty daughter of eighteen who, appearing in the room, rested her head on his arm. I had the picture.

He had chosen to desert, but had no money. As a gesture I handed him 100 lire from the fund and took a receipt from him, complete with his name, rank and German Army number. Back at Vico Breve, these too were entered in our cash book. Our organization was broadening.

So was our household, by one. Concezio, the Carugno son, had returned home from the partisan band in the mountains. Angelo and Anna then decided to sleep downstairs as a precaution against night alarms, and thus finally the head-to-toe nightly ordeal for Dennis and me ended.

Frequently now, old Angelo, perhaps through stress, lost his temper with Anna. In these the pathetic little man finished up looking foolish. Quiet, patient Anna always seemed to be right. Yet, for all his peculiarities, we had learned to respect him as much as Anna. They were both marvellously warm, genuine, self-sacrificing and now quite courageous human beings.

6

THE ROUND-UP THAT DIDN'T

On the cold clear afternoon of Sunday, 5 December, Joe Pollak and I delivered clothes and blankets to nine British soldiers hiding in a large cave two miles from Sulmona. It was a tranquil spot, until without warning a flight of Royal Air Force Hurricanes, and on their tail another of Spitfires swooped low over our heads and, to the ear-splitting thunder of rockets, strafed German petrol dumps a mile away. We waved, jumped and cheered. The planes banked steeply and roared off low over the mountains as huge columns of black smoke curled into the sky from the direction of the dumps.

I returned briskly to Vico Breve, Joe Pollak dropping off at a farmhouse on the way. Sunday evening being *Festa*, the other escapers in the immediate vicinity and their *padrone* had gravitated to the Carugnos'.

Angelo and his son Concezio were was pouring wine when I arrived. Besides Dukate, Smith, Wilson and Furman from Vico Breve, Bernard Rosen from several streets away was here in the kitchen with his young *padrona*, as well as Iride and Maria, and Lolla from Duke's home.

The Vico Breve door flew open. '*Tedeschi! Tedeschi, vengono chiapan*'! *Via! Via!*' screamed Maria, framed in the doorway. Germans were surrounding the *quartière*. They had entered the house next to hers.

Duke shot past her and, with Lolla at his heels in the dark, doubled down Vico Breve, to slip back to the Carabbias' home around the corner.

Out of the Church lane door Rosen dragged his young *padrona* by the arm, but at the foot of the lane they ran smack into helmeted Germans. Quickly she slapped and kicked Rosen, shouting '*Ubriaco! Vergognia te!*' Then, to the Germans, '*Mio marito, sempre ubriaco. Sempre vino, vino. Managgia!*' She had found her drunken husband and was dragging him home. The Germans let them pass.

Maria vanished. From the open front door Iride reported that Germans were clustering at the top end of Vico Breve. They were entering old Maria's house. When powerful flashlights lit up the entire lane, Iride slammed the door. All the eight front doors flush with the street on Vico Breve were now in full view of the German searchers, and all the escapers living on the lane were trapped here in one house. A quick crossfire of opinions concluded that no one could risk leaving. The loft was no place to hide, with the trapdoor so visible, but we had no options. 'Come on! Upstairs!' snapped Dennis. 'God, what a crowd.'

Angelo and Anna, serious but calm, switched off the kitchen light as we clambered up the stairs. Up went the ladder, up went the trapdoor, and up the ladder went Furman, Smith, Wilson, Concezio and myself. From the loft, I looked back down for Rendell. He stood uncertainly in the room below, seemingly straining for some alternative or planning to create a diversion.

'Get up here!' I yelled. He looked up and then, giving up whatever idea he had, climbed up into the loft. Now Iride appeared at the foot of the ladder, looking up and wringing her hands. For a second I wondered how poor Angelo and Anna were reacting down in the kitchen.

'Look,' I hissed to the others, who were confused in the strange loft, 'We can't just stand here. They're bound to see the trapdoor. Our only chance is down under the eaves there. Get down ... pull that straw over you.'

Where the sloping roof met the floor on each side, a narrow planked ledge, running nine inches below the level of the loft, could hold three stretched end-to-end. We were six. Concezio and I smothered the radio in loose straw and then, like John, Gil and Pat on the far side, squeezed down on to the ledge overhanging Vico Breve seventy feet below.

'Dennis, the ladder.' I had pulled it up but it still lay uncovered on the floor. With the bedroom light from below catching his face as he held open the trapdoor, Dennis still gazed down at a tearful Iride.

'They're getting closer,' she sobbed in Italian, '...two more houses, *Madonna mia!* I must go.'

High time too, I thought. Dennis closed the trapdoor. In the dark he kicked the ladder behind posts and pulled straw over it, then slithered down on to the far end of my ledge and swished straw around. We fell silent.

Outside heavy boots clanked on the cobblestones. Across the way voices argued. A door slammed. Another rattled violently as gruff Germans demanded entry. A minute's quiet followed before boots clattered on the street again, coming closer.

Almost immediately below, soldiers battered on a door till it opened. They pushed inside. Through the thin walls heavy steps sounded on the stairs. They were next door. Italian voices protested as the soldiers searched. Only this morning, thank God, we had moved two Englishmen out of there. Now the boots descended again.

Our door was next. Hardly breathing, we listened. Old Angelo and Anna, would they panic? When found, we would be dragged off as prisoners. Bad enough, but for them ... and young Concezio here. They'd be dead ducks. The trapdoor over there, certainly the Germans would see it. Even with no ladder, they'd get up here somehow, shine their flashlights, see the straw. Would they prod, or just open fire?

Directly below now, soldiers stomped about, shouting. For a second the swinging beam of a torch from the street flashed on the eaves beside me. In the dead stillness of the loft we lay rigid.

'*Aprire! Aprire!*' shouted a harsh voice in the street as boots kicked the door. It opened and the searchers rushed in. Now for it.

From the ledge, heart pounding, I listened for the first footfalls on the stairway below. Yes, there they were, indistinct, now louder. On the landing, they would search the rooms first, but the boots were still climbing, even louder. How come? The stair was short. I twisted my head. No, the heavy steps were not directly below. In fact they were sounding through the wall on Dennis's end of the loft ... on the long stair in the tall house next after ours. From the Carugnos' directly beneath us, still no sound came.

A woman screamed, but it was not Anna. A man remonstrated in Italian. They must be the neighbours who bring in the stewed *pepperone* every night. Furniture crashed and doors banged. Germans sounded angry as they retreated downstairs.

Once more boots hit the street. Others issued from a house opposite. From the commotion rose a garble of German. Probably our house this time. No, they seemed to be moving down the street away from our door.

For fully ten minutes we lay silent, not daring to move. Quiet had descended on Vico Breve. Cautiously we eased from our cramped positions. No one spoke. Instinctively we were waiting for a signal from below. Could the searchers really have missed our door? And with all of us cornered here?

Finally light footsteps climbed the stairway below. Following a gentle knock on the trapdoor, Angelo quietly called to his son. Concezio crawled over and lifted the trapdoor. By some miracle, Angelo mumbled, the Germans had missed our house, and the street was quiet.

We rose from the ledges. Concezio whispered to his father. Light from a candle appeared. Through the opening, upside-down on the end of a pole, rose a familiarly shaped round white pot with a round handle.

'Concezio, you're brilliant!' breathed Gil, setting it down on the floor.

After twenty minutes, with no sound of the searchers returning, but still hardly accepting our luck, we descended quietly to the kitchen. On a struggling fire Anna was calmly brewing coffee. I passed my arm around her shoulder and she turned her head; she was paler than usual.

'*Il Signore m'a sentito,*' she murmured, instinctively raising her eyes as she crossed herself. The Lord had heard her. I nodded. Since this appeared to be the only house not searched, no other explanation came to mind. Her hand was steady as she poured the hot coffee.

'The Jerries are probably as angry as hell,' Furman was saying. 'They may come back. We're too many here. If the street's clear, I'd say we should go back to our own billets.' John was being considerate.

'Yes, but we don't know,' said Dennis. 'I don't think we should even open the door.' In fact, at the bottom of Vico Breve, German sentries still waited in the shadow, watching silently.

The only safe hideout, Concezio said, was up in the loft of the nearby church, whose entrance stood on the lane leading from our back door. If we left by this door at dawn, we would avoid Vico Breve, which might still be under surveillance. Leaving Angelo and Anna downstairs, we filed quietly upstairs and, with the ladder in place to the open trapdoor, stretched out on the beds.

At 5.30 am Concezio reported the lane clear. We crept out in the semi-dark, slipped through the church gate and followed Concezio along cobwebbed passages and up a narrow spiralling stairway. Clambering over solid old beams and joists, we halted on the planked flooring of the belfry. Concezio went home.

With draughts blowing in every direction, the belfry was freezing. While the others huddled on the floor, I opened a bottle of brandy I had grabbed from a drawer as we left the Carugnos'. William DiCarlo had given it to me for emergencies. 'Yes, I think this rates as an emergency,' said Gil, shivering as he put the bottle to his mouth.

Despite our incredibly lucky break, the situation was awkward. Certainly we could not return to our families on Vico Breve. Yet to make for our lines in the south would be foolhardy.

In the afternoon Concezio returned with Joe Pollak. The Germans had caught nobody. Their officer-in-charge had held a list of addresses, even knew the nationality of the man hiding in each house. Who had given us away? *Pazzone* felt sure it was the girl who had lost an arm; she had been seen with Germans. This had logic to it – revenge against the Allies whose bombs had dismembered her.

'Let's all go to Rome!' Joe said. As we thought about this, he hastily supplied us with good reasons why we should. There was a train from Sulmona at six o'clock that evening.

'We can be in Rome tomorrow morning,' he added.

My first reaction was against leaving Sulmona. The escapers had come to depend on Dennis and me. So had *Pazzone* and his gallant helpers. Yet, what good could we do if we lacked freedom of movement and an available billet? While all except myself were warming to the Rome plan, I had to admit the impossibility of staying on usefully in Sulmona. I conceded.

Just as Concezio appeared with hot soup and bread, Joe darted off happily to make plans. With his fluent Italian and a permit ostensibly signed by the local German Commandant, giving 'Giuseppe Bernardini', medical student, special permission to travel to Rome for examinations at the University, Joe could talk his way through a dozen enemy *rastrellamenti*. He returned at 3 o'clock, accompanied by Iride and her sister Maria.

Everybody was jabbering at once, Iride saying she had arranged accommodation for a few nights at her uncle's house here in Sulmona, Joe telling us about trains. Finally establishing order, we made our plans.

From the station, a mile distant, a train left at six o'clock. It was a freight train but it took passengers. Provided the road was clear, we could gather at the Carugnos', have the other fellows' belongings brought over and set off quietly after dark at half-past five for the station. But what about buying tickets? Since German troops patrolled the trains, would they not examine passengers before boarding? If the journey passed without mishap, what chance did we stand at the other end of clearing the police check on all individuals entering Rome? Even with our identity cards, we were rather a motley crowd to be escorted solely by Joe Pollak.

At Iride's insistence, Joe translated our jumbled discussion. Now her voice rose above the others to declare that she and Maria would come to Rome with us. She would buy the tickets, do everything. If we reached Rome, she would take us to a certain small hotel.

While Iride and Maria rushed off to prepare, Joe left to apprise Duke of our plans. At half-past four Concezio led the five of us down to the door of the church. When he signalled from the gate that all was clear at his home, we slipped along the stone wall to Casa Carugno one at a time.

Laden with parcels of food and the few possessions of their recent guests, the other *padrone* were here waiting. Edging over to the coal bunker, I wrote a letter to the 'Allied Troops' specifying the magnificent help of the Carugnos. After Dennis and I both signed it, I pulled Anna aside and, handing her the letter, told her to present it to the Allies when they arrived. Laying her grey head against my chest, she began to sob. It was the first time I had seen her show emotion. Unconsciously a strong affection had grown between us; she had treated Dennis and me like sons.

In the midst of these difficult farewells, Duke, Iride and Maria arrived. Half of Vico Breve had congregated to wish us well. They were grand people but it was time to go.

We assembled in small groups. Old Angelo insisted on escorting Duke and me to the station. Last night, faced with the near certainty of German arrest, he had behaved magnificently. Now his whole manner was cocky and bold.

To final '*Auguri*', our little cavalcade slipped out of the back door and moved off at intervals on a detour route to the station. The night was clear and starry; the moon would rise later. A fine night for aircraft, I thought, while we hurried along, with old Angelo almost running every few steps to keep up with us.

As we entered the bomb-shattered station yard and crossed lines toward what in the dark looked like our train, a steam whistle blew. Up ahead, Joe shouted to us to hurry. We passed the message back to those behind us and, with a last farewell to Angelo, ran the remaining 300 yards. As the last of us clambered on board the train began to move.

We were off. *Addio*, Sulmona. The train picked up. Running alongside the open door of our wagon in the darkness outside was a figure. I looked. It was old Angelo, bareheaded, waving his cap at us and shouting a last '*Buon viaggio, buon fortuna.*'

Rome – Open City

7

ROME ONE WAY

To the click of wheels crossing points, the train stumbled its way out of the Sulmona yard on to the single track heading west. With windows along each side, the crowded carriage appeared to be an old type of coach from which all seats and internal fittings had been removed. A dim light fell from one masked electric bulb. In the far corners passengers had already settled with blankets and coats. In the middle others lay across mounds of freight and baggage. Nearby a child whimpered.

At the rear end of the coach Joe Pollak and Iride stood talking to an official or conductor, buying tickets for all eight of us. I was glad now that Joe had come along; we might need his fluent Italian and quick wits on this improbable flight to Rome. Before leaving Sulmona Iride had pointedly asked Joe to stay behind, but he had ignored her. Now, it seemed, Iride disliked having to share the spotlight with Joe. Too much depended on her, but right now she was our angel.

Up forward, Maria had settled beside me on two soft sacks, behind which a tall wooden packing case made an uncomfortable backrest. Feet away, Duke lay full length on the floor. Farther back John Furman, Gil Smith and Pat Wilson leaned casually against baggage.

A bright flashlight beamed from the forward door. Behind the light a uniformed German guard approached slowly. His flash picked out the face and ran over the clothing of each passenger. I pulled Maria's head on to my shoulder and stuck my chin in her hair. My eyes were half-closed when the German halted right beside us and held his light a foot from our faces. The beam switched to Duke's upturned face on the floor. He was yawning. The German moved on. Maria's eyes closed.

As the rumble and clatter of the wheels jolted us on, I could not sleep. On reflection, two months ago we should have collected food and headed south right at the start. Well, we hadn't. At least in and around

Sulmona we had done what we could for the other escapers. If *Pazzone*, like Dr Scocco, was forced into hiding, hopefully someone else would carry on.

None of us could know that, back in Sulmona an hour after we left, a reinforced detachment of Germans again raided Vico Breve. This time the Carugnos' home was a target. Bursting in, they searched it from the kitchen up and into the loft where we had all hidden the night before. Subsequent interrogation of old Angelo and his gentle Anna was vicious, as the Germans remained thwarted in their search. But they did not crack and, after hours of terror, were left shaken but physically unscathed in their dishevelled home. Wisely, Concezio had moved out in time.

Though officially the train was due to arrive in Rome at half past six in the morning, it had not done so in months and, when our aircraft had been over, had frequently been twelve hours late.

Another German guard appeared and checked on us. I avoided his eyes and slipped my arm around Maria. He moved on. I left my arm around Maria. She was a pretty girl, only twenty. In coming with us, she was blindly following Iride, her dominating half-sister.

It was light now. At least our own bombers hadn't been over. Joe Pollak crouched beside me. 'Iride says we're five stations away from Rome Terminal,' he said. 'She thinks we should leave the train at Palestrina, two stations before Rome and walk the rest. They check everybody's documents in Rome station. Not worth the risk.'

'Yes, but what about the road-blocks?'

'We may be able to bypass them.'

'Okay, warn the others.' I moved to a window.

At the fourth station before Rome, no passengers left or came aboard. 'Twenty minutes from the city,' an Italian said. At the next small station a trickle of passengers left the train, but I observed no police check, not even a ticket collector.

The train chugged out again. Our group collected their scant belongings. Shortly, however, the train braked, and halted with no station in sight. On one side lay an open field, beyond which, a hundred yards away, a tarmac road ran parallel with the railway line. Over a wide expanse of flat country beyond, the only signs of habitation were two distant farms.

When, ten minutes later, the train still had not moved, Iride whispered that it would be safer to get off here – a bit unorthodox, but they would think we were tired of waiting for the train to reach Palestrina. We signalled the others. Joe opened a door. Each of us jumped down on to the grass by the track. Up and down the length of the train, heads extended from every window, including those of five German soldiers in the adjacent coach. All eyes turned to watch as four British, two Americans and one Czech carrying awkward paper bundles picked their way across the open field. We reached the deserted roadway as a whistle blew and the train began to move. We waved. All waved back.

Seven miles ahead lay Rome. Light-hearted at having left the train without incident, we set off at a good pace. After only a mile banks of cloud blew up from the south and heavy rain started to fall. We ran to a nearby farm house. Here a woman allowed us to enter her kitchen. We dived into our packages of bread, cheese and salami from Sulmona, while Iride got the woman, who was studying us curiously, to make some ersatz coffee. Shortly, when the rain stopped, we filed out and took to the road again.

Two miles of steady walking brought us to a village just as another heavy shower started and we made for a large shed. Iride went off to reconnoitre. When she returned, by which time several villagers stood gazing at us, she brought the disturbing information that 500 yards beyond the village was a road-block manned by both German and Italian military police. She had seen them. No, there was no alternative road, and a detour, besides being lengthy, would probably draw suspicion. While we huddled, uncertain of the next move, more villagers gathered to stare.

'Look,' said Pollak, turning from a hasty conversation with Iride. 'She thinks she can get us right past the police at the road-block. We have identity cards. Our families are starving. We're coming to Rome to buy what we can. It's risky, but she thinks it'll work. She and I are going down there to check it some more. When we come back, if it looks like a fair risk, we'll signal you from the bend in the road down there.'

Six minutes later Gil Smith and I, ambling past shop windows, spotted Maria waving at the corner.

'Iride says you're going straight through the roadblock. Say nothing. Just produce your identity cards.'

'Sounds bloody unlikely to me!' muttered Gil, as Maria ran ahead to join Dukate and Furman. We followed a distance behind.

Three hundred yards ahead, on a long straight road large cylindrical drums blocked the highway. Iride stood with three uniformed figures. Apart from our group the road was deserted. Out ahead Pollak, Wilson and Rendell approached the critical spot. At the block two of the three men had moved over to the side of the road, leaving Iride talking to one tall figure wearing an Italian police uniform. Before him the trio halted, fumbled in their pockets. Then, to our immense relief, they walked on. Staying at the block with the Italian police officer, Iride looked back toward the rest of us.

Now Dukate and Furman came up with Maria. The policeman examined their cards and they too passed through.

Here goes! For the third time I checked my inside pocket to feel my Identity Card. The two figures who had moved off the road, a German military policeman and a civilian, were in conversation and paid little attention to the block. The Italian policeman, in a long buff greatcoat bearing Fascist insignia and an impressive mustard-coloured helmet, seemed remarkably tall for his race. He looked down at Iride as, with her hair tossing, she talked rapidly, presumably giving him the hard-luck story of us stupid simple *contadini*.

In front of a large rusted drum of concrete, we halted. '*Carta d'Identità*,' said the Fascist, stretching out his hand. Silently we presented the folded cards. He examined them, looked at us and studied the documents again. He hesitated. With a nervous laugh, Iride made some crack. Throwing us a quizzical look, he handed the documents back and nodded his helmet. We stepped through the opening between the drums. *Molto gentile, Signor. Tante grazie. Arriveder...*'

Tensely conscious of eyes on our backs, we kept walking, looking straight ahead. After showering gratitude on the policeman, Iride caught up with us. How she had carried off this coup we did not stop to ask.

Farther along the road we were overtaken by a horse drawing a two-wheeled farm cart. Iride waved the driver down. Yes, he would take us to the first tram terminus on the outskirts of the city. We clambered on, dumped our modest belongings in the back and took off at a trot. When we caught up with the others, we pulled their baggage on board. The small cart could carry no more passengers, but the driver agreed to return for them.

We trotted on briskly. Scattered farms soon gave way to roadside cottages and in turn to more built-up sections of shabby tenements and stores. The sun reappeared and Gil slapped my knee. Behind our broad smiles was more than a tinge of excitement. We were now riding along a street named Via Prenestina, about to enter the ancient heart of the most renowned empire in history.

Our cartwheels rattled to a stop in a cobbled *piazza*. Ahead, bearing the bold letters SPQR, stood a trolley car. The generous farmer went back to pick up the others. Once all reassembled, we clambered on to Iride's choice of a tram car.

Street traffic grew heavy as our tram, filling up with passengers at each stop, headed into modern Rome. On a signal from Iride, we eased past the other passengers to the rear tram door and stepped off into a noisy struggling crowd. On broad Via Cavour Iride turned into a doorway beside a polished brass wall-plate announcing 'Albergo Vulcania'. We followed her into a small hotel lobby. A good-looking, dark-haired girl came running downstairs and greeted Iride. As she listened to Iride's urgent explanation, her face at first registered astonishment and concern. Then, breaking into a sparkling smile, she beckoned us to follow her.

Upstairs, she ushered us into a spacious room. We gaped. To us it appeared elegant, the washhand basin with shining chrome taps, and a large double bed covered by a silk spread. As Iride left with the receptionist to check more rooms, each dusty face registered joyful disbelief. After prison camps and unsanitary Abruzzi slums the contrast was strong.

Gil ran the water. 'My god, hot!' he exclaimed.

Gina, the attractive receptionist, returned with her smartly dressed brother, Elio. He looked like a good type. With their father they ran the hotel. Hot baths? Right away. And our grubby clothes, how soon could they be cleaned? One big pile, Elio instructed. He would fix it. Chasing the girls out, we stripped down and stacked everything except our outer suits in the corner. Within an hour we had soaked in hot baths.

Elio warned us that we must be quiet and only move about with the utmost caution. Only a few nights ago the Fascist-controlled Metropolitan Police had checked the hotel and reviewed the guests' Identity Cards which Gina kept in a bunch at the reception desk each night. Ours were down there now. If the '*Metropolitini*' – by which diminutive this force was known to the average Roman – called again, the presence of several guests from Sulmona in far-off Abruzzi might occasion deeper inquiry. But for the time being Elio was prepared to risk this, as they had many transients each night. Germans? No, he said, the hotel was out of bounds to Germans. Food? No, the hotel did not serve meals; Iride would arrange to bring in food from a nearby restaurant.

Strange kind of hotel, I thought. Yet Iride knew it so well. When Elio left, we exchanged looks.

'Sounds like a shack-up joint to me,' observed Duke.

Joe Pollak had already gone out to look around. Now he returned with toothbrushes and razor blades.

Iride came back with a gentleman she had met on her previous trips on our behalf, M. De Vial of the Vichy French Ministry. In fluent

English he greeted us warmly. To each he handed 2000 lire. We signed a simple receipt.

'Oh, don't worry,' he said, 'they will repay me.'

'How can we find clothes?' asked John Furman.

'I'll let you know. I'm sure they can arrange it.'

Who were 'they' we wondered when he left.

Since entering the hotel we had smothered Iride with praise for the magnificent way in which she had piloted us to Rome. We were indeed grateful. Now, however, we sensed a new imperious air about her. When she and Maria were leaving to collect our first meal from a restaurant Gil Smith asked her to include a bottle of wine. Abruptly, she refused. We must have nothing to drink lest we become noisy. The last tense 48 hours had been virtually without sleep. Unwinding now in the warmth of this large bedroom, we were fatigued. Finally Pat Wilson, who still knew little Italian, showed his annoyance. She stamped her foot, but the expressions of the others, including Dennis, remained blank. She turned almost pleadingly to me. I gave her a slow wink, at which she tossed her long hair and marched out with Maria.

Half an hour later they returned carrying trays covered with napkin and, sure enough, a bottle of Chianti. Hungrily we shared modest portions of veal and spaghetti. With one glass of wine we toasted the two girls and thanked them again. Tired out, we rose to go to our rooms. Dennis looked uncomfortable. Six of us were sharing rooms. Iride had put Dennis by himself.

8

THE LADY SPURNED

In the morning Iride ordered that none of us budge from our 'common' room. Since our laundry had not yet returned, her remonstrance was somewhat irrelevant.

Despite her, Joe Pollak, the only owner of a spare shirt, went out early. In his absence Iride berated him all morning. He should be sent back to Sulmona. He was untrustworthy and dangerous. We let her rave on. Resourceful Joe was a threat to her sole command. Like us, she was probably wondering what would happen next. To keep her dashing Dennis, she must control the group; we were her captives.

We admired her for all she had risked of late, but something had changed her. Gil and I tried to joke with her, flatter her, but she was burning inside. Dennis and she were avoiding each other. I made a silent guess. Her cosy little scheme with Dennis last night must have misfired. In Sulmona, I felt sure, Dennis's idea had not gone beyond an innocent light-hearted, and useful, flirtation.

After lunch she started again. Dennis and Duke after a while became short with her. Aggravated, she turned to me for support, demanding that Joe be sent back to Sulmona forthwith. When I began to explain in a conciliatory tone that, at least for the present, we could not send him back, she flew into a temper. To prevent a worse scene, Joe, when he returned, kept out of her way.

In late afternoon an elderly French Monseigneur called, accompanied by a small bespectacled German Jewish gentleman. Pat Wilson, John Furman and Gil Smith urgently needed new suits and all of us required basic accessories, in order to appear more natural in Rome. The Monseigneur agreed and the little man soon filled his notebook with sizes for suits, shoes, shirts and hats. To supervise the buying, I was elected to go along with him the next morning. What about payment? No need to worry, said the Monseigneur. 'They' would look after that. That mysterious 'they' again!

Just as the quiet little German left, a young priest entered, pale, puffy-faced and fat. Nervously he clasped and unclasped pudgy hands until, sweeping into a deep bow, he fell on one knee before the Monseigneur and kissed his hand. Then he was introduced to each of us. His hand felt cold and moist. I did not care for Father Pasquale Perfetti. Iride had met him before. He was in touch, he explained, with many escaped prisoners both within and beyond the city, and was also helping many fugitive Jews.

When the old Monseigneur bade us goodnight and left, Iride immediately drew Perfetti into the hotel corridor. At an angle through the open door I watched her. She looked stern as she talked. While her arms gesticulated, the priest nodded and wrung his hands. Then she left him.

Perfetti signalled me to come outside. In Italian he explained that Iride was upset over the way we were treating her; she was having difficulty controlling us. Could I, who, Iride had said, was more understanding, try to make the others be reasonable? When I told him the other side of the story he smiled. I assured him I would keep Iride calm. He left, just as Elio and a maid brought back some laundry.

When Duke and I found we could dress completely, Elio offered to take the two of us out for a walk. Iride raised no objection and we left on our first exploration. Street lamps shone brightly and shop windows, trams and trolley-buses were lit up. Clearly Rome had no black-out: surprising, even if Rome was an 'Open City'. From the air it must be a beacon in the night. But maybe that was the idea, to protect the city against accidental bombing.

Though Elio spoke no English, we talked easily in Italian as we mixed with other pedestrians, and Duke could follow us quite well. The stroll felt good as Elio led us from Via Cavour on to a wide thoroughfare, Via dei Fori Imperiali. This was not ancient; it had been constructed by Mussolini as a grand avenue from – and he pointed behind us – the Colosseum, just dimly visible, then running the length of the ancient Roman Forum, barely discernible at a lower level on our left as we walked, to what now emerged in front of us, a huge ghostly white mass of statuary, the King Vittorio Emanuele II monument. Even more fascinating, just ahead but cordoned off by Italian Police, was the Piazza Venezia, almost familiar-looking from prewar newsreels of a frenzied Mussolini electrifying the cheering Fascist crowd from his famous balcony.

At 9.30 the next morning the little German Jew took me off to buy clothes. Since my German was worse even than his English, we struggled along in Italian.

'I take you to my headquarters ... someone else then go with you.' A tram ride and brief walk brought us to a red brick building on the corner of Via Sicilia. As my escort knocked on the heavy timber door, I noticed the number '62', the address Iride had given us back in Sulmona.

A square panel opened revealing a bearded face. The door swung and, when we entered, the owner of the beard, a Capuchin monk in long mauve-coloured robes, led us silently into a room where twenty people sat waiting.

'Jewish refugees,' whispered my little man. 'Say nothing and wait.' He disappeared. As I sat, a monk appeared at the door every few minutes and invited the next person forward.

My man reappeared and waved. In a rear office I was introduced to a smiling young Yugoslav Jew, who had himself been a prisoner of war in Italy. We set off. In a large department store my companion was joined by the manager, also Yugoslav. After an hour in the men's clothing department we walked out carrying four suits, three raincoats, seven hats, shirts and ties. My guide hailed a *carrozza*, a horse-drawn open carriage. We piled in with our parcels.

While this December day was cold, the sun was out and Rome looked bright. Noting my curiosity, the Yugoslav amiably explained our route, past the high ancient Egyptian obelisk in the centre of the Piazza del Popolo, through a high archway into Piazza Flaminio and then, veering uphill to the right, entering a long avenue arched by trees and rich with statues, at the end of which the sun played on a beautiful marble fountain. In the hubbub around the archways of Porta Pinciana German uniforms were everywhere.

Back at the hotel, all the clothing fitted and, with the return of the remaining laundry, each of us looked passable.

M. De Vial arrived and, when Iride was out of the room, announced that, upon hearing about Dukate and Wilson, the American Chargé d'Affaires in the Vatican had arranged for them to be admitted to the American College, an extraterritorial property on the Gianicolo Hill close to the Vatican. Not Vatican proper, he explained, but safe, and it had a mixed population of American clerical students, Jewish-American refugees and escaped prisoners. Duke and Pat elected to go. Gil Smith was keen to go with them. One more would probably be accepted, M. De Vial thought. He would confirm later, he said as he left.

This was the break-up of the gang, but it was only a matter of time anyway. We couldn't expect to move around as a group.

I was glad the College proposal did not apply to me. Rome had looked good this morning. It had been exhilarating to walk the same pavements as the Germans and mingle unnoticed with well-dressed citizens.

Iride overhead talk of a move and, seeing that no one volunteered information, remained coldly silent. De Vial had emphasized that no one must know about the American College. Beyond that, since apparently this morning the tension between Iride and the others had worsened, I began to feel that we would have to cut loose soon. If a move came, somehow we should tactfully avoid giving her details. She had shown glimpses of a vicious side; since her motivation was more venturesome than dutiful, her volatile streak could be dangerous.

When Joe Pollak returned, his face told us he had important news. Iride left the room. Joe had snooped around St Peter's Square, observed the Swiss Guards on duty at the Santa Marta entrance on the left of St Peter's. 'They're tough. Stop everyone, ask a lot of questions.' He had stopped two priests. 'I struck it lucky with the second one. I told him about us, that I had to make contact inside. He took me across the Piazza to a side entrance, into the Holy Office building. It's "extraterritorial", whatever that means. He went off and came back with a big tall priest called Monsignor O'Flaherty. I understand he's the important fellow in the background. He's mixed up with a whole crowd of escapers around here. He's got a British Major working with him. His name's Derry.'

'Did you see him, Joe?'

'No, but I mentioned I'd been in Chieti and Sulmona. He told me Major Derry had been in Chieti. So I told him our story.'

This had to be the Sam Derry we all knew.

'Apparently this Irish Monsignor and Derry are running quite an organization. I told him what we had done in Sulmona; he wants to know more about it, wants one of you to report to him on the whole situation there.'

'Well done, Joe,' said John. 'Sam Derry and this Monsignor must be the people De Vial was talking about.'

Elected, as the senior in rank, to report, Dennis left in the morning for St Peter's with Joe Pollak. Iride did not openly protest, but resumed her sullen silence. The night before she had thrown more biting insults directly at Joe in front of us. Joe had held his tongue and left the room.

Now, when she and Maria brought in a late breakfast of coffee and rolls to the large bedroom, she ignored our attempts to be cordial. The pretty face had vanished. She looked hard. Disgusted with her bursts of temper, Dennis had made it clear that her attentions were not appreciated. Now he had gone out, and with that detestable Joe!

M. De Vial arrived to pick up Dukate and Wilson. The American College would take Smith too, he said, and Gil quickly gathered his things. As all three again thanked Iride and Maria, Iride unfroze temporarily and smiled.

'You will come in my car,' said M. De Vial. His illegal passengers followed him out.

Like myself, John Furman had no desire to go into seclusion. Back in Sulmona, weakness following his dysentery had stopped him from being active. Now he had regained his strength and already he spoke fair Italian, albeit with deliberate London modulation. Some ability in German he had too, far ahead of mine. A chartered accountant by profession, John was precise, clear-thinking and resourceful by nature. I admired him, and the longer I knew him, the better I liked him.

As we sat speculating, our ideas ran along similar lines. The Derry-O'Flaherty business sounded interesting, and we were restive.

The door opened and Joe stood in the opening alone.

'Where's...' I began, but Joe was waving us outside. Something was up. We entered my room and Joe handed me a note from Dennis. He was not coming back. Joe would explain. An opportunity had been offered, and he had felt it wisest to take it. Would I explain to Iride how sorry he was not to see her again. I shook my head and passed the note to John.

'We're in for a happy evening!' he remarked. 'But what's the story, Joe?'

'We got there all right and met Monsignor O'Flaherty. He took us up to his private room in the German College and Major Derry joined us. Dennis gave them the run-down on Sulmona, and they had us stay for lunch. Funny, German nuns serving lunch! Sam left, and Dennis, well, told the Monsignor about Iride. He was embarrassed by her attention, but didn't want to hurt her after all she had done. O'Flaherty phoned somebody, then told Dennis the American College would take him too, tonight. The other three were being brought to his office at seven, so he might as well wait. No point in coming back here.'

Derry was keen to see us. He had suggested we call on him the next evening after dark.

'Come on, let's face it!' As I entered Iride's room, she stopped combing her long dark hair. She sensed something. Quietly I explained. Dennis had been taken to a safe hideout, had been given no chance to come back. He was eternally grateful, and this was goodbye. To my surprise, she betrayed no emotion, shrugged her shoulders and, with a weak smile, resumed combing her hair. John had followed me in. Joe was outside. I admired his restraint, but something had to be done.

'Joe, come on in.' Hesitantly he joined us.

'Let's all go out to dinner.' Iride forced a smile.

Later, seated around a corner table in the busy Ristorante del' Opera, near the Opera house, Iride ordered our dinner. This was our first venture into a restaurant. The black-market steak and the rich *zabaglione* were good. On the way back to the hotel, in a jovial mood in spite of the chill night air, I held Iride's arm. If John, Joe and I had to move off somewhere soon, I asked her gently, what would she and Maria do? Probably go back to Sulmona, she answered easily.

I felt lighter as we turned into the warm Albergo Vulcania and left our identity cards with Gina at the desk.

1. "*Campo di Concentramento* P.G. 21 at Chieti, safely isolated near the Adriatic coast of Central Italy" (p.7).

2. Captain Dennis Rendell, of the 2nd Parachute Regiment, at Sulmona Fair in November, 1943. Two German soldiers look on (see p.9).

3. "A big tall priest called Monsignor O'Flaherty... the important fellow in the background" (p.52).

4. Sir D'Arcy Osborne, British Minister to the Holy See (see p.57).

5. "Major Samuel Ironmonger Derry, MC, RA of Newark, Nottinghamshire" (p.57).

6. "John May was of medium build, with strong features, heavy eyebrows and a shock of greying hair standing up almost straight" (p.66).

7. The author with "Gina, the pretty young hotel manageress with whom I was becoming increasingly friendly" (p.73).

8. "Their niece, Dedy, was bright-eyed and spoke faultless English" (p.76). With the author, January, 1944.

9

IRISH PROTAGONIST

The evening of 10 December was dark and wet when three raincoated civilians stepped off a 34 trolley-bus.

'This way,' whispered Joe Pollak, fastening his coat collar and leading us from the deserted bus station. But John Furman and I paused in awe. Before us stood St Peter's Square. My eye traced the dark outline of the high colonnade encircling the immense *piazza* and, through the heavy rain, strained to make out the façade of St Peter's at the far end. The famous dome was hardly visible.

'Come on! Don't stand here! Look, over there.' Joe tugged on my sleeve. Nearby two German soldiers carrying automatic rifles paced slowly between sentry boxes. Halfway round the outside of the left colonnade, Joe led us across a quiet street to a massive door built into a high stone wall. He knocked. A small door set in the big one opened. '*C'abbiamo un' appuntamento con Monsignor O'Flaherty,*' said Joe briskly. A civilian porter waved us through into a paved courtyard and led us across to a dark building, up steps and into a long narrow lighted room. From a group of four men seated around a table at the far end a tall figure rose quickly and came toward us. Major Samuel Derry was beaming. We shook his hand.

'Look, stay here for a minute or two till I finish with these chaps.'

The door behind us opened and a tall, bare-headed figure in a long black cassock appeared. He walked up to Joe and spoke to him in Italian. Joe introduced John and me. We shook a large powerful hand. As he greeted us with a mellow Irish lilt, his friendly blue eyes were studying us through steel-rimmed spectacles. A broad grin emphasized a strong jaw and an irregular ample nose. He disappeared in a rustle of silk.

The group around the table included one Italian. From the alternate

English and broken Italian, they were working out the cost of maintaining two English escapers in a flat. Finally they reached agreement, and the small Italian, whose thin face and narrow black beady eyes did not impress me, departed.

The atmosphere livened as we exchanged greetings with two exceptional Englishmen. Captain P.J. ('Pip') Gardner VC had been a prisoner with us in Chieti. A live bearer of the Victoria Cross was rare. Lieutenant Colonel Robert 'Tug' Wilson DSO had come ashore from a British submarine behind enemy lines north of Naples, in a canoe loaded with explosives, and demolished ammunition dumps and a railroad tunnel. Weeks ago they had come to Rome hoping to enter the Vatican. At the Santa Marta gate they had tried to rush the Swiss Guards, only to be unceremoniously ejected. The little Italian who had just left, Nebulanti, was fixing them up with a flat and a cook.

When Sam Derry indicated his wish to confer with us, Gardner and Wilson joined a waiting escort and left. Pollak discreetly moved to the other end of the long room with a newspaper.

Back in the Chieti camp Sam had been the enthusiastic head of the Escape Committee. As in every prison camp, no escape could be attempted without the unqualified approval of this vital committee. We had soon covered events in Sulmona and asked Sam how he came to be here.

'The first day at the Sulmona Camp,' Sam recalled, 'I had an absolute "sitter" of a chance, but just then the SBO [Senior British Officer] called for me and I had to pass it up. Then I heard about you fellows. I was desperate.'

The first night on the train from Sulmona had been trying. Each coach was heavily guarded. After sitting all day in a siding near Rome, the train resumed its journey north at dusk. A guard let Sam go to the lavatory at the rear of his carriage where two guards had their backs to him in the poor light. A window two feet from him was open.

'I hopped up on the sill,' Sam continued. 'Couldn't make out a thing ... and jumped. I was lucky. I hit the ground with a tremendous thud, but it was grass.'

Friendly *contadini* gave him a haybarn and put him in touch with scores of other ex-POWs. A local priest who 'knew' somebody in the Vatican took a letter from Sam, listing names and numbers. The priest returned with another, Father Perfetti, who brought an anonymous English letter, along with cash and clothing which Sam soon distributed. A week later he sent back a statement with receipts.

This orderliness had impressed both Monsignor O'Flaherty and Sir

D'Arcy Osborne, British Minister to the Holy See, both of whom were concerned by the burgeoning traffic of escapers coming into Rome. Some senior-ranking officer could assist them in organizing and controlling this traffic. Through continuing diplomatic communication facilities, via Switzerland and Spain, Sir D'Arcy initiated a speedy security check on a certain Major Samuel Ironmonger Derry, MC, RA, of Newark, Nottinghamshire. Clearance came back quickly.

Thus Sam accepted a courier's invitation to come into Rome to visit a British diplomat. To pass the road block, a farm cart carried him buried under a load of vegetables. Monsignor O'Flaherty, dressing him as a priest, had smuggled him right into the Vatican, to Sir D'Arcy. There he learned that Monsignor Hugh O'Flaherty of the Congregation of the Holy Office, previously an official Vatican visitor to Allied POW camps and well remembered by many, had been besieged since the September Armistice by liberated POWs converging on Rome, many expecting to penetrate the Vatican's neutral territory.

In response the Monsignor had assembled a network of friends – priests, foreign seminarians, Roman nobility and a Maltese lady called Mrs Chevalier – to find temporary homes in Rome for these fugitives, with remarkable success except for supporting funds. Into the breach had come his long-standing friend who had opposed the Fascist régime from the start, Prince Filippo Doria Pamphilj, who, with a cash gift of 150,000 lire, had facilitated the expansion of Monsignor O'Flaherty's organization to meet the growing demands. 'He's not just involved with our chaps,' Sam said. 'Rome's full of Jewish refugees from all over Europe; he's hiding them, too.'

By October Monsignor O'Flaherty had been forced to seek financial help from the British Minister who, while a consummate diplomat, relented enough from his strict posture of observing the Vatican State's neutrality to develop streams of funds from the British Foreign Office via Switzerland, Spain and through a Barclays Bank manoeuvre with a financial entity within the Vatican.

But a military man of rank was required. Sam was that man.

'Need any help?' asked John.

'Certainly do!'

'Bill and I are ready. Our Italian's pretty good.'

'Excellent!' Sam beamed. 'I can use you right here in Rome. Let me fill you in.' Sam leaned closer. Joe, at the end of the room, was still reading.

'Incidentally, I wasn't at all sure of Joe when he popped up here. Remember the fuss with him and some of those Cypriots at Chieti, before the Ities moved them away? But after what Rendell, and now you, tell me, I imagine he's okay. Now the dope – for your ears only.'

Inside Rome 150 escapers – British, South African, some Americans – were hidden with families, in religious colleges and special flats. Outside the city, to date he had records of over 2000, whom they were trying to keep supplied. He was setting up a card index record for each one. Answering messages alone took time and he had little to work with.

To operate, he was sharing the Monsignor's room in the adjoining building, the German College, which was not Vatican proper but extra-territorial. It allowed him to come and go by the same door we had used tonight, without going near the Swiss Guards.

'Don't tell me you go out into Rome yourself,' I said, eyeing his huge frame and ill-fitting navy blue suit.

'Oh, certainly! I've been visiting some of the boys, but mostly after dark. I have to take somebody along. My Italian's lousy!'

The odd ones and twos scattered with families in town were super-vised by some Maltese and Irish priests. Without ration cards and bread coupons, food had to come from the black market. Each man was paid a hundred lire a day. Whenever possible, every two weeks, they paid the landlady, who had to buy the food. The hundred lire left nothing over.

'Two weeks ago we managed to rent two big flats in the city. They're rented in Italian names, real names. At the moment the two flats are housing twenty-four!' One, the 'Opera Flat', on Via Firenze near the Opera House, held ten British and South African soldiers. The other, on Via Chelini in the Parioli area, was fancier and housed fourteen officers, South African and British, along with a cook, an Austrian Jewish girl, who was hiding as they were. It could take more in an emergency, but Sam preferred to keep reserve space.

'Main problem is feeding them,' Sam continued. 'They need an awful lot of food every day and it has to be black market. We've got a Maltese woman, a Mrs Chevalier – we call her "Mrs M" – who collects the sup-plies every day. She's got good black-market friends. Also has a bunch of daughters. Manages to keep some of our escaped fellows in her big flat too.'

'She buys food for all these?' I asked.

'Every day, for thirty odd! I pay her, of course, and it costs a lot! It's damned bulky, a huge job to distribute. That's what I'd like you to do, for a start. It'd really help.'

We readily accepted. Joe would return on the morrow for directions. Sam handed us 3000 lire each, our 'month's allowance', and a few thou-sand extra for expenses for which we would account later.

'Sam, one quick point,' I said. 'Rendell probably mentioned the possibility of using Joe back in Sulmona. What d'you think?' I smiled apologetically at Joe.

'No, not now anyway,' replied Sam. 'He'll be better here.' Joe sighed.

In the middle of a large *risotto* in the Ristorante del Opera, we spotted Iride and Maria dining in the far corner. With them sat a man. Good! If they had friends in the city, our responsibility was lightened.

10

ROMAN FLATS

A grocery store and a butcher's shop flanked No. 12 Via Imperia. Through an archway and up three flights of stairs Furman and I followed Pollak. At the flat marked No. 9 Joe rang the bell – three short rings and a long one. A very young girl opened the door. Behind her appeared a short woman in a long dressing-gown.

'*Buon giorno*,' began Joe. 'Mrs M? We're from Major Derry.'

The woman's face lit up. She beckoned us inside and shut the door.

'I expected you.' Mrs Chevalier smiled as we introduced ourselves. Two young girls, who had been screaming at each other, fell silent.

'My daughters, Gemma and Mary,' said Mrs Chevalier, slightly embarrassed. Probably in her late forties, she was still an attractive woman; her hair was tidily set and she wore lipstick. Her silk robe was neatly wrapped around a full figure.

Two other girls appeared and inspected us. Matilda, younger than Gemma, was slim, serious and shy. The other, about twelve, was an imp. Pouting, she ran off with a high-pitched laugh into a room where an older female voice angrily silenced her. The voice appeared drying her hands on an apron. Rosie, Mrs M's oldest daughter, ran the kitchen and tried to manage this large family for her mother. She was plain and did not care.

'Come and meet Grandma, the seventh female in the house.' We followed Mrs M into a large kitchen, where a bright fire burned in a wide grate. Baskets of vegetables and fruit stood on the floor, and large chunks of red meat lay on the table. In the corner by the window an old woman sat in a low chair peeling potatoes. Mrs M's mother, as she looked up, smiled faintly and resumed peeling.

'Some family,' I said, confused.

'Oh, that's not all.' She led us to another door in the corridor and pushed it open. Four men lay in one huge bed, their faces turned to us. 'Good morning!' said the four in unison. As Mrs M introduced us to her four private escapers, they climbed out of the bed fully dressed.

'They hop into bed every time someone comes to the door,' she explained. She had sheltered them here for weeks. Two were survivors of the British submarine *Saracen*, sunk off the west coast of Italy six months before, and one was an anti-aircraft gunner from Northern Ireland. The fourth, a sergeant parachutist, had never been taken prisoner; after dropping behind the lines in northern Italy and completing his mission, he had worked his way south. On the way he fell ill and was cared for by peasants. Later a priest brought him to Rome, to Monsignor O'Flaherty.

'You should've seen him when he first arrived.' Mrs M shook her head. 'He was pitiful. Had scabies, lice and a high fever, all at once.'

'That's true,' said the parachutist, 'and in two weeks she had me all fixed up.'

Since the flat had only two bedrooms, it was hard to see where everybody slept.

'At night,' Mrs M explained, 'we make up three beds in the sitting-room and two in my room for the girls, and another two in the kitchen for Grandma and Rosie.' She made it sound easy.

Near lunchtime Mrs M's only son Paul came in. He was twenty and employed by the Swiss Legation, in that part which for the duration of the war was 'caretaker' for British interests in Rome, and was actually located in the spacious residence quarters of the British Embassy. The Legation, he informed us, had a supply of Red Cross food parcels, sent earlier in the war for distribution to some British subjects who were too old for internment camps, but hard up financially. When some escapers started calling looking for help the Legation decided to issue one parcel every two weeks to anyone who risked going personally to get it. We noted the address. The parcels contained valuable food items.

In the sitting-room Mrs Chevalier explained how she ran things. Except for a slight Maltese accent, her English was faultless.

'I've a very good butcher friend, Giovanni, whom I can trust. You passed his *macelleria* coming in. It's seldom that he can't give me all the meat I need. A baker down the street gives me plenty of bread without ration coupons. Giovanni gets his friends to buy sugar and other difficult stuff on the black market. They don't know what he does with it. The girls here go out in the morning to buy the uncontrolled things like potatoes, fruit and vegetables. Major Derry sends me money in advance, and I send him an account.'

Each morning the food, divided according to the number of mouths in the two flats, was packed into two large suitcases and, if required, into additional straw carrier bags.

'The biggest problem is delivering the stuff,' Mrs M went on. Carrying large cases attracted attention, and the local police were alert for black marketeers. The system was hit or miss. Father Borg and Brother Robert had taken them today. Monsignor O'Flaherty sent different people. Sometimes, when nobody arrived, two of the older girls had to step in, but it was too onerous and too risky for them.

'We'll start tomorrow,' said John. Gemma would take Joe Pollak to the flats today to learn the route.

Following directions from our friendly waiter at the Ristorante dell' Opera, John and I set out to explore the Red Cross food parcel situation at the Swiss Legation.

At Porta Pinciana curiosity drew us to the famed Via Veneto. Here Germans abounded. Outside the impressive Hotel Flora stood steel-helmeted German sentries. Further down the street, the even more elegant Hotel Excelsior was also heavily guarded, not surprisingly as it was headquarters of the German SS, the élite *Schutzstaffeln*. From the news kiosk across the street we assessed the sentries' sharp uniforms and sidearms. Next down the curving street, the American Embassy was also manned by Swiss.

Half a mile away Via Montebello was quiet when we opened the solid door in the wall of the British Embassy building. A polished brass plate explained the caretaker occupancy of the Swiss. Inside, when we declared our identity, a receptionist ushered us upstairs to the office of a Captain Trippi. This distinguished old gentleman, we soon found, was rather deaf. He barely smiled as he made notes.

'D'you have many British fellows coming here?' I asked, to make conversation, but at that moment he seemed particularly deaf. He looked up, handed us a note authorizing the issuance of two Red Cross parcels and directed us downstairs to a storeroom.

Below, an attractive blonde Swiss girl fetched two of the familiar oblong parcels and wrapped them in brown paper. To our delight, she handed each of us a packet of twenty Player's cigarettes. Promising to do more business in two weeks, we left. Outside in the quiet street, nobody appeared to be watching. This was too easy.

★ ★ ★

When Furman, Pollak and I arrived at Mrs M's at 10 the next morning,

Rosie and Mrs M stood in her kitchen over baskets, sacks, food and scales, as they packed supplies for each flat. At 11 am Furman and I picked up the two heavy suitcases and Pollak two carrier bags. Gemma, from a window, signalled that the street below was clear of strangers. At the front door Mrs M stopped us.

'Wait till I signal you,' she whispered. 'Fascist neighbours here ... one bad family right across the landing.' Slowly she half-opened the door and slipped outside. She looked up and down the narrow well of the stairway, waved, and we staggered out with our burdens.

With much switching of hands, we boarded a tram at Piazza Salerno and stood beside our cases on the rear platform. At the first halt, jostling through a waiting crowd, we switched to a packed 'Circolare Rosso'. A mile north along Viale Regina Margherita and the tree-bordered Viale Liège, at busy Piazza Ungheria, we transferred again, to a small tram this time, half empty. Alighting at a deserted halt, we dragged the cargo down a long flight of steps to Via Chelini which ran through blocks of modern apartment buildings. A hundred yards further, with Joe ahead of us to check the entrance, we turned into a lobby.

To reach Via Chelini we had travelled to the very northern end of Rome, to the Parioli, which, built on the most northerly of the Seven Hills, was clearly a superior residential quarter of the city.

In answer to Joe's three shorts and a long on the bell, the left ground-floor door opened quietly. Inside, perspiring, we dropped our loads.

Herta, an attractive blonde girl who had answered the door, led us with all but one suitcase through a wide hall and down a narrow stair to a clean, well-equipped kitchen in the basement. A sophisticated cook, I thought, and then remembered she too was in hiding. As Herta tackled the contents, we came back upstairs.

In a living room across the hall part of the flat's complement of four-teen officers in civilian clothes rose from armchairs and sofas to meet us. Three South African officers had once been with us at Chieti. Major D'Arcy Mander, the senior officer, and Captain MacAulay, a British Army medical officer, were new to us. A South African sergeant, Burns, and four British soldiers helped to run the place.

'Simpson, any way of getting these to Sam Derry?' asked Major Mander, holding out some envelopes.

'I'm going this afternoon.'

Reappearing at the door, the lovely Herta lifted the cover of the peep-hole and checked the outside lobby. We left with the one full suitcase and some 'empties'. Two long tram rides brought us south across the city to Rome's giant railway terminal. Past the Opera House on Via Firenze, we turned into an entrance between a barber's shop and the Hotel del'Opera. At the top of one flight of dark stairs, Joe gave the 'V' ring on the first door. It opened an inch. An eye peering out recognized Joe and the cases. The door opened.

The flat was spacious, if dismal, and appeared adequately furnished. From various rooms men joined us in the kitchen, where the appointed 'cook' was already checking the supplies. Sergeant-Major Billett, the South African Warrant Officer in charge, was a tall, heavily built fellow with whom nobody there would probably take liberties, but he was soft-spoken and good-humoured, and the other men, British and South African, seemed to like him.

Yes, they told us, the place was all right, the confinement was boring, the grub was good and they were short on smokes.

After dark, Sergeant-Major Billett and another South African sergeant went out, when they had an escort, to buy odd things. All twelve, however, were rigged out in fair-fitting civilian suits.

Joe volunteered to take the 'empties' back to Mrs M's. I boarded a No. 34 bus for St Peter's. After these exertions I had one question for Sam. For this job each morning, could the 'old firm' stand the price of a horse-drawn *carrozza*?

11

BUTLER EXTRAORDINAIRE

A bright December sun tempered the cold breeze as I gazed for the first time in daylight at the scene in Piazza San Pietro at the stately grey façade of St Peter's and Michelangelo's massive dome rising to a glistening sphere of gold, topped by a simple cross. The graceful colonnade, four columns deep, flanked the wide-stepped approach to the basilica, before sweeping out in symmetrical arcs around the long circular boundary of the piazza, right down to where I stood, humble and awed as I noted the girth and height of just one grey column rising from its base, some twelve paces around in circumference. Atop the colonnade scores of saintly figures seemed in motion across silhouetting white clouds.

Down in the geometrically cobbled piazza people strolled in the sun. Dotted among them were German soldiers. Reluctantly I moved on. Close by, two German military police patrolled back and forth along a white line painted on the cobblestones across the entrance to the piazza.

At the high doorway of the Sant'Ufficio beyond the colonnade I entered through the small inset door. The courtyard inside was unattended, but I found the office where we had conferred several nights before. Neither Sam nor the Monsignor were here, but a young Italian offered to escort me to the Monsignor's room. He led me across another cobbled courtyard into a tall building opposite. Past long corridors, heavy doors, spacious lobbies and a silent library, we climbed some stairs and finally arrived at a door in a bright corridor. The youth knocked, announced me and departed. Sam and the Monsignor were bustling around opposite sides of a table set for lunch.

'How on earth did you get up here?' asked Sam, looking surprised.

'Oh, we're getting around. Hello, Monsignor.' The powerful handshake was here again. 'Actually I came to deliver these letters from Major Mander and Mrs M.'

'Good. You'll stay for lunch, won't you?' invited the Monsignor, as Sam began opening and reading the letters.

'Thank you, if I'm not intruding.'

A nun entered silently, carrying a laden tray. The Monsignor spoke to her in German, and she hastened off again, to return with more cutlery and dishes. Sam poured two glasses of Orvieto wine and held one out to me. I hesitated.

'Don't worry, Bill. The Monsignor here doesn't mind us drinking his wine, but he never touches it himself.'

The Monsignor pulled up a third chair and beckoned us to sit down.

'So you've met the Chevaliers,' Sam resumed.

'And their four lodgers. Don't know how that woman does it. We made our first deliveries this morning.'

'Yes? How are all the lads in the flats?' asked Sam.

'Oh, they're all in good shape. If the weight of those rations is any indication, they do all right. We changed trams five times this morning. D'you mind if we try hiring a *carrozza* tomorrow?'

'Certainly not, if you think you can get away with it,' Sam replied.

In the middle of lunch, the door opened.

''Ello everybody! Ow's yer knees an' things?' said a loud Cockney voice.

'Hello, John,' said Sam, rising to meet the newcomer. 'Bill, meet John May. John, this is Bill Simpson, one of the fellows helping us with the flats.' John May was of medium build, with strong features, heavy eyebrows and a shock of greying hair standing up almost straight. He looked formal in a white shirt, grey tie, black jacket and grey striped trousers.

'Ah, you're the fellow oo's been spending fousands of lire on clothes, eh?' he exclaimed.

'What exactly do you mean?'

'Yesterday I received a bill for 20,000 lire for clothes you bought for yourself, Smith, Dukate and the others. Spent far too much, you did. Oo the devil d'you think's going to pay for it all?'

I felt my blood rising but, as calmly as possible, explained the arrangements we had made with the French Monseigneur and with the Jewish helpers brought to us by M. De Vial.

'They gave us to understand we could buy what we needed at reasonable prices, and I personally went along and bought this stuff in good faith. Now, if there's to be any argument about the bill, I'm sure the matter can be adjusted as soon as I and the others are in a position to do so.' Who was this jerk anyway, I was wondering. John May began to smile. Sam and the Monsignor seemed amused too. I took my cue.

Lunch over, the Monsignor led me out of the room, ostensibly to show me the rear view of St Peter's dome from a corridor window.

'Bill, don't you worry about John May. He's Sir D'Arcy's butler. He has his own way of needling people. He's a fine fellow really, and he's working very hard with us.' From the Monsignor's tone, he had a high regard for May. Besides acting as liaison between the Minister, Sam and himself, May had important contacts on the outside. The tall, grey-haired priest took off with fast silent strides to keep an appointment.

When I re-entered the room, John May looked up from the papers he and Sam were discussing and turned with an obvious effort to be cordial. Apparently Captain Henry Judson Byrnes, of the Royal Canadian Army Service Corps, an ex-prisoner now legally inside the Vatican, was aiding by developing the card index Sam needed.

'What about this "Open City" business?' I asked. 'I see Germans all over the place.'

'Lot of nonsense! Certainly, they've stopped major troop movements through the city, but that doesn't matter to them anyway. Most of the Germans you see are on leave here from the Front, but the city's loaded with SS and Gestapo. The Hotel Flora and the Excelsior are their head-quarters; they make no bones about it.'

'Furman and I passed there yesterday.'

'Oh, you did? Well, Via Veneto's a good place to stay away from.'

'Did the Monsignor tell you about his party at the Hungarian Embassy last week?' May asked. I shook my head.

Rome's Gestapo already knew of the Monsignor's leading role in helping Allied escapers. Efforts to catch him red-handed had so far failed. Cautioning from Derry and May he ignored. At the Hungarian reception the German Ambassador to the Vatican, Baron Ernst von Weizsäcker, had given him a clear warning. While respecting his position, the German authorities found his activities unacceptable. They would permit him a safe return to the Vatican that night, but he'd better not step outside again.

'He laughed it off as a big joke,' said Sam, shaking his head.

The door opened, and a tall young priest entered. Father Owen Sneddon came from New Zealand and among other duties now made regular broadcasts in English on Vatican Radio. These were peppered with names and numbers. The War Office in London monitored and notified families that the 'names' were alive somewhere.

'Bill Simpson? Funny, you're the reason I came over. Here's a letter.'

'For me?' As the priest turned to talk to Sam, I opened it. It was from

Dennis Rendell. Up in the American College, he and the other three were quickly going crackers. The place was all right, but life was disgustingly dull. They wanted out – fast. Could I possibly find them a billet outside in the city, and how soon? I had thought this might happen, but not quite so quickly.

The Monsignor returned, pulled open some drawers and tossed me some pairs of socks, cigarettes, a tie and a pot of jam.

'About all I have left, Bill. Your *benedetti Inglese* have ruined my wardrobe.'

With a full briefcase I left. The Monsignor, whose timely arrival had saved me from having to explain Dennis's letter to Sam or John May, accompanied me out. Yes, he chuckled, he had given away all his regular clothes, all except one pair of white golf trousers.

In the busy evening tram I pondered Dennis's call for help. Joe, John and I were still sleeping in the Hotel Vulcania, thanks to the patience and friendship of Elio and his sister Gina. I couldn't bring them back there. Since the Monsignor and others had taken trouble to place Dennis, Pat, Duke and Gil in the American College, I couldn't let the Monsignor, or even Sam, know they were dissatisfied. Sam would be annoyed, embarrassed. I'd have to find a place and then present a plan to Sam.

At Mrs M's the following morning Joe Pollak and I were preparing to deliver the rations ourselves – but by *carrozza*. Joe went off to find one. Twenty minutes later Gemma shouted from the window that a *carrozza* had stopped along the street. Joe came upstairs. When Gemma, watching the street, and Mrs M on the stairway signalled that the road was clear, Joe and I moved downstairs with the two heavy cases and one overflow straw carrier with cabbages sprouting over the brim, and walked along to the *carrozza*. When we were on board with the cargo, Joe told the driver where to go and we were off at a trot.

The *carrozza* followed the same route the trams had taken. Since the main danger now lay in the local Italian police, who were on the alert for black-market traffickers, we sat far back under the canopy. The bulky cargo at our feet was obvious. In the Piazza Ungheria a traffic policeman stared at us, but nothing happened.

For the Chelini flat the *carrozza* drove us to the front door. The driver agreed to wait while we delivered half the cargo. Outside the Opera flat, Joe paid off the driver – 300 lire and worth it. We had completed our deliveries in half the time, with little effort.

Inside the Opera flat today, something was amiss. The men were subdued. The night before, Sergeant-Major Billett explained, the other

South African had gone out to buy a few things and had not returned. By now they assumed he had been picked up by police. Perhaps Rome was not as easy as it looked.

12

ENTER RENZO LUCIDI

Back on the pavement in front of the shops on Via Cavour, near the
Hotel Vulcania, I recognized a smart young man I had previously met
with Elio in the hotel. He was walking towards me with a slightly older
man in an overcoat. I was going to walk straight on, but he spotted me,
stopped, shook hands vigorously and to my surprise introduced me to
his companion, Signor Renzo Lucidi. Crowds were passing, and for a
moment I felt uncomfortable.

'Don't worry, we're old friends,' Signor Lucidi explained in good
English, probably observing my concern. 'He knows how I feel politically. This morning he told me he'd met some Englishmen down here at
the Vulcania. I begged him to let me meet you.' Lucidi's English was
fluent. I relaxed. He was about five-foot-seven, stockily built, dapper,
with bright blue eyes under his grey felt hat. 'My wife's French,' he
went on, 'and used to be a secretary in London. She'd be delighted to
meet you. Won't you come around to our flat for tea this afternoon?'

I hadn't 'come for tea' anywhere in years. Now to hear this in perfectly natural English on Via Cavour in enemy Rome – but Lucidi was
smiling at me, waiting.

'Why, er, of course, I'd be delighted.' I liked the look of him. He
agreed to pick me up at the hotel later.

At 3 o'clock Lucidi and I boarded a crowded bus and soon were
walking across the many tram lines in Piazza Flaminio, down a quiet
side-street lined by high blocks of flats, till we turned into No. 18 Via
Scialoia. A lift took us to the top floor, where we entered the only door
on the landing. At the end of a long dark hallway we arrived in a bright,
well-furnished living-room. A tall vivacious woman with bright red hair
rushed forward, arms outstretched, and planted a large kiss on my
cheek.

'Welcome to our home! So wonderful to see you,' Signora Lucidi exclaimed excitedly, 'and look, I am wearing this in your *honneur.*' Stepping back, she fanned out her pleated skirt to show off the bright colours and design of its Scottish tartan. 'You are the first Briton to arrive in our home, and Renzo told me you are a Scot.'

Behind her stood a tall dark-haired, bespectacled youth, dressed in a tweed jacket and grey trousers. Signora Lucidi then introduced me to her son Gerald. As we sat down midst a battery of questions, a handsome young fellow, about eleven years old, came into the room. Maurice was their younger son.

Conversation was fast. I briefed them on our group from Sulmona. Renzo, 38, was half-Italian and half-Danish. While in Paris learning the hotel business, he had met and married Adrienne, the effusive Signora Lucidi, whose son Gerald was by a previous marriage. Later, in Venice, Renzo's rather vocal anti-Fascist sentiments had ultimately forced him into liquidation of his small hotel there. Then he had entered the comparatively young Italian film industry. Until a few months ago he had been earning a good living as a film cutter and editor. He looked highly intelligent and capable. Even as he took charge of the tea tray which their maid Pepina brought in, he had a business-like air. Meanwhile Adrienne cut in frequently with derisive shafts against Fascists and bursts of venom against Germans.

'How long have you been staying at the Vulcania?' Renzo asked.

'About two weeks, but I don't know how much longer John, Joe and I can stay there. We're paying our way, but we're a definite risk to them.' Adrienne and Renzo looked at each other for a long moment, the first silence since I had entered.

'Why don't you all come and live here with us?' said Adrienne, more calmly. 'We've got enough room, and we'd be happy to have you.'

This was a surprise. The flat was comfortable, and the atmosphere obviously convivial.

'Are you sure?' I asked.

'Of course,' said Renzo, nodding emphatically. 'When can you move in?'

'I'll tell John and Joe tonight. I'm sure they'll want to come. You're very kind but, if you don't mind me saying this, we must put this on a business basis.' Since most of the film studios had moved to Northern Italy following the Armistice back in September, I suspected that Renzo had no current job.

'I must admit,' Renzo said, 'we're no different from others in Rome right now. We're living on what we've saved, and we're rapidly running

71

out.' I mentioned our allowance. With a quick mental calculation, no doubt of black-market prices, Renzo concluded that he could work it out.

'What about your other four friends from Sulmona?' asked Renzo. 'Have you heard from them?'

I had not divulged their present hide-out. Now I mentioned the letter I had just received from Dennis, and confessed I did not know where to begin to find them a place.

'Renzo, what about Père Meunier? You know, at the French Seminary?' Adrienne asked. Renzo pondered, but Adrienne was becoming excited again.

'Yes, I must ask him,' she went on. 'Already he has some French Jews hiding there. Perhaps he could take your friends too.'

After arranging to meet Renzo the following afternoon, I thanked them warmly and left. On the way downstairs I felt dazed; Adrienne's non-stop conversation in staccato English and pungent French accent was overpowering. So also was the sudden turn in events. At the hotel later, John and Joe were equally happy over this bit of luck.

The next morning the black-market food delivery went without incident. This time our *carrozza* driver was such a pleasant and seemingly tactful old man that Joe asked him if he would like to be hired by us every morning. He nodded eagerly and agreed to be near the *macelleria* each morning at 10.30.

Back at the Lucidis' that afternoon the news was good. They were ready to receive the three of us. Furthermore, Adrienne had been to see her old friend Père Meunier, who had agreed to accommodate Dennis and Co. at his Seminary, located in a quiet piazza in the heart of old Rome near the Pantheon.

Elated at the thought of 'liberating' the other four, I shot off to St Peter's. I found Sam Derry and proceeded to tell him about Dennis's recent letter.

'Let's face it, they aren't happy up there. Life's dull and they've been used to moving around.'

Sam shrugged and waited for me to continue. I gave him the news of the Lucidis and of the French Seminary.

'Sounds good, Sam, and, who knows, this Father Meunier may have space for more. If you could get them down here, say, tomorrow night, we'll be here to take them off.'

'I don't know how the Monsignor'll feel about this. He went to a hell of a lot of trouble.' Sam's frown lifted. 'All right, 6.30 here tomorrow.'

True to his word, our old *carrozza* driver parked at Via Imperia at

10.30 the next morning. He asked no questions and the flats were all quiet.

Shortly after Joe and I arrived at Sam's office near St Peter's at 6.30 pm, Dennis, Pat, Duke and Gil appeared with a priest. They looked slightly sheepish as they said goodbye to Sam and left with us. In heavy rain Joe took one pair and I the other. Keeping just in sight of each other, we picked our way in the darkness along a detour through a short road tunnel leading away from St Peter's and the German sentries. Once through the tunnel, we loaded our charges on a tram.

At 7.30 pm the small, rain-soaked cavalcade arrived at the Lucidis' flat. Adrienne's enthusiasm for her Allied guests was extraordinary. When Renzo and his two sons escorted their new charges off to the French Seminary, Joe and I returned to the Vulcania. To allow Renzo further time to get organized, we had postponed our move.

John and Joe handled the food delivery from Mrs M's the next day to release me for a planned excursion with Gina, the pretty young hotel manageress with whom I was becoming increasingly friendly. She took me across the city to keep an appointment with her brother's tailor. We descended from a tram on to an attractive tree-lined road bordering the River Tiber.

At the tailor's home Gina did all the talking; I stood like a dummy while the elderly tailor manipulated his tape. From a surprising selection of woollen cloths, I chose bolts for a grey suit and long black overcoat. In two weeks they would be ready.

Most young Italians, though back in civilian clothes, had walked around for months in their Army boots. To dress more like them, Furman and I still wore Italian *Alpini* ski-boots acquired in Sulmona. However, the new Republican Fascist Government, via radio and newspapers, had recently ordered all young men to report back to the Army. The boots were a liability.

By lunchtime I was wearing brown leather shoes and a broad-brimmed grey Borsalino felt hat to conceal my light-coloured hair which, on a recent visit to a barber with Joe Pollak, I had left to grow longer. In my pocket a new Italian identity card and German work pass, courtesy of Monsignor O'Flaherty's forgers, boosted the confidence of Guglielmo Del Monte, a clerk displaced from his native Naples.

* * *

John May let it be known he would cash cheques for us at the Allied rate of exchange in the occupied south of 400 lire to the pound. To him, this offered an opportunity to convert accumulated Italian currency which was losing value.

'But where do we find cheques?' the four at the French Seminary asked.

'Simple,' I explained. 'Two years with the National Bank of Scotland at least taught me that legally any piece of paper will do. Write the name and address of your bank, then "Pay to the Order of so-and-so", enter the amount in figures and words, and sign it. In the UK it needs a tuppeny stamp, but your banker will provide that.'

Pat Wilson, ex-National Bank of Detroit, confirmed that it was this easy. May hadn't mentioned American cheques, but I felt confident he would cash them too.

Finally checking out of the Hotel Vulcania on Friday, 18 December, Furman and I arrived at the Lucidis' flat in Via Scialoia at seven. Renzo welcomed us but, as we dumped our small cases and shed our coats in the hallway, the sound of male voices came down the hall. I looked quizzingly at Renzo. He just smiled and pushed us along to the open living-room door where Rendell, Wilson, Dukate and Smith sat with Signora Lucidi and her two sons.

'What the...!' I began. As several started to explain, they were drowned by the shrill, French-accented English of Adrienne.

'Father Meunier became worried today. Last night the German SS raided some religious colleges in the city. They found refugees hiding and took them away. They have arrested some of the priests too. Father Meunier naturally suspects his Seminary may be next, might even be raided tonight.' For this reason he had pleaded with the four men to find another hide-out, even if only for the time being. Knowing no other place, they had come back to the Lucidis' only a few hours before.

'But heavens, Renzo, you can't make room for us all,' I said, a little embarrassed. 'Maybe John and I should go back to the hotel.'

'Don't think of it,' said Renzo. 'I assure you tonight there will be beds for all. Remember, I'm a hotel man.'

Somehow he and the maid Pepina produced an exceedingly good supper, amply accompanied by wine and cognac. Later, by the time someone declared 'last hand' in a noisy poker game, Renzo had conjured up six extra beds, complete with sheets, pillows and blankets.

With Christmas only days off, Renzo and Adrienne generously insisted that, if we felt comfortable, we should all stay over Christmas.

Initially Renzo was concerned about John, Joe and me going out and coming in at least twice a day, but he soon realized we were discreet. Joe, however, had to be restrained from using the Lucidis' telephone in the evening to chat to new friends.

'You may not believe it,' Renzo had explained seriously, 'but practically all telephone lines in the city are being tapped. The Fascists have a huge staff doing this.' We must, he said, use the phone only for serious emergency, and then with great caution.

On the Sunday before Christmas, when John and I returned from a conference with Sam Derry and Monsignor O'Flaherty, a large group had gathered at the Lucidis' for afternoon tea. In addition to Dukate, Wilson, Rendell and Smith were two new male guests. One, Galeazzo Pestalozza, was well-groomed, looked scholarly and spoke English easily. The other, *Professore* Gentiluomo, a lecturer in philosophy at Rome University, was, Renzo explained, a leader of Rome's underground Communist Party. His slight build, gentle manner and dapper appearance hardly suggested his political colour, but I was learning. Undoubtedly each of the politically inspired anti-Fascist underground movements, from Monarchists to Communists, had its intellectual leadership as well as its stalwarts. Adrienne, too, had Communist leanings and on many occasions had held intense political discussions with Gentiluomo and other notable anti-Fascists around this very table.

Renzo pulled me aside with Galeazzo Pestalozza, who explained that he lived with his sister, his niece and an old English lady, Miss May, who had been his niece's governess for 15 years. Her age had permitted her to continue living with the Pestalozzas during these war years. She wanted us to come to tea on Christmas Eve. I agreed we would.

On 23 December Monsignor O'Flaherty's room was crammed with hundreds of small parcels, all wrapped in gaily coloured paper and tied with red silk ribbon. In the centre stood a middle-aged English lady. Miss Stanley, an enthusiastic aide to the Monsignor, had prepared all these Christmas gifts for the men in hiding. Protected by the titled family with whom she was a governess, she had avoided internment by the Fascists. Squeezing in were priests – Maltese, Irish and New Zealand – mustered here to distribute these gifts throughout the city.

While afternoon teas at the Lucidis' were quite special, unfortunately their tea service was sadly depleted. Early on Christmas Eve John and I went shopping and, to our great satisfaction, found a full china tea set as a Christmas present for Adrienne.

The Christmas Eve food delivery to the two flats was extra heavy. The now-reliable *carrozza* was in Via Imperia on schedule, but it took two cautious trips up and down stairs at Mrs M's before the Christmas supplies were all loaded. As the *carrozza* moved off, John and I were half-buried in canvas and straw bags packed around us. Inside the suitcases at our feet lay five fat turkeys. Mrs M was determined that all the men would have a bright Christmas.

At each of the flats we dumped off these loads which included bottles of Frascati wine, cigarettes and the special Christmas parcels from the Monsignor's headquarters. Our elderly *carrozza* driver, responding to a double fare as a Christmas bonus, wished us a cordial '*Buon Natale*'.

Up in the residential area on the Parioli, the Pestalozzas occupied an attractive modern flat on the third floor of a six-storey building. As Furman, Pollak and I, with the Lucidis, entered the long living-room, an old lady, pale and thin, with grey-white hair brushed from a centre parting straight down each side of her face and pinned severely around her small head, came forward excitedly to greet us. Tears in her eyes, she hugged and kissed us.

'What a day ... what a day!' she sobbed, as she tried hard to smile. John and I were the first British she had seen since 1940. In the lapels of her dress she wore two miniature Union Jacks.

Galeazzo's sister Giovanna was a trim woman in her mid-thirties. Their niece, Dedy, was bright-eyed and spoke faultless English. Tea was a grand performance by Miss May. She had spent days preparing it. Mince pies too.

'Miss May's been starving us for a week for this,' Giovanna reproached.

'You've no idea how much this means to me.' Miss May looked happy now. In the confusion when Italy declared war in 1940, she resigned herself to seeing the war out with her friends here. A married cousin also lived in Rome. But it had been a long, trying time, sitting here helpless, reading the endless Fascist propaganda, listening to them crow over the brave Italian Forces and brag about bringing England to her knees.

'You must come back on New Year's Eve,' she said, when we rose to leave. Galeazzo nodded in his chair. 'Bring the other four chaps too.'

'What about the curfew?' I asked. Recently the local German Command had imposed a strict seven o'clock curfew throughout Rome.

'Oh,' exclaimed Miss May, 'bring enough food and drink and stay till the morning – all of you!'

At 12 Via Imperia on Christmas morning Mrs Chevalier served us brandy instead of tea. The house was a circus. Christmas gifts had already been exchanged among the family and the three British 'lodgers'. Even old grandma was hobbling around happily. In the kitchen Rosie laboured over the Christmas dinner. On every sideboard and shelf in the dining-room dishes groaned with cakes and fruit.

From Mrs M we collected some extra titbits and left to wish the flats a Merry Christmas. In the Chelini kitchen the beautiful Herta looked determined as she struggled with this Christmas challenge. At the Opera Flat several unlikely cooks jostled each other in the demanding act of squeezing a large turkey into an undersized oven.

At Via Scialoia, in the afternoon, the Lucidis' festive table was magnificent. Renzo, Adrienne and the maid Pepina had gone all out. With dishes of vegetables passing while Renzo skilfully carved a giant roast turkey, we realized our luck in having such considerate hosts on Christmas Day. If only our families back home, gnawed by uncertainty, could know this. While we had been prisoners, one postcard a week on average had reached them through the Swiss Red Cross. Since our escape they knew nothing. Home and family were undoubtedly on our minds, certainly on mine. Yet, if the real essence of Christmas was a conscious thought, it found no expression.

On this fourth wartime Christmas overseas it occurred to me how little active thought I had given to religion, in spite of having grown up in an exemplary atmosphere of Christian faith. My father, running a highly respected printing, stationery and publishing business, turning out a weekly newspaper, while bringing up a family of one girl and four boys with the saintly, unfaltering labours of my good-humoured mother, had always given priority to his responsibilities as an Elder of Ashton Church in Gourock. Church had been a central influence in most of our local youthful activities. Ingrained in me remained an acceptance of faith, derived in a private undemonstrative Scottish Presbyterian sort of way from a tradition nurtured more by behavioural example than through intellectual curiosity.

Even in the final disaster of Tobruk I hadn't turned suppliant, although I had welled with profound gratitude when, onto our casualty-strewn gun-site, suddenly from nowhere arrived a real live Red Cross ambulance big enough to take all the severely wounded to hospital. At Chieti, during the last months we were there I had taken to attending Sunday services led by a Methodist chaplain. But that was it.

★ ★ ★

The Wehrmacht had recently cancelled all leave to Rome for the troops but, in any case, this type of regular, decent, run-of-the-mill German posed no problem to us. The real threat to our hidden escapers came from the shrewd plain-clothes Gestapo units whose strength in the city was growing daily. A numerically strong Republican Fascist police force was also becoming feared in the city, under the ruthless command of its Chief, Colonel Pietro Koch. Half-German and half-Italian, he was collaborating fanatically with local German SS.

Back in mid-October Italian Fascist police units, who until then had virtually ignored anti-Jewish regulations, had, under pressure from the German SS Command, rounded up a thousand Jews, mostly from the small ghetto area in old Rome. All, old and young, had been trucked north, to destinations and a fate undisclosed. Thus all remaining Jews in Rome were in effect fugitives, and most were in hiding. The SS had taken over the huge Third Wing of Rome's giant civil prison, *Regina Coeli* (Queen of the Skies) and were jamming it with daily hauls of political prisoners.

Meanwhile, Monsignor O'Flaherty and John May were wide awake. Intelligence pipelines to the Monsignor's office were multiplying. John May had a responsive civilian contact right inside the Italian Police Headquarters flashing immediate warning of scheduled raids whenever possible.

At the German College on Boxing Day the Monsignor closed a thick file of papers and turned around to Sam Derry and me.

'Between you fellows and all my Jews, I can't get my own work done,' he complained.

'Still going out, Monsignor?' I asked.

'Only if it's critical. Sam keeps lecturing me. I don't move far from the steps of St Peter's. I know they're watching me. Have you been inside St Peter's yet, Bill?' I shook my head.

'Come on down with me now, then. I've just time to show you quickly.'

'Tell Bill about your last prank on the police,' said Sam, as we left. Along the corridor, I prodded him for the story.

'Oh, Sam's talking about one night two weeks ago. I had to take a big bundle of clothes to a man in the town, about a mile from here. He's a fine fellow, helps me a lot. Had some new arrivals in another house. They needed the clothes badly.'

Although he had waited till dark, he had soon noticed he was being followed by plain-clothes men. Walking fast to the house, he dumped the clothes and asked if it had a back door. No, but his friend had a big coal cellar with a chute. The policemen were standing outside the gate. Down in the cellar, he changed into dirty overalls, stuffed his cassock, collar and hat into a coal sack and covered himself in coal dust. Crawling out through a manhole on the pavement, he walked off, bent over, with the sack on his back. The plain-clothes police ignored him. 'These foolish police,' he said. 'They kept watch on that house, without going inside at all, for two whole weeks. I just heard from my friend, only yesterday, one of them came to the door with extra police waiting outside, demanding the tall priest they had seen enter two weeks before!' He was still chuckling as we ascended the broad steps before St Peter's.

The massive centre door stood closed. 'It's only opened on special festivals,' the Monsignor explained, leading me through a diminutive door to the left. Inside the almost deserted basilica, its very magnitude was striking. After the briefest stops at Michelangelo's masterpiece, *Pietà*, and the giant beckoning figure of St Peter, with his extended toe worn smooth by centuries of pilgrims' touches, the Monsignor steered me down the long north aisle, defined by columns rising in parallel discipline to bear the massive ceiling. Directly under the great dome, the ornate bronze canopy over the high altar was art beyond me ... Baroque ... Bernini. The Monsignor moved me on to return up the south aisle, slowing only to point out the bust of 'your old Scottish hero, Bonnie Prince Charlie', the ill-fated young Pretender, Charles Edward Stuart.

'Of course, you Presbyterians ... barely a religion at all.' His blue eyes were laughing behind his steel-rimmed glasses. I let the friendly crack go by. Even in a less public place, I would not have dared a dialogue, far less a debate, with this profound cleric whose learning reflected two decades within the Curia.

His quiet commentary had been continuous and rapid, on chapels, balconies and choir lofts high on the walls of the spacious transept. Now, in the long centre of the basilica, he pointed to the brass inlays in the stone floor, marking from the east entrance the comparative length of other main cathedrals, Notre Dame, Chartres, St Patrick's in New York, Canterbury.

The fast tour was over, as we parted outside on the wide steps, but leaving me in awe of this museum-like cathedral.

13

ROYAL OPERA HOUSE

Early on New Year's Day a boisterous group of four British, two Americans and one Czech, with Adrienne and Renzo Lucidi, quietened enough to slip out of the Pestalozzas' Parioli flat into the cold clear dawn of 1944. Having arrived there before the curfew on New Year's Eve, loaded with cooked chicken and ham, cheeses and rolls, abundantly augmented by Gordon's Gin and Orvieto Bigi wine, by midnight spirits had been predictably high. Aided by mild flirtations and a noisy roulette table, the exuberance had held through the first curfew hours of 1944.

At noon at the Lucidis' Adrienne appeared from her room looking especially chic in a silk suit and gay-coloured broad-brimmed hat perched on her red hair. Renzo had reserved a prominent box at the Opera House for New Year's Day. The night curfew had moved all performances to the afternoon.

Outside the Opera House our party gathered – John Furman, Joe Pollak with a girl friend, Gina from the Vulcania and the Lucidis. The other gang of four had gone to meet the Pestalozzas.

Furman tugged my sleeve. Across the street stood, of all people, Iride, with the short, red-headed Free Frenchman Henri Payonne. John, Joe and I moved across to greet them. Lucidi, curious, joined us and met Iride. Payonne he pulled aside, invited to tea soon, and, hearing his good Italian, gave him his phone number. They had just come from Sulmona and were at a nearby *pensione* on Via Massina d'Azelio.

With the awkward explanation of having to make curtain-up at the Opera, we followed the Lucidis into the theatre. In the foyer a resplendently liveried usher led us upstairs to our box. Germans were everywhere, in the corridors and on the stairs. Inside the large plush box with its red velvet walls, we seated Adrienne and the two girls in front and settled down in chairs behind them. This opera house, though far from the largest in the world, was reputed to be the most beautiful. Our box was ideally situated on the first tier above the stalls and the second to the left of the Royal Box in the centre.

Renzo passed us programmes, on rich parchment with gold-embossed lettering and long silk cords. To view the theatre, I stepped forward past the ladies. Most of the seats were already occupied, and the remainder of a well-dressed capacity audience was still filing in.

The Royal Box, twice the height of the others, was notably empty. As I stood reflecting on the absence of the Italian Royal family who had fled to Allied territory down south, the box between us and the Royal Box started filling up with high-ranking German officers. Seated closest to them in the open curving front of our own box, Adrienne too had seen them. In fact, from where she sat, she could have leaned over and touched the nearest German. With her profound hatred for the Nazis, she was finding it difficult to remain calm.

John Furman, craning over to see what was going on, pointed. Down the centre aisle walked Captain 'Pip' Gardner and Lieutenant-Colonel 'Tug' Wilson, being ushered to orchestra stalls accompanied by two smart-looking ladies. Now, in the left of the stalls, Rendell and Dukate, with pretty Dedy della Campana between them, were waving at us. All around them sat German uniforms. To avoid the curious glances of the Germans in the next box, John and I moved back just as the brilliant giant chandelier, hanging from the centre of the frescoed ceiling, began to dim. As it darkened completely, there remained for a few magical moments only the subdued illumination within hundreds of red-walled boxes rising in tiers around the perimeter of the horseshoe auditorium. The lights vanished.

The conductor on his podium below stood erect, baton raised. His arm dropped and the orchestra began the slow first bars of the Overture to Puccini's *Tosca*.

At the end of the first act, after the great soprano Maria Caniglia, tenor Beniamino Gigli and tall bass Tito Gobbi took several curtain calls, the audience began to move. Renzo suggested we go down to the bar and join the grand promenade so traditional at the Opera House. As we came out at the rear of our box, seven German officers issued from theirs. They glanced at us as they moved away. We followed them. One, surrounded by the others, was clearly a big shot, some high-ranking general. As we followed behind them, I had to admire their appearance, tall, erect and perfectly groomed.

Following the second act, with the ladies remaining in the box, we four men ambled downstairs, again on the heels of our German

81

neighbours. Puccini's opera, I thought, was eerily evocative of our present situation. Rome, the locale of the historic plot, was dominated by local mercenaries of a foreign despot, Napoleon, a century earlier; the city trembled under the brutal command of its wicked police chief, Scarpia.

At the end of the last act, while the adoring audience called back the stars time after time, I whispered to Renzo.

'These programmes are pretty special. I'd like to keep one as a souvenir.'

'Good. So?'

'I want it autographed.'

'By whom?'

'By the German General in the next box!' Renzo looked askance, then, as he got the point, grinned.

My first intention had been to ask for the autograph myself, but, as I edged forward to the front of the box I realized that, with the ladies here, it might look out of place. I bent over Adrienne's ear.

'Adrienne, pass my programme across and ask the General for his autograph,' I whispered. She looked around at me, shocked.

'You're joking!' she breathed.

'Certainly not.' I winked at her. 'You're closest to him.'

Suddenly she understood. A mischievous look came over her as she nervously adjusted the angle of her big hat.

Red lighting returned to the boxes and the giant chandelier again lit up the whole theatre. Below us in the orchestra stalls, most heads were turning to stare up at the German General's box, just as Adrienne, flashing a glamorous smile, gave the programme to the General three feet away. Would he be so gallant as to autograph it, she asked in French.

Standing beside Adrienne, I watched the General's face light with pleasure as, slightly embarrassed, he took the hastily proffered pen of one of his aides and scrawled his long signature across the front of the programme. The General, rising, passed the programme back to her, then bowed from the waist. Adrienne nodded in acknowledgment and sat back again. Her gloved hand was shaking as she passed me the programme.

On the bus back to Piazza Flaminio, inside the large pocket of my coat, I fingered the souvenir programme bearing the strong clear signature 'Mackensen', that of General Eberhard von Mackensen, Commander of the German Fourteenth Army.

Rome – City of Terror

14

THE LADY SETS A TRAP

The telephone broke the early morning quiet of the Lucidis' flat. Furman, Pollak and I were asleep in three similar beds in one room. Adrienne's voice on the phone through the half-open door sounded urgent. A moment later, dressing-gown flying, she burst into our room.

'Joe! Joe, wake up! Iride's on the phone. Important news from Sulmona. Wants to see you at her *pensione* right away.'

'Tell her I'll phone her later.'

'No, no, she insists on speaking to you now, right now!' Grudgingly Joe went to the phone in the hall.

'*Va bene, capito. Vengo fra poco.*' The receiver clicked. Joe returned to bed.

'What's her trouble?' I asked.

'Oh, something about Sulmona. I'll see her later.'

In ten minutes the phone rang again. Adrienne answered. She slammed the receiver and rushed into our room.

'Get out!' She was scarcely coherent. 'Henri says, "Throw away the three packets you have; they're dangerous!" Quick! Via!'

This was vague, but we jumped up and threw on our clothes. Across the hall Renzo was interrogating Adrienne. It was Henri Payonne, the Frenchman, who had called. The 'three packets' were obviously Furman, Pollak and myself. Rendell and the others had returned to the French Seminary two days ago. Something was wrong.

While Renzo still tried to make sense out of Adrienne, the three of us raced downstairs and out. A safe distance down Via Flaminia, deserted at this early hour, we considered the best course to follow.

'Is Henri staying with Iride?' John asked.

'Well, he's staying at the same *pensione*,' said Joe. 'He came to

Renzo's for tea yesterday. I was there. Said things were rough in Sulmona. Iride was coming to Rome, so he came with her.'

How did Iride know the Lucidis' phone number? Perhaps she had watched Payonne dial. Even if it was a false alarm, we couldn't return to the Lucidis' until it was cleared up.

'Dammit, I'll go to her *pensione* now,' said Joe, fidgeting.

'No,' said John. 'Could be a trap. Henri didn't call for fun.'

Joe and John left for St Peter's to check with Monsignor O'Flaherty. He might know something. In the meantime I would make for the Pestalozzas' to see if they would accommodate us, then deliver the rations to the two flats myself. We would meet later at the Chelini flat. A startled Miss May in her nightgown let me into the Pestalozza flat, and a sleepy-eyed family appeared as I explained. They readily agreed to accommodate us.

'Should I phone Renzo, to tell him you'll be here tonight?' asked Galeazzo.

'No, you'd better not. Renzo's flat may be raided. Their phone may be tapped. We'd better wait.'

At Mrs M's at 10.30 am, when Gemma shouted that the *carrozza* was waiting, and with Mrs M watching the stairway, I lugged the two bulky suitcases downstairs, loaded up and took off. The Opera flat was quiet. Inside Chelini, I waited. At one o'clock Furman arrived, alone. He looked grim.

'Joe's been pinched!' he muttered. We moved over out of earshot. They had met the Monsignor, Sam Derry and John May. Everyone smelt a rat. John May, who had dealt with Iride on her trips from Sulmona, thought highly of her and couldn't imagine her laying a trap. While suspicious too, he agreed with Pollak that the air had to be cleared. Sam and the Monsignor felt we should await developments, but Joe wanted to have done with it.

Leaving behind everything except his identity card and some spare cash, Joe set out accompanied by a young girl selected by the Monsignor. She would wait outside the *pensione* when Joe went in.

At noon the girl returned, agitated. Two minutes after entering the *pensione*, Joe had come bolting out the front door chased by a German soldier and a plain-clothes man. They caught him, bundled him into a car and took off.

At the Pestalozzas' in the afternoon, Renzo was waiting. As yet nothing had happened at Via Scialoia. Joe's capture angered Renzo.

'We might have prevented this,' he said. 'You know the state Adrienne was in after Henri called.' In her excitement she had omitted to

CONNOTATI E CONTRASSEGNI SALIENTI

Statura ... 1.78
Corporatura Norm.
Capelli biondi
Occhi grigi
Contrassegni

FIRMA DEL TITOLARE *Del Monte Gug Nicola*

IMPRONTA DEL DITO INDICE SINISTRO

9. "A new identity card... described me as Guglielmo del Monte and bore the stamp of the City of Naples" (p. 100).

10. "'How can we find clothes' asked John Furman" (p. 48)... "a chartered accountant by profession, precise, clear-thinking and resourceful by nature" (p. 53). Furman found the clothes but was later arrested.

11. The author in 1946.

12. John Furman, Sam Derry, "Barney" Byrnes and the author,
September, 1944, at 18 Via Scialoia, Rome...

13. ... and reunited at the 40th Anniversary of Rome's Liberation.

14. Renzo Lucidi relives the past with Colonel Sam Derry, DSO, MC…

15. … and with the author, Rome, June, 1984.

16. Monsignor O'Flaherty takes leave of the author in New York in the 1950s.

17. Anniversary of the Liberation of Rome. Pope John Paul greets the author and his wife.

convey part of Payonne's message, that she should meet him at the Railway Station at ten o'clock. Renzo had chased Gerald and Maurice out of the flat to watch from outside. He didn't know where to find us.

Adrienne did meet Payonne, along with another girl who had come with them from Sulmona. This girl had been with Iride the night before when Germans, with a plain-clothes Italian, burst in and arrested Iride, whose family in Sulmona had been arrested along with others – all for sheltering Allied prisoners. The police had traced her to Rome and wanted to know from her where to find 'Giuseppe Bernardini' (Joe Pollak). Throughout most of the night they had questioned her. Somehow Iride had obtained the Lucidis' phone number and in the morning, in the presence of her menacing captors, had phoned Joe. The other girl, after convincing the police that she was not implicated and having been released, quickly warned Henri in his room and mentioned the phone call. Henri had rushed to a phone to warn the Lucidis.

I told Renzo not to blame Adrienne. Her panic was understandable.

'You're not moving out of your flat, are you?' I asked him.

'Certainly not. In fact, I'd better get back to it. Adrienne and the boys are there. But you and John stay away for a day or two.'

★　★　★

'Look at this,' said the Monsignor, when I entered his room at the German College the next morning. 'From Iride.' Addressed to 'Patrick', Derry's code name, in translation it read:

Dearest Patrick,

Yesterday at midday, I was arrested and I got the news that my mother, sister and my baby as well as Flora and her family and the famous 'Dino' (who knows Joseph) had also been arrested and were in the hands of the German Command. We were betrayed by ... Captain MESSENGER who is not a Captain but a simple Red Cross Orderly who has divulged everything. They are here looking for Joseph and at all costs must take him.

I begged Joseph to come to me because I am very sick, but I am guarded. I think that the arrest of Joseph will be the saving of all of us. I won't talk unless threatened that I endanger the life of my baby by not doing so – in which case I shall poison myself. I beg you, however, to save the lives of my baby and my poor mother.

You must not believe that if they take Joseph that it is a betrayal – he is of no interest to them – they only want to know who supplies the money and I repeat that they will never know from me – I prefer death – I am only afraid that Joseph may talk if he believes himself betrayed.

Iride

We felt badly about Joe.

Sam ended a huddled conversation in the far corner with a short, thick-set man whose face was familiar, the wild-eyed, rugged Yugoslav, Bruno Büchner. We had met twice at the Chelini flat.

'Who's this Bruno anyway?'

'Always pushing some new mad sabotage plan,' said Sam. 'We have to dampen his ardour.' Sam was pacing up and down rubbing his large hands.

'But how does he tie in with the flats?'

'He's mixed up with Nebulanti,' Sam said, adding that he mostly worried about Bruno, not about his loyalty, but because he knew so much about the set-up. Because of other stunts he had pulled off, the SS apparently had a price on his head.

''Ello, me old cock-sparrer,' announced John May, dressed trimly as usual in his formal black and grey morning wear. ''ow's yer knees an' things? Seen any good operas lately?' I handed him the home-made cheques from myself and the gang at the French Seminary and he cashed them.

Sam was pressing the various priests to find new friendly billets in order to reduce the numbers in the flats and have them as transient quarters.

Lucidi, I assured him, was canvassing his political friends. That afternoon we were taking three from the Opera flat out to a family recommended by Father Perfetti at Tor Pignatara.

15

GESTAPO JACKPOT

Inside the Via Tasso prison on 5 January Gestapo interrogated a newly arrested young Italian active in the Communist underground. They beat him up brutally. The next morning plain-clothes Republican Fascist agents of the Gestapo visited the captive's widowed mother, introducing themselves as Resistance friends of her son. They had a plan to pry him free, but needed help from other friends of his. Could she put them in touch? Desperate, the mother volunteered the name of one close friend of her son. But could he be trusted, they asked. She assured them on this. In fact, she understood he was looking after two escaped English officer prisoners of war in a flat in the Parioli.

In no time the Gestapo agents learned the name and precise location of the young cook at Pip Gardner's flat. They phoned there, referred to the chat with the youth's mother and asked the unsuspecting cook if they could get together to plan his friend's release. The cook checked with Nebulanti who had happened by. He invited them to come right over.

In Gardner's flat the agents, well-briefed on the Communist underground, convinced the cook and Nebulanti of their authenticity as fellow conspirators. So much so that, before they left, they heard gratuitous mentions of two large flats, both housing large numbers of Allied escaped prisoners. Further rough interrogation in Via Tasso dragged from the youth confirmation that the flats existed. The addresses he did not know.

At noon on 7 January two carloads of Gestapo agents and uniformed German SS, one carrying the battered young man from Via Tasso, pounced on Pip Gardner's flat and grabbed Gardner and Tug Wilson, Nebulanti and the cook. When the Gestapo confronted the young cook with the horrible sight of his friend and threatened him with the same fate unless he divulged the addresses of the two big flats he caved in.

At 2 pm two contingents of Gestapo and heavily armed SS troopers roared out of SS headquarters, one headed for the Opera flat on Via Firenze and the other for the officers' flat on Via Chelini.

Two hours before, Furman had left me at the Opera flat after we delivered supplies. I continued alone through a heavy drizzle in our *carrozza* with the groceries for Via Chelini.

'Rough morning for deliveries,' said Major Mander. 'Where's Furman?'

'Gone to see Derry. He'll be here before two. If the Monsignor has a new address for us, we'll take two of your chaps away this afternoon.'

The doorbell rang, the usual 'V' sign. Major Mander and the others slipped back out of sight into the living room and the pretty Herta opened the front door an inch to observe, then wider to allow two young men in civilian clothes to enter.

'Hello, Burns,' I greeted the South African sergeant, who a few days before had transferred from here to a friendly family nearby. 'Who's your friend?'

Sergeant Burns pulled me aside and Major Mander joined us.

'This chap's Sergeant Eaton, American Air Force,' said Burns quietly. 'He's living in the house I've moved to. Been there five weeks. No one to talk to. Never goes out. He's gone a bit nutty, and the family asked me to take him off their hands. Doc MacAulay's here, so I thought I'd bring him over.'

Major Mander fetched Captain MacAulay, who promptly took the young American into a private room. Herta let Burns out of the flat. Just before lunch the doctor joined us in the living-room.

'This chap's in a bad state. May be connected with his plane crash. He could become violent. I've a small quantity of morphine, but that won't last. He should really be in a hospital under proper care.'

'Fair enough,' I said, 'but how the devil do we fix that? No one here can take him to a hospital, explain his trouble and book him in!' At the same time, it was clear we couldn't just take him to a hospital entrance and leave him.

Major Mander wrote a number on a scrap of paper.

'This is Brother Robert's number. He's one of the Maltese brothers who come here. Maybe we should have him standing by to take this fellow to a hospital if necessary. Let's have lunch; it's ready. You can hop out afterwards and call him.'

At two o'clock, leaving on this errand, I ran into John Furman in the street. He had the address of a new billet for two. I told him about the American airman. I'd be back shortly.

'OK, I'll wait for you.'

The rain had stopped when I entered a phone booth in Piazza Ungheria. I asked the operator for the number. It did not respond. Several attempts were unsuccessful. Back to the flat I headed. What could we do with our deranged American?

At the ground-floor door of the Chelini flat I gave the 'V' ring on the bell. But footsteps sounded on the nearby stairs, and since the strict rule was to avoid being seen entering or leaving the flat, I walked quickly outside. Across the wide, normally deserted street, a small cluster of people stood watching. I walked away for a few minutes and came back. As I approached the door of the flat for the second time, the old female janitor of the building was standing nearby in the narrow lobby. Often we had seen each other, without ever exchanging even a nod of recognition. I raised my hand to ring the bell.

'You're going in there?' she hissed in Italian.

I nodded. Why did she look so scared? My finger almost touched the bell when she hit my arm.

'No, no, *Via! Via!*' she rasped. '*Sono tedeschi la dentro!*'

I looked at her incredulously. Germans inside? What was she talking about? But she was wringing her hands, and repeated in an urgent undertone that armed Germans were inside. She was serious, and frightened. I turned on my heel and strode outside. 300 yards down the street, I turned to look back. My chest was beating hard. What had happened? Outside nothing seemed amiss, no car, no truck. When I rang the bell the first time, no one had come to the door ... or had I walked away just in time?

Now the small gathering of people on the other side of the street took on significance. They were gazing across at the flat. The arrival of German soldiers on this quiet street must have caused a flurry. But I had been away only twenty minutes. And John Furman must still be inside.

I was in a quandary. Major Mander had left the flat just ahead of me. Should I try to alert him? But how? I made a detour to the top end of Via Chelini and approached from the other direction. When the building came back into view, doubt vanished. By the curb at the entrance stood a large German Army truck. Across the street the group of spectators had grown to 50 or 60. I joined them. Several pairs of eyes turned on me. I was uncomfortable. Whatever misfortune had befallen, I could not alter it by standing here. Mander might not return for hours. Others who often visited the flat I did not even know. The first need was to alert Derry and the Monsignor.

What was going on behind these drawn shutters on the ground floor across the street? Out in front, all was still. The German truck stood unattended. More of the spectators were staring at me now. So I took off.

Half an hour later at St Peter's I ran all the way up to the now familiar room, where I found Sam and the Monsignor.

'Chelini's had it! And John along with it!' I blurted out. Their faces fell. I filled in the sparse details I knew. It was a quarter past four. There was no way of stopping anyone going there that night, Sam said, but the word would be around before morning. He wondered if anything had happened at the Opera flat.

'Who could have done this?' Sam paced the room. 'Nebulanti? Bruno maybe? Who?'

'Bruno's probably been grabbed too,' I said. 'He was in the flat when I left.'

'I just can't believe that either of these two turned us in,' said the Monsignor.

'Bruno and Herta'll get a rough time,' murmured Sam, almost to himself. 'If they make them talk. Well, at least they don't know who Mrs M is, but Bruno knows about us here, Monsignor. They'd give their eye-teeth to know what's going on. If they feel they've got a case, there's nothing to stop them from raiding.'

Just let 'em try it!' interrupted the Monsignor, with a grim expression. 'If any of these scoundrels ever dare to come near this room, I'll beat the...!'

His vehemence surprised me; but he was deadly serious.

Sam had reason for concern. The security of this room, in fact of the whole organization, was now in jeopardy. Until we found out how the Germans had traced the Chelini flat we could be sure of nobody. Was there an unknown informer? If so, it would be even more necessary now to compartmentalize each cell, to avoid any one operator knowing the activities, even the identity, of another. This would be restrictive.

Even if in time we were to find a more direct explanation of today's raid, the almost certain capture today of Bruno and Herta along with fourteen British and South African officers and one unbalanced American was a major setback. The tongue-loosening methods of the Gestapo were legendary. The former POWs might be spared the rough treatment, but Bruno and Herta were now in deep trouble. The circumstances of their capture could lead to the death sentence and execution. Drastic enough, but what brutality would they suffer in the meantime?

The *Collegio Teutonicum* in which the Monsignor had his room was only extra-territorial, not Vatican proper. Down below the entrance from the street to the courtyard was unguarded. Anyone could enter without obstruction. In spite of the Monsignor's determination, this room could be invaded any time. He had refused to keep firearms. He did, however, keep a coil of rope under his bed. If they had warning, they could escape through the window down to the courtyard.

'Look, it's close to the curfew,' I said. 'The Pestalozzas' is too far away. What's the shortest way to the French Seminary, Monsignor?' While the Monsignor drew directions, Sam suggested I return the next day after calling on Mrs M.

'We should know the worst by then.' Sam was shaking his head.

'Right, I'm fed up about two things. One is John Furman being pinched, and the other is the loss of a very important document.' They gave me a quick look. 'I left my briefcase inside the Chelini flat, in the hall, when I went out to phone. All my worldly possessions and the autographed programme from the Opera.'

In the maze of narrow cobbled streets between Piazza Colonna and the Tiber I located the French Seminary just before the seven o'clock curfew. In answer to the bell, a face appeared at a small grill, recognized me and unlocked the heavy door. Father Meunier appeared and agreed to accommodate me. Upstairs a priest allotted me a small unfurnished room with a metal bedstead.

Somewhat incongruously, laughter came from down the hallway. I opened a door to receive a noisy welcome from Wilson, Rendell, Dukate and Smith. Wine had preceded the supper on the table.

When I broke the bad news, they sobered. 'You need a drink,' said Gil. He was right.

★ ★ ★

At Mrs M's the next morning the news was the worst. The Opera flat and Pip Gardner's place were gone too. One of the Maltese priests had witnessed the Opera flat group being bundled into a German truck.

The big question on Gardner's flat, we thought, was Nebulanti, the man who had arranged it with Sam Derry. He could not be located, although he might have been arrested along with Gardner and Wilson and their young Italian cook. Someone had blown the gaff, someone who knew about all the three hideouts. Presumably the mysterious informer did not know of Mrs M's place, which was obviously still intact. The household here was shaken. Even the impish daughter was subdued.

While we stood speculating, I remembered our friend the *carrozza* driver and ran to the window. Down below he sat patiently with his horse and carriage, as he had done every morning for weeks. The sight of him there, ready for his regular morning hire, emphasized our loss. We had no deliveries to make.

'Gemma, run down with this,' I said, handing her 500 lire, 'and tell him thanks, but we don't need him any more.'

Later, in the German College, Sam and the Monsignor were still trying to work it out.

'Both Bruno and Nebulanti were arrested,' said the Monsignor. I was impressed; his underground informers had worked fast. 'All your boys are in Regina Coeli.' The Monsignor had not yet learned the exact whereabouts of Bruno and Nebulanti, but their arrest obliged us to drop any suspicion that either had double-crossed us. If they had been dragged to Via Tasso, the Gestapo would spare nothing to find out what they, and possibly Herta, knew.

After the nuns had come and gone with lunch, Sam and I sorted out the addresses of the escapers who had until yesterday been handled by Furman. They were scattered all over Rome. Many were recent arrivals, whom we had planted in already crowded homes, on our promise to move them soon. On our plea of emergency, friends had contacted friends who now found themselves in the compromising position of hiding British or American escapers. The dire consequences of discovery featured prominently in the Nazi-controlled *Il Messaggero* and *Giornale d'Italia*. Yet most new hosts soon quelled their fears, swallowed the inconvenience and began to relish their role of participating. But we had to be ready to move the escapers fast.

For me to handle the increased load single-handed was neither practical nor wise. First, Pollak had been recaptured. Now, just as we had built up to a full schedule, Furman was gone. I could be next, any time. I had to have a partner who at least would know and be known to the various *padrone* hiding our men.

'Sam, there's only one person I know for the job.'

'Who?'

'Renzo Lucidi. He's a hell of a good chap, and he's anxious to do more for us. So far we've kept him pretty much in the dark, but I'm sure we can trust him. I'd like to bring him in full-time.'

'All right, bring him along next time. In any case, I don't want you bogged down too much. I want you available for emergencies, as they turn up.'

Just as Sam handed me money to pay the latest arrivals to the end of January footsteps in the corridor stopped outside the closed door. No caller was expected, but we had no time to get out of sight. The Monsignor got up quickly from his desk. The handle turned, the door swung open and there stood Major D'Arcy Mander of the Green Howards.

'Did you go back to Chelini?' I asked him.

'I certainly did,' said Mander. 'At six last night I rang the bell and a stranger let me in, a civilian. Just inside I met a German soldier! They asked me a few questions, put me in the front room and told me to wait. They both left the room. I looked around. The window-sill was only six feet from the ground outside. The window wasn't even locked. It was dark. I eased it open, hopped down into the front garden, vaulted the wall and made off.'

Sam grinned.

'You didn't have time to find out how all this happened?'

'No, afraid not.'

He had gone to another address in the Parioli, where friends took him in.

* * *

The Pestalozza family, when they heard of the German raids on the flats, were upset. Miss May sobbed over John Furman's imprisonment.

Renzo Lucidi was delighted to become part of the Organization. As there had been no sequel at Via Scialoia to the panic over Iride, he now felt his flat was safe. Back there for lunch, we divided my list of names and addresses in two, according to location and set out on a round of those billets which Renzo did not know. 'Are we going to visit your famous Mrs M?' he asked, as we came out of one block of flats in the late afternoon.

'Yes, we'll go now.' From our earlier descriptions of the daily suit-cases with meat and other precious black-market rations, Renzo, as a typical small-family negotiator in the black market, already held the mysterious Mrs M in awe.

After a noisy welcome from the Chevalier family and a brief chat with the four escapers there, Renzo arranged to call frequently to collect meat, cheese, sugar and other things which now he found it impossible to buy.

The next afternoon the matter-of-fact and self-composed Renzo was clearly intrigued as I led him through the portico off St Peter's Square, and thence to Monsignor O'Flaherty's room in the German College. Sam and the Monsignor gave Renzo a warm handshake.

'Bill,' began the Monsignor, 'we've an awkward situation. Two Englishmen, Major Fane-Hervey and Flight Lieutenant Garrad-Cole, are hiding in the Swiss Legation – the old British Embassy. When I had no place to put them, as a temporary thing Brother Robert persuaded Secondo, the little caretaker – he was caretaker for the British too – to smuggle them into the empty part that isn't used. If we could get away with it, we could keep a whole army in there. Trouble is Sir D'Arcy feels it's not quite playing the game.' The British Minister could be embarrassed diplomatically if these officers were discovered. They had to be moved quickly.

I undertook to shift them, and the Monsignor briefed me on signals for recognition at the Legation the next day. Renzo volunteered to accommodate them for the time being at his flat.

'Good,' said the Monsignor, 'then noon tomorrow.'

Sam gave me a sign and I moved across the room. The Monsignor took Renzo outside, ostensibly to show him the Vatican grounds from the corridor window.

'Bill, you may not see me for a while.' Sam's voice was lowered. 'But still make this room your headquarters. We can communicate through the Monsignor, and John May'll be back and forth all the time.'

'Fine, but what's up?'

'For your ears only, things've become a bit sticky around here. The head fellow of the German College has told the Monsignor he knows there's a questionable foreigner staying here. He's embarrassed and wants me out. It makes sense. In any case, after all these arrests, this room isn't secure. So I'll be dressed as a priest tonight. The Monsignor's going to walk me past the Swiss Guards, counting my beads, into the Vatican.'

He would not be given asylum in sovereign Vatican territory; that would raise questions. He would be staying unofficially in part of the British Minister's quarters in the Santa Marta Hospice. From now on we would communicate in writing. John May or a priest would act as courier. To be safe, we would employ the code names which we had recently given to all members of the Organization. Sam was 'Toni', the Monsignor was 'Golf', Brother Robert was 'Whitebows'. I was simply 'Bill S'. Renzo became 'Rinso'. Renzo and the Monsignor re-entered.

'Bill, you won't be able to use the street door to the German College after today. They're closing it up tight.'

Then how, pray, do I get in?'

'Through the Vatican, past the Swiss Guards.'

'What?'

'It may be a little tricky,' began the Monsignor, 'but it should work out.' He drew on paper my new route to his room. It entered the

Vatican proper through the Santa Marta archway located to the left of the façade of St Peter's and constantly protected by Swiss Guards. Once inside, it turned sharp left across 100 yards of Vatican territory, only to leave the Vatican gate again through a high wrought-iron gate. Then across extra-territorial ground to the German College. Simply, the roundabout route crossed a corner of the Vatican State.

'Now, as you come up to Santa Marta, two Swiss Guards on sentry duty will stop you first. When you've passed them you'll run into two more about 20 yards further in, right under the archway. These two check your credentials and papers. After that you turn left inside.' His finger followed the diagram. 'You stop at a window over there and pick up a pass. That's to let you go back through the Vatican on your way out. Then walk on through a big iron gate – another sentry there – and come all the way down to the German College here. Got it?'

'Oh, sure! It's easy, except for one small detail. You've been telling me for weeks that the Swiss Guards are loyal to the Vatican's neutrality, that they're rugged soldiers, that they screen everybody thoroughly, that, because of the new Republican Government orders recalling Italians to the Army, they won't let any young Italians into the Vatican. By what magic do I get past the Swiss Guards?'

'Shouldn't be hard,' said the Monsignor. 'Just show them your Identity Card and say you've an appointment with me. Your Italian is good enough.'

'And if they don't let me past?'

'Ask them to phone me, and I'll come down and meet you.' The Monsignor seemed confident. Instinctively I trusted his judgment. Renzo and I started to leave.

'Sam, does Captain Trippi at the Swiss Legation know about Fane-Hervey and Garrad-Cole?'

'Heavens no!'

'Just wanted to know. Have an exciting time in the Vatican.'

★ ★ ★

To avoid curiosity at the Swiss Legation, I first visited Captain Trippi upstairs, enquiring as an excuse about Red Cross food parcels. The supply, he said, was exhausted. In his cautious 'neutral' manner, he hinted that the entrance to the Legation was now under surveillance. No point in escaped POWs calling here any more; the help he could offer was too limited. Obviously he did not tell me that the German Embassy had recently delivered a stern warning to the head of the Swiss

Legation; unless assistance to the known traffic of Allied escapers to the Legation ceased forthwith, the German authorities would take action against the Swiss official responsible.

Already Mrs M's son had warned us that plain-clothes police were watching the gates regularly. One Swiss male was known to be pro-Nazi. A British parachutist hiding at Mrs M's had ventured to the Legation and had left with a plain-wrapped Red Cross parcel, only to be arrested farther along Via Montebello.

Halfway down the spiral staircase from Captain Trippi's office I spotted a diminutive man at the back of the entrance hall. Secondo Constantini, the caretaker, recognized my look and almost imperceptibly motioned me to come through a rear door. A good distance behind, I followed him across an open courtyard neatly planted with small trees and entered a stately mansion beyond. From a large hallway I continued, after Secondo, into a spacious drawing-room, darkened by drawn draperies descending heavily from a high, richly moulded ceiling. Clusters of furniture under drab dust-covers formed a bank on either side of me. It was musty, eerie almost. In the dead hush, I instinctively stepped quietly.

'Good morning, Simpson!' shouted an English voice. I was startled. Through the bank of white sheets, an erect figure in a silk dressing-gown emerged, blocking my way, but he was smiling as if he enjoyed my momentary fright.

'I'm Salazar,' he announced. 'I expected you.' Major Derry and the Monsignor had omitted to alert me to this English-looking, moustached older man, Count Sarsfield Salazar. Officially with the Swiss Legation, but living on these premises with some British credentials, he was one of the 'Committee of Three' – with Monsignor O'Flaherty and butler John May – who had formed this Rome Organization after the Italian surrender. His code name was 'Emma'.

'Carry on upstairs there,' he pointed. 'Secondo has your charges ready.'

In a room upstairs was Major Fane-Hervey, 4th Royal Tank Regiment, in a decent-fitting suit. RAF Flight Lieutenant Garrad-Cole, standing six feet four, broad-shouldered with a head of blond hair, looked even less Italian than the other. His suit did not begin to fit. Garrad-Cole recalled meeting Monsignor O'Flaherty in a prison camp in Italy a year earlier. When he told the Monsignor that he had been recaptured after an escape attempt, the Monsignor had promised him that, if he ever escaped again and came to Rome, he would have him outfitted by the finest tailor in Rome.

'If he said so, he'll do it,' I assured him. 'Just wait.'

Secondo led the three of us downstairs and along the inside of the high wall of the Embassy grounds, to a wooden door at the end. A servant brought along by Secondo slipped outside to check the road. When he waved, I went out first, and my two charges, each carrying a small bag, followed a few yards behind me.

'We're going on a tram,' I said. 'It's only a ten-minute run. Just follow me. Do nothing. Keep a few feet apart, and get off when I get off.'

At Via Scialoia an extravagant welcome from Adrienne Lucidi preceded a good cold lunch. The Lucidis would still have preferred not to lodge any escapers, but, prompted by Adrienne who was impressed by Fane-Hervey's charm and his rank of Major, the highest British rank she had yet encountered, Renzo suggested that Fane-Hervey remain there, while Garrad-Cole could no doubt be squeezed in with the others at the French Seminary, to which sons Gerald and Maurice escorted him.

16

APPUNTAMENTO CON MONSIGNORE O'FLAHERTY

An SOS for more cash from the French Seminary crowd had me off to St Peter's with their improvised cheques. For the first time I would have to run the gauntlet of the Swiss Guards. My new black coat, grey suit and broad-brimmed felt hat instilled confidence. Moreover, a new Identity Card, turned out by the Monsignor's private forgers, who were working full-time fabricating an ingenious array of documents, looked genuine. It described me as Guglielmo del Monte and bore the stamp of the City of Naples.

Outside the Santa Marta archway a Swiss Guard stepped forward and lowered his halberd.

'*C'ho un' appuntamento con Monsignore O'Flaherty*,' I said, and showed him my Identity Card. He let me pass. At the inner end of the long archway another sentry examined my card. Again I mentioned my appointment with the Monsignor. He looked me up and down and pointed to the office on the left where I obtained a written pass. I walked on and crossed a courtyard to the *Collegio Teutonicum*. A German nun answered the door-bell, and a porter guided me upstairs.

'More room now,' said the Monsignor. 'Sam's inside with the British Minister. I got a note from John Furman from the prison. I've passed it on to Sam. John must have bribed someone with an outside contact.' They were still in *Regina Coeli*.

'Anything about Bruno and Nebulanti, or Herta?'

'Not directly. He infers that all three were taken to Via Tasso.'

'D'you think the Germans would have the nerve to come up here?'

'Who knows? If they could build up enough justification, I don't think they'd stop at raiding the Vatican itself.'

'And risk the consequences, politically?'

'That's the only thing holding them back.' The Monsignor began to smile. His eyes flashed. 'You know, the Swiss Guards realize this could happen. There aren't many of them, but they'll die to a man before a single German sets a foot in here.' He went on about the responsibility of the Church for all peoples, including Germany's large Catholic population. Hitler and his Nazis were the problem.

It was clear that this independently minded official of the *Sant'Ufficio*, the Holy Office, which oversaw so many facets of the central church's activities and world affairs, had determined, based on his first-hand knowledge of Nazi *kultur*, to wage his own humanitarian battle of defiance. Apart from the Allied escapers, he was busy protecting some 2000 Jews within the city. Yet, as Sam Derry had hinted, the key to the Monsignor's activity was the word 'independent'. He was on his own as far as his Vatican superiors were concerned.

The higher echelons of the Vatican deemed the protection of their sovereign state to be a matter of the highest priority in relation to its worldwide influence. The natural corollary of guarding its neutrality in the war put them in numerous dilemmas. Pope Pius XII was facing agonizing choices. He was fully aware that Hitler was prepared, if obliged to pull out of Rome, to invade the Vatican City and abduct the Pope by force. A desperate Führer might evaluate 'possession' of the Pope and, ideally, a concomitant acquisition of Vatican art treasures, as outweighing the adverse shock which such action would send across the globe. Clearly, Vatican policy sought to avoid identifiable breaches of strict neutrality.

Moreover, the Vatican's ultimate enemy was Communism. Years of authoritarian Fascist rule in Italy had spawned a host of resistance groups and underground political parties. Of these, the most numerous, most radical and most potent were factions collectively organized under the Communist flag. In the event of a German pull-out from Rome, the despised new Republican Socialist Government, set up by the Germans at Salò in northern Italy, with the recently retrieved Mussolini as its puppet head, would be impotent as a force for public order. Even the briefest transitional vacuum in exercised control of Rome would, it was feared, risk a Communist insurrection, a power grab in the capital which could spread like fire across the country. Interwoven with these perplexing possibilities were anxieties for the physical preservation of Rome itself.

The Monsignor had risen and pushed back the table, thus clearing the full length of a thin carpet. At one end he put down a black shoe and, at the other end, he dropped three golf balls. Taking a pitching wedge from a golf bag and holding the club with a wide grip halfway down the shaft, he proceeded to chip the balls toward the shoe. The first two just missed; the third went in.

'But take all this work you're doing, Monsignor, all the risks, helping our chaps, hundreds here in the city and some three thousand you and Sam are financing outside? I mean, this has some military value.' Apart from the instinctive desire to stay free, each escaper, by keeping out of enemy hands, would one day rejoin our forces and resume military service. Even now, just the existence behind their lines of thousands of free British and American ex-POWs was a security problem to the occupying Germans causing them to deploy ever-increasing police strength.

While born an Irishman with no great love for the English, the awful cruelties the Nazis had committed under the excuse of war disgusted him. He was lining up the balls for the fourth time. Out of the last six, four had landed in the shoe.

'What's your handicap?' I asked.

'I haven't played much recently, but it's around one or two. I used to play a lot with Ciano, Mussolini's son-in-law. I practically taught him the game.'

He turned on the radio. The BBC's three o'clock news from London was far from encouraging,

'Bill, *quando vengono questi benedetti Inglese?*' he pleaded with a note of desperation. When would the blessed English come?

The Monsignor had good reason to be worried. In the last five months he had deeply involved a score of younger priests as his aides, and almost every close friend he had in Rome was working for him. Now German security measures were intensifying. Arrests were leading to more arrests. Each time one of his friends was imprisoned, the Monsignor felt a personal responsibility. How much longer could he expect them to take these risks? How much longer before the *benedetti Inglese* arrived?

"Ow's yer knees an' things?' announced the arrival of perky John May. Silent German nuns served tea, as I exchanged the unconvincing-looking cheques for a bundle of Italian currency.

I took my leave, back through the Vatican corridor with the return of my official pass and out again into unpredictable, fascinating Rome.

17

ANZIO LANDING

'Early this morning, Allied Forces landed on the west coast of Italy at a point between Ostia and Gaeta. No further details are ...' The dramatic announcement came from the radio in the Lucidis' living room, on the nine o'clock morning News from London. Gerald and I stared at the radio. Had we heard correctly on this Saturday morning of 22 January, 1944? Ostia was only 20 miles away; Gaeta lay some 60 miles further down the coast. Where was the landing? Gerald ran to tell Renzo and his mother. Left alone, my impulse was to drop everything and head south. If the landing had in fact taken place, the enemy must have been taken by surprise; the time to reach our troops was now, before any battle lines existed. Almost as quickly I realized that free choice was no longer mine; in these last seven weeks in Rome I had become too deeply committed here.

If this was a major landing whose objectives included the capture of Rome, then in no time all this could be over. If, on the other hand, it was only a feint or if the Germans were able to react in time to contain the landing force, wherever it was, then our work in Rome would become doubly complicated.

The Lucidis burst into the room, Adrienne overjoyed, Renzo sceptical about the accuracy of the news. From a back bedroom, Major Fane-Hervey appeared. His initial reaction was that, at least until something further developed, we should stay put.

Renzo rushed off to the French Seminary to tell the gang hiding there, and to take them the cash which had been the reason for my early morning visit here. I headed for Mrs M's. On my way there, the tug of war raged inside me. Just what was I doing riding in a trolley-car across Rome when I could be hiking my way south, however unprepared, perhaps with slim odds of avoiding recapture but with the chance of reaching Allied lines or advance mobile units, wherever they might have landed? For sixty miles south along the Latina coast the land was fairly flat. The obstacles previously discouraging us were no longer present, if the BBC communiqué was accurate.

So what if I had become part of this quasi-military but still amateur underground? After all, it had few rules, was led by a self-effacing, albeit magnetically strong Irish priest and Sam Derry, a Major, an energetic leader, and backed by the British Minister, but an escaper just like the rest and now involuntarily holed up in the Vatican. We were running by the seat of our pants. I was just an escaper, like the hundreds of others hidden across the city, like the five irrepressible American and British officers in the French Seminary, the four British other ranks in Mrs M's where I was headed. After all, once you escaped, it was every man for himself, with the duty of trying to rejoin Allied lines. Why don't I just get off, I argued, head south and chance it? Somebody else could supervise Mrs M's crowd and the others hidden at more than a dozen addresses I carried, and their nervous *padrone* could, well...

The other end of the rope took over: poor Monsignor O'Flaherty, already up to his eyes and overburdened, John Furman gone, Joe Pollak God-knows-where, Nebulanti and Bruno incarcerated. If these other *padrone* didn't have my visit on time with the bi-weekly allowance to help feed their dangerous guests, who would fill in?

My internal debate went on as I changed trams, realizing that with every minute of indecision the practical chance of a successful flight south was evaporating. Call it conscience, a vague sense of duty to this weird organization, to the other escapers under my wing, especially when I had no way to communicate quickly with Sam Derry; whatever this confused mixture of loyalties, I concluded finally that I'd be wrong to just disappear. I'd stay.

By the time I reached Mrs M's, the household had heard the news and was greatly excited. All Rome was on edge. Rumours flashed that the German Command in the city was in a state of panic and confusion, but shrewdly that very afternoon, a large contingent of German staff officers appeared at the Royal Opera House outwardly cool and unperturbed.

Towards evening, as further speculative reports filtered through, it became clear that the points of landing were the beaches at Anzio and Nettuno, 50 miles south of Rome.

At the Pestalozzas' after the curfew, *Radio Londra* and *Radio Roma* fed us snatches of news. During the night the heavy drone of German planes flying south grew in intensity. The enemy was reacting quickly.

This steady throbbing of hundreds of aircraft engines was to continue for several nights.

By Sunday afternoon it was known that the landing, enjoying the full element of surprise, had been unopposed at first. One lone reconnaissance column of armoured vehicles had reached Castel Gandolfo in the Alban hills, only 12 miles from Rome, but had returned quickly to the zone of the beachhead. Now two German Panzer Divisions were rushing from the north of Italy to oppose the landing.

By Monday the surprise phase of the landing, we guessed, was over, still, to our chagrin, without a major offensive strike from the beachhead. Even if Rome, which by the indefensible nature of its physical terrain was admittedly of little military value, was not an immediate objective, there had to be some strong strategic motive behind this operation. Either Anzio was intended to outflank the enemy's Gustav Line, which had proved impenetrable against Allied attack all winter, or at least the landing force was supposed to threaten or cut the Germans' two main supply routes, Via Appia and Via Casilina.

The traffic of German armoured units moving south was heavy and the nightly German aerial attacks intensified. The situation became unsettling. Was our landing force about to lose its offensive initiative and, instead of striking, become involved in a slogging battle to defend its beachhead?

Every hour of the day Fascist-run *Radio Roma* blared out bulletins declaring the Allied landing a failure and claiming that the increasing German strength around the now-contained perimeter of the beachhead was preparing to sweep the Allied forces back into the sea. By the end of the fourth day, even the BBC was less reassuring. While still confident that such a defeat would not occur, we nevertheless recoiled from the thought of the political repercussions in Rome, if the worst did happen.

On the fifth day the Commander of the German 14th Army, General von Mackensen, our recent neighbour in the Opera House, launched a major attack against the extreme west sector of the Anzio perimeter. The Allied defences held. This was the turning point; from then on the danger of losing the beachhead faded.

Yet our disappointment was acute; the prospect of quick liberation had evaporated. Editorials in Rome newspapers were venomous. Headlines and comment called the operation a fiasco abortively conceived in Allied stupidity, and proclaimed afresh the unconquerable prowess of the Nazi-Fascist forces. One widely published photograph of a captured detachment of Scottish infantrymen bore the caption, 'The Famous Gordon Highlanders Reach Rome ... as Prisoners of War!'

Bad news leaked out from *Regina Coeli*. In their temporary panic, the German SS had moved their most important captives, including John Furman, and sent them north by train.

Since the Anzio landing, heavy German ground transports had been flouting the German 'Open City' declaration by driving in convoy through the eastern part of the city. The Allies could no longer overlook this vital traffic. With ground fighting deadlocked south of Cassino on the Gustav line and defence of the precarious Anzio beachhead an imperative, Allied air power focused on interdicting enemy buildup of matériel. Limited only by overcast winter skies, Allied bombers pursued this objective wherever air reconnaissance and ground intelligence led them. Thus, the sky above Rome now vibrated frequently as American high-altitude raids pattern-bombed airfields and arterial roads close by.

Twice, targets lay well inside the city, like the gigantic Italian barracks, Castro Pretorio, often used now as a German staging area. The densely populated area around Piazza Bologna had also suffered. Concerned over public reaction, the local German Command withdrew from view all non-essential troops. Over Rome Radio and in the daily *Il Messaggero*, Rome Commandant General Kurt Mälzer's staff declared that no German military personnel were now in Rome, except for a 'few security details' required to prevent outbreaks by 'misguided' elements.

18

GOOD MORNING, GESTAPO

The bulge in my inside pocket as I left the Monsignor's room came from 100,000 lire in cash, February's 'pay' for the thirty-three escapers on my list.

On an evening when the Pestalozzas had invited normally frequent guests in to play bridge, I had agreed to spend the night at the Lucidis'. There, at supper, in addition to the family, were Major Fane-Hervey and a new face to me, a smartly dressed young Pole. From Genoa, where he had been studying shipbuilding at the time of the Italian Armistice, he had come to Rome. Now he was deeply involved in a Socialist Resistance movement, through which he had met Renzo Lucidi. Already he had found several safe billets for our escapers. Because of the constant risk, he rarely stayed in one place more than a few days. By coincidence, he was here tonight, complete with a packed briefcase holding galley proofs for the next issue of his Resistance newspaper and two revolvers.

After supper Renzo and I split the list of escapers, wrote out pro-forma receipts ready for signature the next day and divided the pile of cash. I placed my cash and receipts in my briefcase. Renzo hid his bundle in a cache above a fireplace in the hallway. With an early start we should cover all the billets in one day.

We retired, Fane-Hervey to his room beyond the living-room and I to the spare bed in Gerald's room, next to the dining-room. In minutes, I was asleep.

'Bill, wake up! Bill, Bill, get up! Do something! Germans!'

Adrienne's frantic whisper in my ear woke me with a start. Leaning over in a dressing-gown in the early daylight, she was shaking me.

'What?'

'Germans, here, in there!' Adrienne pointed to the dining-room. 'They're taking Renzo!'

I sat bolt upright. Adrienne rushed out of the room and slammed the door. In seconds her burbling French was screaming above other voices, harsh male voices, in the dining-room. What was going on? My watch said 7.45. Gerald still slept. I jumped from the bed and scrambled into my clothes. Strangers were in the next room all right. What had Adrienne said? Taking Renzo away? Had they come to find Renzo or Fane-Hervey and me? Whatever the reason, it took me no time to decide I'd rather be anywhere else than here. Discovery would be certain, at any moment. I had to get out of this trap somehow, and take with me this pile of money and these damning receipt forms. Throwing on my overcoat, I grabbed my hat and briefcase and tiptoed to the bedroom door.

'But where is my husband?' Adrienne's shrill French through the wall was almost hysterical.

To the left of my door lay the dining-room. If I could just slip across twelve feet outside the bedroom without being spotted, the long darkened hallway straight ahead would cover me all the way to the front door. If I ran into more Germans outside on the landing.... I had to take the chance.

My hand shook on the doorknob as I eased open the bedroom door and listened. The voices seemed to be inside the dining-room to my left. Ready! Go! I tiptoed quickly across the exposed twelve feet.

'*Halt! Halt!*' bellowed a voice. I froze. I bent down as if to tie a shoelace and rose again slowly, heart thudding, as a short plain-clothes man strode up and peered at me.

'*Ché siete?*' he asked. So he was Italian, not German. As soon as I spoke, he'd spot my accent. Who am I? My mouth was dry. My voice would hardly come.

'*Guglielmo del Monte,*' I forced out.

'But who are you? What are you?' Behind him now appeared a helmeted SS man gripping a machine-pistol. What could I say? As I stalled, Adrienne rushed up.

'*Guglielmo del Monte,*' I repeated. Then finding my voice and pointing at Adrienne, '*Sono il nipote della Signora qui.*' Adrienne caught my look.

'Yes, yes, he is my nephew,' she confirmed.

The plain-clothes man looked suspiciously from me to Adrienne and back. I tried again. What was 'aunt' in Italian? '*Si, si, mia ... tante,*' I stammered.

'*Tante? Ah ya! Si! Ya!*' He indicated that he understood. '*Tante! Ya, tante!*' he went on, heading for the kitchen. By mistake the word I had used was *tante*, the German word, instead of the Italian *zia*. But a lucky mistake; the man was German, not Italian.

Ten minutes ago Renzo had been awakened by a loud banging on the front door and had answered it in his dressing-gown. The civilian and two uniformed Germans had pushed their way inside, demanding Signor Renzo Lucidi. Renzo, only too aware of Fane-Hervey, the Pole and myself asleep in the flat, had immediately declared himself. In quick response to their command, he had thrown on a suit and all three had escorted him downstairs into a waiting car. Leaving him there with other armed SS men, two had, to Renzo's dismay, returned upstairs to search the place. In the car below Renzo prepared for the worst. Why the Germans had come for him he did not know, but with two British escapers and an armed Pole to explain away...!

The searchers reappeared from the kitchen, marched down the corridor and disappeared through the front door. I stared. I could hardly believe it.

What about Fane-Hervey? I ran through Adrienne's bedroom and found him in his room.

'What's going on?' he asked.

'Didn't they come in here?'

'Who? All I know is that I woke up with somebody shouting *"Luce! Luce!"* It was dark, so I didn't move. But he shouted again, so I got up, walked over to the lamp there and switched it on. Right beside me was a German. Bit of a shock! But he was just as surprised. He mumbled something about *"Ché siete?"* Not knowing what the hell to say, I just said. "Paula". He sort of nodded, looked around a minute and left.'

'Look, Fanny,' I said, 'get dressed, double quick. Something's crazy around here. Let's get out, fast!'

Back in the lobby 10-year-old Maurice stood dressed.

'Maurice, run downstairs to the street – don't take the lift – and see if they've left anybody on guard. Come right back.' He raced off.

'Non c'e nessuno!' he announced minutes later. Nobody down there.

'Fanny, I'm off. Hurry up! I'll wait for you on Via Flaminia.'

Five minutes later, as I paced up and down Via Flaminia waiting for Fane-Hervey, I still could not make sense out of the last half-hour. Renzo had been arrested. Why? Apparently we, the escapers, were not the reason. In that tight corner too, Adrienne had been wonderful; she had kept her head and played her part. The Germans had been bluffed, but they could be back. Should Adrienne and the boys stay or get out?

I was in a fix again. I had lost my valuable partner. Parcels of cash and incriminating receipt forms written in English lay hidden in the Lucidis' hallway.

Fane-Hervey arrived. After a brief post-mortem we separated, I to warn the Pestalozzas, Fanny to seek shelter at Signor Esmé Simpson Almagia's magnificent villa on nearby Via Stanislao Mancini.

Thus we did not see the car which at that moment swung into Via Scialoia and screeched to a halt before No. 18. The same two Germans leaped out and ran upstairs to the Lucidi flat. Where were the other two men, they demanded.

'They've left,' said Adrienne.

'Who were they?'

'Just two friends who came to play cards last night. They were caught by the curfew, so we put them up for the night.'

'Where have they gone now?'

Gerald, now dressed, joined them.

'They've ... gone off to work.'

'Work? But this is Sunday! What kind of work?' Gerald, noting his mother's confusion, stepped forward.

'We don't know them very well. In fact, they were a damned nuisance last night. We don't know where they've gone, and don't care!' The German seemed already to have forgotten the earlier 'nephew-*Tante*' alibi. He and the soldier then proceeded to search every room in the flat. In the kitchen they found the Pole, who had avoided discovery in the initial raid, and questioned him at length. Feigning embarrassment and guilt, he slipped his arm around Pepina's waist and 'confessed' he was her lover. Secretly last night she had let him in to spend the night with her. Even Signora Lucidi did not know he was here! He had planned to leave early in the morning, but the surprise arrival of his interrogators had put him on the spot, and Pepina too.

With a nod of manly understanding, the short German agreed not to give them away and they withdrew from the kitchen.

The cache above the hall fireplace, where the money and receipts were hidden, escaped their notice. However, in searching Gerald's room the short German found a current issue of *Avanti*, the Communist party newspaper, which Gerald had left by accident on his dressing-table. It was the first piece of incriminating evidence to surface. They pumped Gerald about it. Calmly and cleverly, he parried their questions. They seemed satisfied and started for the door. Then the short German hesitated, turned back, grabbed hold of Gerald and led him off with them.

Adrienne barred their way at the door. Why were they doing this? Why had they taken her husband away? The German volunteered that during the night the SS had raided the home of a certain Professor Gentiluomo, a leader of the local Communist Underground. They had arrested him and in the course of searching his house had come across an address book. When this was studied at SS Headquarters, detachments had been sent out immediately to arrest every person whose name appeared in the book. One of the names was Renzo Lucidi.

Later in the Monsignor's room at the Vatican, I related the bad news of Renzo's arrest.

'It's midday, nobody's been paid, and I'm down 50,000 lire!' I was concerned about the loss of the money, but the Monsignor was only amused.

'You're more Scotch than I thought,' he chuckled. 'I'll send word to Sam. Stay for lunch and in no time at all you'll have your money again.'

'Five months ago,' he said, 'the loss of 50,000 lire would have been distressing when I had to rely on my wealthier friends for help. Now money's no problem. Mind you, Sam's watching it carefully.'

From the autumn of 1943, when Prince Doria's gift of 150,000 lire was 'heaven-sent', the organization's budget had escalated. I curbed my curiosity about the source of funds. There was no need to know that Sam Derry was now dispensing three million lire per month, including sizeable deliveries to groups of escaped POWs far north of Rome. Prompted by Sir D'Arcy Osborne, the British Foreign Office had provided credit guarantees to the Vatican Bank to facilitate the release of substantial sums,* and was arranging additional funding through Switzerland. Harold Tittmann, the American counterpart to the British Minister, was contributing his share. The Monsignor explained Mr Tittmann's position. The United States, for political reasons, did not actually have a Minister to the Holy See. Instead, President Roosevelt had appointed a Personal Representative to the Vatican in the person of Mr Myron Taylor. In Mr Taylor's absence back in America, Mr Tittmann was the Chargé d'Affaires.

John May plunked a bulky envelope in front of me. '50,000 smackers! 'Ow's that for service, guv'ner?'

'Thanks, John. Tell Sam the money may not really be lost, but I'm damned if I'm going back to the Lucidis' to look for it.'

May waited while I wrote a quick letter to Sam, giving him, among other items, the new address of Mrs M's three escapers. Her butcher friend had taken them to his own home.

At the Pestalozzas' in the late afternoon the family was on edge.

*FO 371/44215

Adrienne Lucidi had suddenly appeared on their doorstep, in a state of collapse. They had put her to bed. While full of sympathy, they were logically concerned that her open arrival might have compromised them; she might have been followed.

Dedy filled me in on the return visit of the Germans to Via Scialoia only minutes after Fane-Hervey and I had left.

Entering the bedroom where Adrienne lay, I tried to reassure her. She seemed to be in a state of shock.

'Bill, if anything happens to Renzo or Gerald,' she stammered, clutching my arm, 'my heart, it's weak.'

'Don't worry, Adrienne; they'll come out of this.'

'If the worst happens,' she concluded, 'promise me you'll look after Maurice, poor boy.'

'Of course Adrienne, absolutely. But don't feel this way. Now that we know why Renzo was arrested, things aren't so black as you imagine.' I hoped I sounded convincing.

To avoid further suspicion falling on Renzo and Gerald if the Germans returned, Maurice and Pepina were keeping the flat open at Via Scialoia.

Two days of zig-zagging across Rome, with help from Mrs Chevalier who knew some the *padrone*, accomplished the pay-out of February's allowance to the thirty-three escapers on my list.

★　★　★

Mrs. Chevalier was about to be used again.

Even as Lazzaretto Hospital filled up with German casualties from Anzio, Surgeon Professor Urbani had acceded to an urgent request from Monsignor O'Flaherty. Hiding on a farm near Subiaco, 40 miles northeast of Rome, Private Anderson of the Cameron Highlanders had contracted appendicitis.

In the Vatican, the Irish Minister, Dr. Thomas Kiernan, tried to observe the neutrality of his country. His wife and daughter Blon felt less constrained. By noon Father "Spike" Buckley was speeding the Irish Minister's official car, bearing diplomatic corps license plates, to Subiaco.

By the time Spike carried his charge into the hospital, his condition had worsened to peritonitis. An hour later, wheeling Anderson away from the operating theatre, the Professor, on Spike's assurances, consented to Anderson being moved.

Spike carried the still unconscious patient to the Irish car and thence up three flights of stairs to a bed in Mrs. Chevalier's dining room.

In the morning I arrived to find Mrs. Chevalier barely composed. In case of prying eyes, Spike had supported the then semi-conscious Anderson in a walking position climbing the stairs.

'What agony!' she said.

The following morning, in the Monsignor's room at the Vatican, I was blowing off angrily about the utter stupidity of some irresponsible fool who had let Anderson leave the hospital when I was quietly interrupted.

'Bill, it was I who told Spike to do it,' said the Monsignor. There was a moment of embarrassed silence. 'Urbani had no choice,' he said. 'He had four other critical cases waiting – all Germans.'

Of course the Monsignor was right. The worst passed. The Professor moved Anderson to the residence of the American Monsignor McGeoch where he received proper nursing.

* * *

At the German College, soon after Lucidi's arrest, the Monsignor asked me to handle two new arrivals whom he had put up temporarily in a religious college not far from St Peter's Square.

'It's a good place for transients but I don't want to keep them there. The janitor Paolino, a grand little fellow, has done a lot for me lately. The building has a fine big basement, and he's hiding a bunch of my Jews down there already. I want Paolino to meet you. We'll go over there now.'

Since the College lay beyond the Monsignor's safe area of movement, I suggested that, if he gave me directions, I would find Paolino myself.

'No, I've warned him to be careful. I'll take you.'

'But you're a marked man, Monsignor.'

'Don't worry, I'll look after myself,' he said as we set out.

Of all the religious schools, colleges, seminaries and parish buildings which abound in Rome, I wondered if there was one that did not harbour a group of Jewish refugees, all at the behest of this dauntless priest.

His lively chatter only stopped when we passed the Swiss Guards on duty. As each Guard in turn sprang to attention and presented arms, he touched his broad-rimmed black hat in acknowledgment. The click of heels and the slap of halberds made it clear that, for all his familiarity and informal friendliness, his high rank commanded great respect. It was his first venture beyond the steps of St Peter's in many days. He was enjoying it.

113

As we passed one of the giant fountains in the *piazza*, he turned me around and pointed to the top of Michelangelo's dome over St Peter's. The cupola above it, a small gold sphere, he explained, could hold sixteen adults standing up. The tall obelisk in the centre of the *piazza*, he went on, had originally stood in another part of the city after the Emperor Caligula had it brought from Egypt to Rome. Centuries later, its great height and slim proportions had inspired Bernini to make it the central point in his grand design for St Peter's Square.

'You should write a guidebook, Monsignor.'

'I have, several.'

Beyond the colonnade to the south, a short side-street brought us to the dignified entrance to the college. Down in a basement Paolino beamed happily at the sight of the Monsignor. I met the two Englishmen hidden there and arranged to call for them the following day.

As I continued on to Mrs M's, American bomber formations droned high overhead. In minutes the ground shook and the air 'crumped' to the explosion of hundreds of bombs. Today they were close, up ahead to the north-east.

Excited Italian police stopped my tram before Piazza Salerno. They had cordoned off the area. The huge military barracks of Castro Pretoria nearby, where the Germans were known to be concentrating transport, had obviously been the target, but the high-altitude bombs had not found it. Instead they had created havoc in the residential quarter between the barracks and Piazza Bologna. Right in the heart of this area lay Mrs M's. My anxiety grew as I was forced to take a long detour on foot outside the damaged section.

At Mrs M's the family's nerves were ragged. Houses nearby had been demolished and many residents killed and wounded.

'We must get out of here!' said Mrs M. Her usual calm had gone. This was the third time recently that Allied bombs had exploded close to their home.

Knowing it would be extremely difficult for her to move, with her girls and their grandmother, I tried to persuade her she was probably as safe here as anywhere. Who knew where the bombs would fall tomorrow? Since her three British escapers who might have reassured her were no longer here, I stayed overnight. By the next morning the talk of moving had subsided.

19

TO HELL AND BACK

'Renzo Lucidi and Gerald are out of Via Tasso.' Overjoyed, the Pestalozzas greeted me thus. They had turned up at Via Scialoia late the
night before. As soon as the curfew ended at daybreak, a suddenly
revived Adrienne had rushed home to her husband and son. 'Renzo's
due here any minute,' said Dedy excitedly. This was more than we had
ever dared to hope for. Free, and after only five days. The doorbell
rang. In seconds Renzo was the centre of a tempestuous welcome. Apart
from a slight pallor, he seemed as dapper and self-controlled as ever.

'Yes, they took us straight to Via Tasso. We've been unbelievably
lucky.' Few prisoners had ever emerged from that dreaded jail.

'Did Adrienne tell you about last Sunday morning?' I asked. Renzo
grinned. Waiting under guard in the German car down on Via Scialoia,
he had been sure the Germans would reappear with Fane-Hervey, the
Pole and me.

'You wouldn't believe the murderous plans I thought up while I
waited – to jump the Germans and make a getaway. When they finally
appeared without you, I felt so relieved I was afraid for a minute I had
given myself away.'

In Via Tasso he had been dumped in a cell, alone. Soon afterwards
through a small *sportello* in the cell door he spotted Gerald being
brought in and his spirits dropped. He did not know the reason for his
arrest until taken the next day to a room for interrogation.

'The first thing they asked me was my relationship with Professor
Gentiluomo. Right away I guessed what had happened. I explained that
Gerald was a student of his at Rome University. Then, for good
measure, and trying to look a little peeved, I told them I had recently
sold an overcoat to the Professor and he still owed me money for it.
They prodded me about connections I might have with Communist or

115

Socialist parties in the city, but I insisted I had never been interested in politics and was content to earn an honest living as a film cutter.' After that he was returned to his cell, where he had been left alone until yesterday morning.

'What was it like?' Galeazzo asked.

'Well, miserable of course, practically nothing to eat, and sleeping on the floor. Plenty of bugs. The worst part was sweating over what would happen, especially when I could see what was happening to the others ...' Renzo was clearly hesitating to continue.

'Go on.' Dedy and Giovanna were here. Miss May, luckily, was making coffee in the kitchen. 'It was awful. Day and night, cries, moans and whimpers from these poor creatures being interrogated. That Gestapo stuff, horrible. I couldn't sleep of course. Through the *sportello* I could watch these poor fellows being dragged back to their cells, unconscious mostly, terribly beaten up.' Renzo's expression conveyed more than his words.

'Did you hear anything about Professor Gentiluomo?'

'Hear? I saw him four times a day, twice a day being walked past my cell to the interrogation room, and twice a day being hauled back unconscious. By the second day he was completely unrecognizable. Practically naked, he was covered in blood. His face, well, just battered in. And you remember, he was such a gentle, frail fellow. Yesterday he couldn't walk from his cell. They hauled him out, more of the same. I caught a glimpse as they dragged him back. His left eye...' Renzo was stammering, hardly audible. 'Kind of hanging from the socket.' This was more than the girls had expected; they had known him too.

'Don't ask me how, but even in a place like Via Tasso word gets around from cell to cell.' Renzo's voice was firmer now. 'We all knew in there that, after five days of sheer hell, he still hadn't broken down.'

Renzo had again been questioned, surprisingly simple questions to which he had given straightforward answers. At half past seven that evening a German officer came to his cell and told him he was free to leave. Gerald was freed at the same time. Apparently the Professor, when questioned about Renzo and his son, had by sheer luck explained their acquaintance in the same innocent vein.

As it was close to the curfew hour, Renzo had asked the guards at the exit how he and Gerald were expected to reach home without being re-arrested. A German officer replied that they would simply have to chance it!

'Oh, before I forget, Bill, here's something that doesn't belong to me.' Renzo pulled a fat envelope from his pocket and threw it over to me.

116

Inside were 50,000 lire and a bunch of receipt forms. 'Did everybody get paid? Sorry I wasn't around to help you.' The sincerity of his apology was comical.

'Yes, it worked out fine, with help from Mrs Chevalier. Of course, you'll have to lie low now.' I felt sure Renzo would want to cut loose from us.

'Why?'

'Well, after all, the Germans know you now and . . .'

'Nonsense! I feel fine. I'm ready.'

'Good! We'll call on "Golf" tomorrow.'

The next afternoon at the Vatican Monsignor O'Flaherty was delighted. To John May I handed a wad of thousand lire notes to be returned to the 'Pay Bloke', Major Derry. A large slice of the cash, however, I had retained for Renzo, whose recent adventures had emptied his family coffers.

20

FRIENDS, ROMANS, GREEKS

Three people received a big welcome from the Monsignor and John May.

'Bill,' said John May, 'meet the "Liberty or Death" boys, Ted Meletiou and Angelos Averoff.' These two Greeks, both escaped prisoners, had earlier organized many Greek escapers in and near Rome. Now they had joined our organization. Their Italian was fluent. A resourceful pair, they had somehow acquired from an unsuspecting German headquarters the necessary permits to travel by car anywhere in Italy. Already they had made several long-distance trips for Sam Derry and had brought back detailed information on groups of escapers in areas as far north as Florence.

'And this charming lady,' said the Monsignor, 'is their travelling companion – Scots too – Mrs Mary Boyd.' A pleasant companion, I thought, observing her profile. Mrs Boyd had spent most of the war in a civil internment camp near Florence. When released after the Armistice, she had encountered our Greek friends, with whom she was now sharing heavy risks.

On an earlier trip north Ted Meletiou, code-named Mario, had located a trio of British generals, in hiding on a farm. Derry had sent Mario back with funds and instructions to bring one of them to Rome. To the Monsignor's request for a 'really secure hiding-place', Brother Robert had produced the answer. Signora DiRienzo, Italian by marriage, English by birth, and niece of Lord Strickland, ex-Governor-General of Malta, had a secret room in her large home in Rome. Now Major-General M.D. Gambier-Parry, captured by the Germans while commanding a British Armoured Division in the Libyan Desert in 1942, was the best concealed escaper in Rome.

Evangelos Averoff-Tossiza, an important figure in pre-war Greek politics, had been interned in Italy when, as Prefect of Corfu, he refused to continue in office under Italian Occupation.

Billets? Mario would see what he could do, but in two days he was leaving again with Mrs Boyd with money and supplies to visit several towns and villages up north, particularly areas where large concentrations of liberated POWs were still dependent on the support of local Italians. They were distributing close to one million lire per month of Sam Derry's funds.

Silent on the tram with Renzo, I reflected on the contrasting characters I was meeting on each visit to the Monsignor's quarters, individuals whose diversity in nationality, social station, sex, age, profession, war status, religion, disappeared in their shared objective of obstructing the common enemy. The task in hand called on their capacity to keep free two hundred escapers within the city, and many hundreds more outside.

Some I had met here only once, such as Bruno the Yugoslav in prison, and the two Greeks of today who, with their Italian-speaking Scotswoman, were the long-range operators penetrating as far north as Milan. American Monsignor McGeough of the Vatican, tall and stockily-built, whose genial smile detracted not at all from the notion one gained of his inner strength, concentrated on American escapers of which Rome so far held only about a score. The US acting Presidential representative to the Holy See, Harold Tittmann, found in Monsignor McGeogh a willing liaison with Monsignor O'Flaherty in organizing help to fugitive Jews as well as to American escapers.

Others I encountered whenever we teamed up: the lively Maltese priests, Fathers Borg and Galea, and the natural, unassuming but intrepid Prince Carracciolo. The bright-eyed Princess Nina Palavicini, a charming practical aristocrat, had many activities. In addition to helping Monsignor O'Flaherty and, in spite of being on the Gestapo's wanted list, she made her palazzo near Piazza Venezia available for clandestine meetings of the *Comitato della Liberazione Nazionale*, or CLN. Immediately after the Armistice, when the King and Badoglio fled south, the dozen or so political parties waiting to shake off the outlaw status of Fascist years had formed this umbrella organization.

Young Signorina Vittoria Rossi, besides being intelligent and attractive and acting as our contact-cum-'runner' with fifty ex-prisoners hiding in Montelibretti, sixty kilometres north of Rome, was turning up billets for me with friendly families within the city. These friends were fellow members of her political group, the *Partito d'Azione*. On several walks with her in and out of the Vatican (when my interest in her political views might occasionally have been secondary, even if hers never was), she had explained her point on the wide-swinging political compass. She accepted the CLN as an essential glue to keep in line the disparate anti-Fascist groups. Outside the CLN, the far-right Royalist military leadership, the 'Badogliani', headed by respected Italian generals, and operating radio intelligence with the Allies, were probably the best-equipped organization to maintain public order, if required. Politically, however, because of the King's years with Fascism, the principal CLN party leaders already discounted the future prospects of the Royalists. Within CLN, far to the right of Vittoria's Action Party, Alcide de Gasperi's Christian Democrats with strong Vatican support were considered in front numerically. Further to the right, the Labour Democrats carried weight; their leader Ivanoe Bonomi headed the CLN. In the centre was the Liberal Party, with uncertain appeal. About equidistant to the left, Pietro Nenni's Socialists had popular drawing power, while Vittoria's Action Party was recognized for its wealth of intellect and its clearly delineated policies, broadly liberal, but still democratic. Farthest left, and of major concern to all other groups, stood the strongly organized Communist Party and an even more radical splinter Communist Junta, calling itself GAP, the *Gruppo d'Azione Patriotica*.

A secretive middle-aged German, Mrs 'K', one of the Monsignor's sources of forged documents, in her luxurious flat on Piazza Cavour, had recently given me a large supply of perfectly counterfeited bread coupons which my numerous *padrone* were now passing off on bakeries around the city, instead of paying black-market prices.

Brother Robert Pace was a gentle, soft-spoken Maltese member of the De La Salle Teaching Order. His code-name, 'Whitebows', sprang from the two white ribbons flowing from the front of his dog-collar. In the thick of the traffic in escapers, he operated boldly with two stalwart young Italian aides, Sandro Cottich, a law student, and Mimo Trapani, a medical student who enjoyed freedom of movement in the city through membership of the Vatican's honorary *Guardia Palatina*.

Prince Filippo Doria Pamphilj, an influential, highly respected, strong-minded yet unpretentious nobleman opposed to Fascism, who had given early financial help to Monsignor O'Flaherty, I had not met. After one German night raid on the Palazzo Doria, where the Prince and his family had hidden successfully, prudence demanded that they live elsewhere under assumed names. False papers provided by the Monsignor's experts confirmed their new ways. The Prince, sharing living quarters in a church property in Rome, was a professor in the employ of the Vatican. His Scottish wife, Princess Gesine, and tall

English-looking daughter Orietta, were relegated to humbler status as third-category employees of the Ministry of Agriculture. Mother and daughter changed new homes twice to deflect attention.

Being technically in hiding did not deter the Prince from working closely with other areas of Resistance, notably with a high official of the Vatican's *Propaganda Fide*, Belgian Monsignor Noebles who, according to the Prince, 'sat in his cold office with his pipe, co-ordinating a steady stream of partisans on demolition plans.'

John May helped discreetly whenever he could, but the pressure on the Monsignor was heavy, so much so that on my visits, now three or four each week, he had me deputizing on some of his appointments, meeting his callers in a bare hallway one floor below his room.

Renzo Lucidi's return meant that we were both available for crises at short notice. With widespread wire-tapping, the Monsignor dared not be too explicit in 'clear' language on his phone. Renzo and I had become his 'Billeting Officers', his street men in Rome. When new escapers turned up, in St Peter's Square or in some church and, by one means or another, their plight was related to 'Golf', he could phone the Pestalozzas' or the Lucidis' or Mrs M's with a brief camouflaged message instructing where and when to pick up what 'packages'. The recipient would indicate to him simply whether the message could be reliably delivered to one of us. This Italian double talk would be flattered to be called code; it was the simple use of our code names woven into standard friendly Italian salutations with the key message sandwiched in.

Meanwhile Sam Derry's accumulation of data on over three thousand liberated POWs located elsewhere in the country was about to prove more valuable than he had imagined. Behind the Allied lines in the south the town of Bari on the Adriatic coast was the operational base of some versatile Allied Intelligence units. One of these, 'A' Force, specialized in sabotage behind enemy lines. Highly trained personnel were either dropped by parachute or put ashore at night from submarines or fishing craft. When missions were accomplished, their secret methods of returning to Allied lines were as diverse as their operations.

Recently an Italian agent of 'A' Force, Peter Tumiati, arrived in Rome after completing his primary mission. Having spent years in political prisons under the Fascist régime, he soon located old friends who led him to Monsignor O'Flaherty. At first the Monsignor was suspicious, but Tumiati finally established his authenticity, and the Monsignor arranged a well-camouflaged meeting between himself and Sam Derry. When Tumiati departed, he carried with him – baked by John May inside a loaf of bread – microfilms of all the intelligence which Sam had been able to accumulate, and of the exact locations across the country of the larger groups of Allied escapers. At the same time, Sam conveyed through Tumiati a strong plea for routes by which organized groups of escapers might rejoin Allied lines.

That Tumiati successfully returned to Bari was confirmed when shortly thereafter low-flying Allied planes dropped food supplies in the principal areas of escaper concentration. On the Adriatic coast 'A' Force operatives landing behind German lines corralled and shepherded groups of escapers from freezing shelters in farmsteads and surrounding woods to prearranged spots on the shore, where, in darkness, small power-boats from Bari evacuated them by sea.

Other intermediaries had given Sam Derry access to an Italian parachutist, Major Umberto Losena, who had landed behind German lines complete with short-wave radio-transmitting equipment and a skilled Italian crew. For the time being this provided Sam with a fast means of relaying back to Bari not only data on newly discovered groups of escaped prisoners in the north, but also whatever morsels of military intelligence came his way. Later Major Losena was caught, tried and executed.

Wisely, Sam, in his letters which I picked up in the Monsignor's room, had so far made no reference to these developments. Monsignor O'Flaherty himself did no more than hint at them. Sam was keeping me fully informed on Rome, and I needed no more. Through interrogation of some of our Italian helpers who had been caught by the German SS in the last month, we had to assume that the enemy's file on Monsignor O'Flaherty and our effective, if unorthodox, organization was growing fast. The Gestapo were undoubtedly anxious to fill in the blanks, particularly as many of their leads pointed directly to the Vatican itself. Thus, with the danger of arrest ever present, the less damning information one possessed the better.

This compartmentalization bred difficulties too. In response to an urgent plea of mine to increase the daily allowance of 100 lire, Sam wrote back that he was reluctant to grant it. If the escapers, he wrote, had their material needs too adequately satisfied, especially here in Rome, they might lose sight of their primary objective, which was to rejoin the Allied lines. Somewhat incensed at this, I wrote him a hot letter, insisting that practically every escaper with whom I was in contact would jump at any feasible scheme which offered the faintest chance of success in getting back to our lines. Without any reliable information on possible points of penetration, the wisdom of even attempting the task now was arguable. This we had agreed several times.

It looked as if we had drawn a complete blank, I went on, in efforts to contact anyone with knowledge of the situation further south. Moreover, I reminded him, two escapers who had recently made the attempt, along routes developed in consultation with him, had both returned with the opinion that it was impracticable, principally because of the snow. These two had come across the frozen bodies of several British ex-prisoners, and some Indians, who had apparently died of exposure and hunger. As usual, a few impolite cracks at the end of the letter turned off my 'steam'.

To his credit, Sam still made no reference to Tumiati and Co., but he did agree to a flat increase of 500 lire per escaper per month, which staved off the threatening and justified 'strike' of many of our *padrone*.

* * *

At the Santa Marta entrance the Swiss Guards were openly hostile. The senior Guard refused to phone Monsignor O'Flaherty and in plain language told me to get out. It was not my day. Earlier, strolling down the east side of Piazza Cavour, on my way to pick up some more bread coupons from the German Mrs 'K', the sun had been warm. Relaxed, I was hardly on the look-out. In fact, I was chuckling over the previous day's lunch with Rendell and Dedy della Campana at the charming Casino delle Rose in Villa Borghese. Close to German SS Headquarters on Via Veneto, it was popular with German staff officers for its cuisine and for its live orchestra – the only one permitted in Rome under the continuing Fascist ban on public music. Through Pestalozza's introduction, I trusted the owner, the head waiter and the bartender. The bouncy orchestra leader, Angelico, seemed to get a charge out of our visits. As the head waiter led Dennis, Dedy and me past tables of German officers to our spot near a blazing fireplace, Angelico had stopped his orchestra abruptly in the middle of a Viennese waltz and burst into the 'Lambeth Walk'. When I turned to his raised bandstand, he was beaming at us, before openly grimacing toward a nearby table of Germans eating with single-minded intensity.

Thus lost in thought as I approached the three high wrought-iron gates of Mrs K's building, I noticed too late the ankle boots of four men standing at the entrance. I pivoted quickly and walked on past the Teatro Adriano. But I had been clumsy. One of the four began to follow me. Round two sides of the large square, he was still there. From the Palace of Justice, on and off three trams, this man with a black moustache and long overcoat still appeared at the rear, making no move to come forward. This was no mere coincidence. I was being tailed. My pockets had money, receipts, names and addresses. If I could not shake him off, at least I must dump these papers.

A crowded trolley bus I had boarded at Piazza Flaminio was approaching its first stop at the top of Via Condotti on Piazza di Spagna. I had muscled up forward. The moustache, never looking at me, was at the back. As one front door opened, I leaped off and sprinted down Via Condotti. When a quick glance back showed nobody following, I turned into Gucci's leather shop, dumped a handful of papers in the hands of an astonished Signor Gucci. 'Hide them quick, and show me some cigarette cases.' I explained why. 'If someone comes in, you've never seen me before. I've asked to see these. I'll leave in a minute. Maybe I've shaken him off.'

On leaving I saw no sign of the black moustache, so I crossed Via Condotti and took refuge in the old Café Greco. When nobody appeared, I checked the street through the reversed gold lettering of the front window. I left and mixed with the shoppers.

Now this obdurate, and irate, Swiss Guard. Retracing my steps down the cobbled approach, I buttonholed an off-duty Guard who, when I mentioned the Monsignor, let me use the phone inside the guard-room.

In five minutes the tall hatless figure appeared under the archway and signalled. As I walked up, the Monsignor argued with the senior Guard. Hands were waving. He was reminding the Guard that anyone who had his approval to enter the Vatican was guaranteed to leave again.

'Even if he is, what does it matter?' the Monsignor was insisting, as I came within earshot. 'If I had given him an Irish passport, you wouldn't have stopped him, would you?' The Monsignor's prestige prevailed and we passed on into the Teutonic College.

'After all this fuss, Monsignor, you're going to like it when you hear the main reason I've come today.'

Once inside the Monsignor's room, I emptied my briefcase – two bottles of Beefeater gin and one of Sarti brandy. 'I told Sam in a letter that Renzo had a bartender friend with a hidden stock of pre-war English gin. Sam asked me to bring some as soon as possible.'

The Monsignor, strictly teetotal, shook his head. 'He'll have it tonight.'

'We had sad news today,' continued the Monsignor. 'I had a note from Bruno. You remember we were worried about him after the raids on the flats? I'd heard the Germans gave him a terrible time in Via Tasso. He wrote me a note yesterday, and somehow got it out. Said he was going to be shot this morning. He wanted me to know that he never opened his mouth once. Well, I got a message an hour ago. Bruno's dead. They shot him this morning.'

To us the loss of the three flats in January was still a mystery.

21

AMERICANS ON THE RISE

Rome newspapers on 10 February carried large pictures of American prisoners under heavy German escort being marched through Rome. The local German Command, with an eye to strengthening Fascist morale in the city, had marched a column of 300 Americans, recently captured at the Anzio beachhead, through the main thoroughfares, from the Colosseum along the Via del Fori Romani to Piazza Venezia, thence along Corso Umberto and up Via del Tritone. Fresh from the battlefield, they were unlikely to have reflected in passing that the Colosseum, these ancient statues and the excavated Roman Forum were the millenial monuments marking man's trek to civilization. While the march breached the Geneva Convention governing treatment of POWs, the Germans had been unable to resist this propaganda stunt.

These new American prisoners were being held temporarily inside an old detention camp near Cine-Città, east of the city boundary. Cine-Città, 'Film City', an independent suburb, had mushroomed in the pre-war years around the new film industry. What we hoped for, more escapers from Cine-Città, happened quickly. Two days after the much-publicized march through Rome, Renzo Lucidi and I rushed to answer an urgent call from Monsignor O'Flaherty to meet him that morning at St Peter's at 11 o'clock. In Piazza San Pietro we spotted his tall figure near the south fountain.

'Six Americans escaped last night from Cine-Città, began the Monsignor. 'They're hiding for the moment in a farmhouse only two miles from the camp. Here's the address. Can you find billets for them?'

'By tonight we will.'

'Good, because they'll have to be moved out of that farmhouse quickly. If not, they'll be recaptured.'

'We'll fetch 'em tomorrow,' said Renzo.

By curfew time we had sufficient temporary billets identified and early next morning, with two wrapped bundles of civilian clothes and cash, Renzo and a young friend, Luigi, set out for the farmhouse where the Americans were hiding. 'Bill,' Renzo had pleaded the night before, when I had planned to go with him, 'please let me do this with Luigi. If we're stopped along the road anywhere, Luigi can pass. You can't! After we get them rigged out, we'll bring them in two lots, straight to Mrs M's. Why don't you wait there, and keep the road clear?' With the probability of police check-points, Renzo was right.

Sure enough, the first batch of three arrived at two o'clock with Luigi at 12 Via Imperia, and twenty minutes later the other three with Renzo.

'Thank God that's over!' breathed Renzo. 'I never thought we'd make it. Look at them!'

The Americans did look a little ridiculous in these clothes. Relaxing now for the first time, they began to laugh at each other.

'We had six suits all right,' continued Renzo, 'but we certainly did a miserable job on the sizes. I thought we'd never get away from that farmhouse. Half the people in the tram kept staring at us. Luckily, we didn't run into police.'

Their attention was rapt as I briefed them on where they were, on how they would soon have better-fitting clothes and Italian identity cards with passport photos. I gave each 3500 lire.

'Now, how about some news?'

From their disjointed opinions, it became clear that, whatever had been the objective of the Anzio landing at the start, unforeseen snags had impeded the development of a major offensive drive.

Four out of the six were infantrymen. They complained that for several days after they landed not one of their armoured vehicles reached shore from the ships lying off, because of some misfit between vehicle tracks and the landing craft. On the tenth night their infantry company had found itself completely surrounded by German tanks. Unable to attack or to withdraw, most of the company had been captured.

Renzo left with two for a friend's flat near the Tiber and two others slipped out with me. Mrs M would handle two temporarily.

In response to an urgent appeal from Renzo, Contessa Borromeo, a strong friend who had already helped a great deal, had persuaded Don Fabrizio Colonna and his American wife, Donna Jane, to take in two of the Americans. Tram rides to Piazza di Spagna and a walk along Via Frattina brought us to the elegant Colonna home. A tall distinguished-looking middle-aged gentleman in tweeds ushered us inside. Upstairs in a wonderfully appointed drawing-room Donna Jane welcomed her countrymen in front of an abundant tea table. Already bewildered by the quick-changing scenes of the day, the two young Americans appeared awkward adjusting to these formal surroundings.

'Bill, you know our position here.' Don Fabrizio's English was perfect. 'We're constantly under suspicion. I'm delighted to have these boys, but it would be unwise to keep them here for long. Now I have a farm, with some outbuildings, out near the city boundary. After a few days, they'd be much safer out there.' I agreed to transfer them anytime he wished, hoping at the same time that his farm might be able to billet others.

As I departed, the two confused but happy Americans were heading upstairs to hot baths and debugging in one of Rome's grandest homes.

★　★　★

For a good lunch, Casino delle Rose seemed handiest. When I arrived alone, it was busy. Perched on a high stool at the little American bar, a lone figure leaned forward to lift his cocktail. With a start I recognized the profile and the blue serge suit: Lieutenant Bill Newman of the American 3rd Rangers, captured at Anzio and escaped near Rome. While moving him recently from the home of an overly nervous old lady to a safe billet, I had brought him here for a good square meal, but I was shocked to see him here now. Apart from the many German officers from the nearby SS Headquarters, most of the civilians frequenting the place were known to be Fascists and German collaborators. For a few of us who now spoke good Italian and were well-dressed, the place was a calculated risk, but for one like Bill Newman, who had first opened an Italian dictionary a few nights before, to come here alone in that ill-fitting blue suit was a little too bold. I took the stool next to him.

'What the hell are you doing here?' I muttered with a false smile.
'Hi, Bill,' he greeted airily. 'Well, I've been closed up in that house...'
'Ssh...'

Quietly he explained that, after a week indoors, he had persuaded the lady of the house to let him out for a walk in the park. He felt hungry and remembered our recent lunch here.

'Just thought I'd try it again!' His cool, casual attitude amused me. I forgot my initial annoyance.

'Nobody likes being shut in, but for God's sake don't come here alone. With that haircut and those glasses, you can only be one thing and that's American! You surely don't look Italian.'

'Neither do you exactly.'

128

'Maybe not, but I'm sort of used to it. Anyway, if you're determined to do the social round, you'll need decent clothes. I'll have Adrienne Lucidi fix you up. Let's have lunch.'

At a quiet table outside on the verandah, conversation revealed that before the war we were both in the insurance business and that by coincidence his firm in the US, the Detroit Insurance Agency, was closely associated with the Royal Insurance Group for whom I worked in Scotland.

While he insisted on finding his own way home, I cautioned him and explained why moving around had become increasingly hazardous.

Roman streets echoed to the cry of *'Rastrellamento!'* Republican-Fascist decrees ordering all Italian males of military age to report for duty still boomed on the radio, filled headlines in newspapers and glared from posters throughout the city. Lending muscle to these orders, truckloads of German SS Police descended each day on some busy thoroughfare, blocked it off and quickly corralled all men caught in the trap. Unless able to produce convincing German-authorized working papers, hundreds of captives were soon in trucks headed to forced-labour camps. Few young Italians dared even to appear on the streets.

Thanks to Monsignor O'Flaherty, my inside pocked carried two long papers printed in both German and Italian, certifying my employment in essential jobs and stamped with the swastika and eagle of *Der Deutsche Kommandant von Rom.*

The Anglo-American quintet at the French Seminary mostly stayed indoors, except for a short walk each day past the Pantheon along ancient cobbled *vicoli* to enjoy the finest lunch in town. First introduced by Renzo Lucidi, every noontime three or four of them walked through the antiquated portcullis-like entrance to the fashionable Hostaria dell'Orso, which was also frequented by Germans.

When Dukate, Wilson, Rendell and Smith, all well-dressed now, arrived inside the dimly lit old bar Felix Oggione the bartender, who had once worked at the Savoy Hotel in London, automatically unlocked his secret reserve and pulled out 'one of the last' bottles of pre-war Gordon's Gin. Each day he allowed them two, maybe three, martinis before lunch. Felix and Toni Prantera, the congenial owner, made these fugitives welcome. Escorting them upstairs to lunch, Toni's wife Giuliana would lead them to a table by a window with a view across the Tiber.

22

RESURRECTED DUO

'John Furman's back!' Renzo Lucidi's eyes shone as he pulled on an overcoat. The Monsignor expected us at 2.30, he said, between St Peter's and the obelisk. 'We don't go near him, just follow his directions.'

Furman had arrived with another escaped prisoner called Johnstone. We would split up and take them to the Pestalozzas'.

'The old boy's crazy,' I muttered as we approached the Monsignor, towering above strolling civilians. Near him stood a scruffily dressed John Furman. With only a brief handshake, I hurried John away from the piazza. Renzo, following signals to the far fountain, walked off with a tall ambling figure wearing an old bashed hat, shapeless coat and trousers high above his ankles. Yes, this was my old pal from Chieti. Once off the piazza, we relaxed.

'John, you look great.'

'So would you if you'd bicycled four hundred miles.'

Where were we going? To the Pestalozzas'. At the Parioli flat, Galeazzo and the girls whooped with joy. Miss May wept.

'Before we sit down,' said Furman, 'we had better shed these rags.'

Miss May produced towels and disinfectant and Galeazzo clean togs. The discards landed in a metal bin outside the back door. The recent tramps emerged from the bathroom transformed.

'First, John, what happened to the flats that day?'

'It took us a while to piece it together, but we did. The Gestapo were damned slick!' He proceeded to describe their clever ruse which had led them to such a big haul. From a camp up north full of recaptured prisoners, where Furman met and paired up with his old friend, Lieutenant 'Johnnie' Johnstone, Royal Engineers, a train of locked windowless box cars was carrying them to Germany. German guards had confiscated all boots and shoes. With a strong knife which Johnstone somehow still possessed and a heavy rusted iron bar which Furman had picked up and smuggled aboard, Sergeant-Major Billett, late of the Opera flat in Rome, weakened a section of the wagon's end wall and rammed it with the iron bar. Through the resulting hole Furman and Johnstone crawled out in the dark out on to the couplings. When the train slowed on a gradient they jumped, somewhere near Verona. The big question was 'To Switzerland, Yugoslavia or Rome?' Rome won. Shoes and old bicycles bought through friendly locals brought them in two weeks to Rome's boundary. A trolley-car carried them unchecked through the guarded road-block. John Furman was ready to start again where he had left off.

'Just deposit me in a quiet corner,' said flaxen-haired Johnstone. His luck had been stretched. 'Fine,' said Galeazzo, 'after I take you to our trusty barber on Via Condotti to have your hair dyed, find you clothes to fit and have your passport photo taken.' Johnstone gave me a questioning look.

'He's right,' I said.

The Monsignor was waiting by the Swiss Guards next morning when Furman arrived. Soon John had a new set of documents. John May dragged him upstairs to a high balcony and pointed out the British Legation quarters in the distant Santa Marta Hospice. At a window, a figure waved. Downstairs again, John wrote to Sam Derry: 'It's worth a sore backside to see your big face again – even at a distance.' With his old confidence restored, John set off to surprise the gang at the French Seminary.

At the Pestalozzas' later, despite the odd presence of a tall young man with auburn hair and eyebrows, John and I reviewed and split up my present roll of escapers. Our real need was for more reserve billets. A few days before, an acquaintance of Mrs M, who was playing both sides at Fascist Police Headquarters, had warned that two of our hideouts were about to be raided. Immediately I had gone to one address and removed the single escaper. Mrs M herself had evacuated the other. That night those homes were raided.

'We're having to use little Paolino's college basement as a clearing house,' I explained, 'but it's not enough.' Paolino's was perfect for fellows still turning up with a country priest, hoping to bust their way into the Vatican, but only temporarily. 'If only we could have another flat, like Chelini.'

Within two weeks John had arranged the 'Brancaccio flat' with room enough for twelve escapers. An Italian helper lent her name to the lease, and the whole deal was registered officially with the documents signed and stamped. By then Maltese priests had brought three more Americans to Mrs M's. Monsignor O'Flaherty had parked four new British arrivals in Paolino's clearing-house. Sam Derry was daily receiving messages from others in the country nearby, pleading to be billeted in Rome. The pressure on us was rising as John strove to complete the preparations for the flat.

Renzo was contacting every safe person he knew, 'selling' escapers. Even the normally lethargic Galeazzo had ferried two of our overload South Africans to a friend of his.

Father Meunier was tipped off that the French Seminary could expect an SS raid and Renzo removed our five officers in a hurry. Through friends of Monsignor O'Flaherty, Gil Smith and Garrad-Cole became the guests of an Italian colonel who was lying low. The Pestalozzas agreed to take in Rendell, Dukate and Wilson. Occupying camp beds and couches in the Pestalozzas' flat, they once more challenged the capacity of old Miss May, as she battled doggedly with the stubborn *carbone* in the little kitchen range.

★ ★ ★

It was hard to believe that the tattered figure running toward me in the Lucidis' living-room was Joe Pollak, the man who had been reported shot near Sulmona. We hugged and laughed. But Joe had not come here alone. On one side of the room stood a young, well-dressed man, benevolently watching the joyful reunion.

'Meet Signor Cipolla,' said Joe. We shook hands. 'I met him this morning when I went to the flat at Via Chelini.'

'Chelini!' I almost choked.

'Yes, I thought our boys would still be there. When we had the flat before, you know, it was officially registered in Signor Cipolla's name.'

I felt distinctly uncomfortable; the name Cipolla I recognized. To change the subject, I invited Joe to sit down and tell me his story. Taking the hint, Cipolla excused himself and left.

'He's the normal tenant at Chelini,' Joe said. 'I really think he's all right. But he told me quite frankly that he's mixed up with the German SS here in the city. Only for business reasons, he says. He certainly didn't do me any harm when I blundered into the place this morning.'

'That may be, Joe, but he's too slick. Better keep clear of him.' In his weak condition, pale and drawn, despite his present momentary high spirits, I could not tell Joe that he had led a possible Gestapo informer right into the Lucidis' flat.

'I've been close to being a dead man two or three times since I last saw you, but right now I feel pretty good.' He did not look it.

'Did Iride really trap you at the *pensione* that morning?'

'She certainly did. When I knocked on her door, she opened it with a big smile and right behind her were two Germans. I bolted, but they caught me outside.'

Back in Sulmona, after much questioning, the Germans took them to Aquila and stuck them in jail. Fifteen friends from Sulmona were already in jail there, all arrested on New Year's Eve. The Carugnos had not been among them, but his friends the Pacellas were there, and the Balassones who gave us all the army clothing and made our identity cards, and Iride's sister, Maria.

'It was that damned fool Messenger.'

Back in Sulmona, a short Australian, a medical orderly, had posed as a doctor. When captured in a roundup on 29 December, his German questioners loaded him with wine. He told them all they wanted to know. On New Year's Eve he had led a party of Germans around the town pointing out houses hiding escapers. The Germans had arrested the lot.

In the cold Aquila jail, after suffering pneumonia, Joe, held as an enemy agent, was recognized by a British officer from the Chieti days. The senior German officer accepted this, and granted Joe POW status.

Before the date of the German Tribunal, Joe found Messenger, gave him hell and showed him the disastrous significance of his treachery. To salvage his future he had only one chance. When called at the Tribunal, Messenger, the Germans' key witness, must declare that in Sulmona he had been in a constant drunken stupor. This would not extricate the Sulmona folks from the nasty hole, but might alleviate sentences.

At the trial, when cross-examined by Joe, Messenger admitted he had been drunk and really didn't know what was going on in Sulmona. The President, a German Colonel, challenged him, but Messenger had acted well and really looked ashamed. The Colonel rejected Messenger's entire evidence. Only three received the death sentence and each managed to escape in time. Others were given terms of imprisonment.

During an air raid while boarding a prisoners' train, Joe got away. On foot and by bicycle he had reached Rome.

★ ★ ★

Monsignor O'Flaherty's face lit up at the sight of Joe, as he waved us forward under the Santa Marta archway, sponsored us past the Swiss Guards and led us up to his room.

'Well, strike me pink!' John May was beaming as he shook Joe's hand.

Fortunately their interest in Joe's exploits provided me with the time to write a longer-than-usual letter to Sam Derry. I reported that the Pestalozzas' boarders were down to three, Rendell, Furman and myself. Dukate and Wilson had met Rome's leading tailor, Ciro Giuliano, who had taken Duke into his own palatial apartment in Parioli and placed Pat Wilson with friends nearby. Moreover, Ciro was willing to cash our homemade cheques at a much higher rate than John May, at 650 lire to the £, but would like some assurance that these cheques would be recognized as valid when the Allies arrived.

Picking up on an idea that John Furman had voiced earlier, I had drawn up a short form of credit guarantee to protect Ciro up to an aggregate cheque-cashing limit of 100,000 lire. If this bore the signatures of Sam, Major Fane-Hervey and myself, Ciro would be happy. I enclosed the simple hand-written sheet for Sam to sign and return on my next call. Since this development would slash my cheque-cashing activity with John May, whom I did not want to embarrass, I preferred that he not be made aware of the financial deal yet.

'Bill, put these in your pocket, for John Furman and you, if you're interested,' the Monsignor said, slipping me two specially engraved invitation cards. 'Sixteenth March is the Pope's Anniversary. He'll deliver an important speech from his balcony. There'll be a huge crowd, so come to my room around 2.30. These cards'll get you in all right.'

Business completed, the Monsignor escorted Joe and me back down to the Swiss Guards. Joe was weak, with signs of possible tuberculosis; Sam had said that he should do nothing but rest for a while.

John Furman at the Pestalozzas' was concerned about Mrs M's. A priest had just dumped three new arrivals on her, and two of her old trio were back. The home of her butcher friend Giovanni, to which the trio had moved, had been raided by the PAI, the Italian African Police force now located in Rome. Two hours before the raid they had fixed a rope ladder to an inside window frame. While the PAI were hammering on the front door, all three of them and Giovanni clambered down the rope ladder at the back of the house and got away.

Being cooped up indoors for weeks was not easy for many of those hidden in Rome. Yet Sam Derry had us delivering written warnings to a few who, once permitted by considerate hosts to slip out for a breather in early evening, had found wine bars and returned in a state less than discreet. Ironically, in a prisoner-of-war camp, misery had lots of company; 'freedom', billeted here in Rome, was lonely and boring. Yet, if only for the security of their risk-taking hosts, we had to insist that they should be patient.

Traffic in and out of the Pestalozza flat was rather constant. My coming and going was the most frequent; it was time for me to move.

'I've just the place for you,' said John Furman when I told him. 'The flat Milner disappeared from last week.'

When John had cashed a sizeable cheque for Milner a week before, the British Captain had left the flat one morning and never returned. Milner was responsible and level-headed, but somehow he had been arrested.

'The flat's darned attractive, and so is the girl who owns it, Flora Volpini. She's, well, early thirties, used to be in Italian films. She usually has one or two journalist types living there.'

When we visited Flora Volpini, I agreed with John's observations. The flat was luxurious and Flora rather lovely. I accepted her invitation to arrive in a few days.

23

POPE PIUS APPEALS

Tens of thousands of Romans jammed the approaches to the Vatican and squeezed steadily into St Peter's Square on the clear sunny afternoon of 16 March. Despite the uncertainty and fears of many months, they seemed to exude an air of optimism, of hopeful expectancy. What message would Pope Pius have for them, and for the world, on this anniversary of his ascension to the Papal Throne?

To push through the tightly packed mass to the Santa Marta entrance looked impossible. I skirted the crowd and joined a small crush of other special guests edging toward a narrow gate. If these were individuals of important status, it was not apparent in this undignified scuffle. Finally the weight of bodies carried me through. Unruffled, the Swiss Guards were examining every invitation card. One glanced at mine and waved me on.

In the Monsignor's room in the German College a group had already assembled. The Monsignor, formally dressed today with a broad scarlet sash around the waist of his black cassock, looked impressive. Soon he ushered most of the group out, to escort them to a good vantage point, and instructed me to wait in the room with one distinguished-looking middle-aged gentleman. From the few words he had spoken, he was obviously English.

'Perhaps we should introduce ourselves. My name is Simpson.'

'How do you do, Simpson,' responded this older man with a smile. 'If you'll excuse me, I feel I must leave it to the Monsignor to tell you my name.' His expression was apologetic.

'I understand, sir.' I began to have an idea.

Twenty minutes before the time scheduled for the Pope's speech the Monsignor rustled into the room again and, urging us to hurry, led us downstairs and out across the now-crowded Protomartyr Square. The Monsignor walked quickly as he led us under archways and along cobbled walks, until we arrived in the Vatican parade-ground, Piazza San Domaso.

The Swiss Guards, today in their full ceremonial uniforms of blue, yellow and scarlet, and plumed helmets of glistening steel, were marching off to their positions outside the Vatican in front of St Peter's. The honorary Italian Palatine Guard formed up and prepared to follow.

'John can't make it,' said the Monsignor. Early in the morning he had relayed an urgent message from Sam Derry. In a village ten miles out a local Fascist gang had discovered four British soldiers. When they tried to arrest them, the men resisted, beat up the Fascists and got away. John Furman had gone with a priest to bring them to Rome.

The Monsignor led us around the rear of St Peter's. Climbing a long enclosed staircase we emerged in the sunlight on a broad crowded balcony which overlooked the packed piazza some two hundred feet below. To our right was the stately façade of St Peter's. High above the huge centre portico, Papal banners draped in the still air from the minute loggia on which the Pope was due to appear.

'We're standing in the Diplomatic enclosure,' murmured the Monsignor, as he halted us in a clear space to the rear. 'These are all the diplomats to the Holy See. I notice the Axis ones are out in strength.'

'Any of the British staff here?' I asked.

'No, the British and Americans aren't appearing, I heard. All this bombing recently around Rome. They feel the Pope may refer to it. Just in case he does, they don't want to be here to give any satisfaction to the Germans.'

With a nod from the Monsignor, I moved to a vacant spot on a parapet and leaned over. In the sun-filled piazza below were packed a hundred thousand people. Up on the little draped balcony on the front of St Peter's tall glass doors opened. A hush fell over the crowd. The clutches of diplomats stopped talking and pressed forward. I looked around to spot the Monsignor, but the diplomatic group had closed in behind me. Curbing my curiosity to look them over, I turned to watch the papal loggia. A white-robed figure moved slowly forward through the glass doors. The crowd began to applaud and cheer. Massed cries of 'Papa! Papa! Papa!' rose in a great crescendo. The Pontiff raised his arms and, as the crowd again fell silent, he spoke. His voice, in Italian, relayed through amplifiers around the piazza, was clear and distinct.

Steadily his high tones became impassioned as, with deliberate yet graceful gestures accentuated by the broad arm folds of his robes, he emphasized his points. The gist of it I could understand – the fervent desire for an end to the ravages of war and, without addressing any nationality, a strong direct plea for the protection of the Eternal City and its preservation in the difficult days immediately ahead.

When his fifteen-minute speech ended, the piazza reverberated again to fanatical cheers and applause. The Pope bestowed his Blessing on the crowd and slowly withdrew.

Attention swung to the centre of the piazza where clouds of pamphlets rose in the air around the obelisk and caused commotion. Directly below me showers of printed sheets fluttered down on a sea of upturned faces. Angry shouts of protest spread among the packed mass, and it looked as if panic might break out. Then, as the leaflets – Communist leaflets, it turned out – stopped falling, the excitement died. The intended demonstration had fizzled out.

The people standing beside me eased back. At the rear of the balcony I again saw the Monsignor still standing with the unnamed Englishman. I rejoined them. The diplomats and their friends, gathering again in groups and no doubt discussing the Pope's message, appeared in no hurry to disperse, but the Monsignor took us both smartly by the arm and walked us off.

'Bill, for the last twenty minutes you've been surrounded by the German Legation!'

Back on the parade square the Palatine Guard and after them the resplendent Swiss Guards marched back to be dismissed. Again the Monsignor's arm moved us quickly away.

'The Hungarian crowd are staring at us,' he explained. 'Come on, I'll show you the Vatican Gardens.'

On the hill rising behind the main Vatican buildings we stood amid groomed lawns and shrubbery while the Monsignor explained points of interest, the railway station to which the single line enters through the Vatican wall at an opening sealed by immense metal doors, the old Governor's Palace, the Mosaic Museum. Turning around, he pointed back to the dome of St Peter's.

'Look, General, d'you see the radio mast over there?'

I looked quickly at the Monsignor.

His roguish smile was there again, as he introduced me to Major-General Gambier-Parry.

'Sam'll be mad at me for this, bringing the General out of hiding,' chuckled the Monsignor, 'but I thought he should hear the Pope.'

Back at the Teutonic College, Brother 'Whitebows' Robert was there to escort his most prized escaper back to the almost foolproof security of the Di Rienzo home.

24

MASSACRE

The militant chorus of the smartly turned out German SS company was stirring, as it marched from Corso Umberto up Via del Tritone past the *Il Messaggero* building into Piazza Barberini in the early afternoon of 22 March. Their marching songs had been equally stirring every day for four weeks at exactly the same time on exactly the same route. This blunt reminder of Nazi police rule had with each passing day fanned resentment among the thousands of Romans whose business brought them to this active commercial heart of the city. The highly organized and restless Communist Party underground just could not stand it.

True to custom, the SS wheeled right with precision into Via Quattro Fontane. With another right wheel into Via Razella, still singing, they marched on up the rising slope of the narrow, deserted street. As the Company came abreast of a garbage cart parked unattended by the curb the cart exploded. When the smoke cleared, thirty-two Germans lay dead.

Chaos ensued. German reinforcements rushed to the scene and surrounded the area. They searched buildings on each side of the street and arrested all the occupants. With no fragment of the cart remaining, the cause of the explosion remained a mystery, except to the small band of Communist GAP extremists who had set the trap with such deadly effect.

Late on 23 March, after a six-mile hike to transfer the two Americans from the town flat of Don Fabrizio Colonna to a home up on Monte Verde, I returned just before the 7 pm curfew to spend my first night at Flora's flat on Viale Liege in the residential Parioli district. Two Italian author friends were there. After Flora had served supper the conversation turned to the latest sensation. All Rome talked of nothing else. Most of the residents of Via Razella had already been released from jail.

Yet Rome waited. How would the Germans react? Several thousand additional German *Feldgendarmerie* had been rushed to the city.

The rumours circulating the next day were gruesome. By the morning of the 25th their confirmation was sufficient to leave no doubt as to the awful retaliation the German Command in Rome had taken under orders from an outraged Hitler. On the 27th a brief announcement in the local newspapers stated coldly that on 24 March 335 Italian 'traitors' had been executed at the Ardeatine Caves in reprisal for the murder of thirty-two German SS storm troopers on the 22nd and the subsequent death of one in hospital. Ten for one! Rome shuddered.

While local German Army commanders had agreed that the quota should be filled from prisoners already sentenced by German Tribunals for capital crimes and from those whose trials for serious offences were pending, SS Colonel Kappler, charged with implementing the order, found on the night of 23 March that the relevant lists prepared by his aides fell far short of meeting the total demanded. Yet he felt compelled to meet both the quota and the 24-hour deadline of dusk the next day, So, early on the 24th the SS virtually emptied Via Tasso and *Banda Koch*'s headquarters and, within the larger Third Wing of Regina Coeli, mustered on the ground floor hall every prisoner named on the lists. Meanwhile, Kappler's men, working against the clock, hastily compiled second lists, randomly naming scores of prisoners held only on suspicion. Repeating their round of the cells, SS guards called out these supplementary names and hustled their bearers to the ground floor.

All that afternoon heavily guarded trucks ferried the selected victims, now bound hand and foot, to the Ardeatine Caves south-east at Domitilla on the outskirts of the city. Each batch was off-loaded, blindfolded and counted. SS officers and storm troopers lined them up, shot them and stacked the bodies inside the caves.

When, at dusk, the requisite quota of 330 had been 'processed', Kappler's men found they had five bound prisoners left over. Rather than risk their survival as witnesses, the SS officers 'processed' them too. Then dynamite charges were exploded, bringing down hundreds of tons of rock and sealing off the mouths of the caves.

Portly Father Giorgio, whose religious college was near the Ardeatine Caves, had heard the rumbling explosions on the fatal evening. Before dawn next morning he crept out to the caves to investigate. The area was deserted, but when he crawled close to the new mass of rocks, he could hear strange muffled sounds coming from inside the crude tomb.

Father Giorgio was just finishing his grisly report to the Monsignor when I arrived.

To make matters worse, Fascist police that morning had arrested Brother Robert while escorting four British escapers. The police, when they saw these men were not Italian, had handed 'Whitebows' over to a German *Feldgendarmerie* post nearby. Through a pious tale of innocently helping human beings in need and after submitting to the indignity of being stripped and searched and referring his inquisitors to the Mother House of his Order, which the Germans now used as a casualty clearing station, he had miraculously been released. Hatless and trembling, he had burst into the Monsignor's room an hour ago. His agitation was understandable. These German Military Police had not known, but 'Whitebows' knew, that Gestapo Headquarters in the city had a description circulating on him. In fact, for weeks now he had been sleeping in different places each night. There and then the Monsignor decided that 'Whitebows' had risked enough. He'd better come into the Vatican proper and stay there.

But this created a problem. 'Whitebows' was handling a good many escapers with the help of his two young accomplices, Sandro Cottich and Mimo Trapani. Both were bold and resourceful.

'You'll have to keep in touch with them,' the Monsignor directed me. 'Be at Santa Maria Maggiore at 10.30 tomorrow. Sandro brought in three today. Two he has placed. The third he's keeping at home tonight, but Brother Robert is supposed to take him off his hands tomorrow. Explain when you see him.'

★ ★ ★

When Joe Pollak met me at Flora Volpini's flat the next morning, introductions caused a slight delay and we were twenty minutes late in arriving at the piazza in front of Santa Maria Maggiore, one of the five great cathedrals of Rome. We searched the almost deserted square but saw no sign of Sandro Cottich or, for that matter, any likely-looking escaper. Guessing that they too might have been delayed, we entered a nearby café which afforded a full view of the square.

Waiting for the *espresso*, Joe was staring down the counter. At the far end stood a short young man, shabbily dressed and timid-looking. His threadbare clothes fitted badly. Under his arm he held a small brown paper package. From his furtive expression, he was clearly waiting anxiously for someone.

'What does he remind you of, Bill?'

From his pocket he pulled a blue tie, held it out full length, folded it and replaced it in his pocket. This he repeated several times as we watched. Maybe this was our man. Something may have happened to Sandro. We moved down the counter.

'You're the British prisoner we're supposed to meet with Sandro aren't you?' asked Joe quietly in English.

'*Non capire*,' stammered the little man, shaking his head. He appeared afraid. This ungrammatical infinitive to say 'Don't understand' was typical. He *must* be our man.

'Now look, you've never seen us before, but we were supposed to meet you here with Sandro. We were late. What happened to Sandro?' Joe went on in English.

'*Non capire.*'

'Now, come on, we're your friends,' I said.

'*Non capire.*'

Joe and I moved back up the counter to our coffee. The wretched blue tie was out again. Impatiently, Joe walked back to him, took him by the arm and tried to pull him away. He resisted and his face registered panic.

'*Ché siete?*' asked Joe switching for no good reason to Italian. '*Dové Sandro?*' Immediately the scared little man talked at great speed in fluent Italian. He'd done nothing wrong. Why didn't we leave him alone? Joe and I headed for the door. With still no sign of Sandro, we returned to Flora's.

When she opened the door to our signal on the bell, she seemed relieved. So were we. Sitting patiently in the living-room were Sandro and one bewildered British escaper. Sandro had waited fifteen minutes in the piazza and, when we did not appear, had come to Flora's flat which he knew. The mistaken identity story amused them.

After depositing the British escaper with a friendly family on Via Imperia, I hurried to meet Dennis Rendell in the Villa Borghese near the Casino delle Rose. I had cashed a large cheque for him with John May, and he needed the money. He had brought Dedy, looking chic in a light spring dress. The sun had warmth as we passed borders of early flowering bulbs and budding shrubs.

Inside the Casino, at the end of the long window-lined entrance lobby, we sat on swivelling stools at the American bar from which most of the restaurant was visible. Eddie, the English-speaking bartender, mixed us martinis. 'Plenty of our friends here today,' murmured Dennis. German and Italian Fascist uniforms were everywhere. The restaurant appeared busier than usual. Emilio, the head waiter, came with menus.

'What's the big party in the centre?' I asked him. He leaned close.

'General Mälzer, his wife and some of the big *Fascisti*. See the officer in the *Battaglione Mas* uniform, on the far side? He's quite a noise around here; been assigned to Mälzer's Command on special duty.'

The *Battaglione Mas* was an élite unit of the reconstituted Republican Fascist security forces. To be held in public, such a high-powered party had to have a motive. It looked as if Mälzer, the German *Gauleiter* of Rome, was trying to smooth over the jagged reaction to the recent massacre, at least with the Fascists.

After lunch Dennis suggested a brandy at the bar. We propped ourselves on three stools with Dedy between us. While Eddie was pouring cognac, General Mälzer and some of his party passed behind us and left. Beyond Dennis a voice spoke in English to Eddie. I glanced over at a smooth, agreeable looking Italian in his thirties. He obviously knew the bartender well. As he continued in English from his leisurely stance within a yard of Dennis' stool, he started across at us, smiling. He was clearly letting us know that he knew who we were. What was his game? During lunch I had noticed him at a large table of civilians next to the German General's. Now his lunch companions, fashionably dressed ladies and well groomed men, congregated behind us and settled into armchairs around a grand piano a few feet back from the bar.

The English-speaking stranger was all but addressing us. Dennis looked at me. I shrugged my shoulders. Dennis turned to him resignedly; there was no point in bluffing. 'What will you have?' Dennis asked him. The stranger nodded amiably and Eddie poured him a glass of cognac.

The normally jovial Eddie, whose expression was our barometer when strangers were around, had a dour look. The *Battaglione Mas* officer from General Mälzer's table was joining the group around the grand piano behind us. More disturbing still, leaning against the piano beside a sultrily-clad young lady stood the tall fair-haired nephew of the restaurant's proprietor. On our first visit Galeazzo Pestalozza had warned us that, while the Italian proprietor was his reliable friend, his nephew was in thick with the local German Command headquartered in nearby Via Veneto.

'Let's get out of here,' I whispered to Dedy. Now the fellow speaking English sat down at the piano and broke into 'Lady be Good'. He was staring right at us as he sang. His friends were beginning to look our way too. This was getting hot, but to rise and walk right out would be too noticeable. 'Dedy, you and Dennis get up casually, shake my hand and leave,' I whispered, appearing to kiss Dedy on the cheek. At least Dedy must be extricated. Somehow I would play along with this until they got out. Dennis and Dedy bade me farewell and walked off down the long foyer. Nobody followed them.

The pianist switched from 'Lady be Good' straight into 'Tea for Two', still staring at me as he sang. The young Republican Fascist officer was deep in conversation, but the proprietor's nephew and three other men leaning on the piano were watching me now and grinning. So they knew too! Well, I thought quickly through my growing discomfiture, so long as they think it amusing I'll play along.

Turning to face them, I pointedly counted the heads around the piano, turned to the bar and told Eddie to pour twelve large brandies – quickly. Eddie looked worried, but he lined up twelve brandy glasses and poured generously. Two at a time I served them myself. Their grins broadened into laughter.

'Be careful! Very mixed company,' muttered the pianist in English when I placed his glass at the end of the piano. The Republican Fascist officer picked up his glass, followed the looks of the others to me and vaguely joined in the 'Saluti,' before returning to his conversation. I prayed no one would attempt introductions.

After an interminable minute of standing there with a cramped smile, while the pianist continued to sing English lyrics, I told Eddie to pour twelve more. Another 1200 lire! Swiftly I passed out this second round.

'Cheerio!' 'Saluti!' 'Cheerio!' came from those around the piano. This was too much. I gulped my brandy, looked at my watch and, just as the prankster at the piano launched into 'In The Mood', I waved to the group and walked away to a chorus of 'Ciao!' 'Addio!' The Fascist officer looked up with a puzzled half-smile.

'Cheerio!' came the loud parting shot in English from the pianist as I reached the exit.

In the crowded security of a tram I mopped my face. Since the group had included Rome's top Fascist collaborators, I could only guess that, in a uniquely Italian way, the mellowness of the social occasion had suppressed their adversarial instincts. But enough was enough; no more Casino delle Rose for me. The cloakroom girl came after me with my Borsalino hat.

Yet the incident had a sequel. Presumably impressed by the quiet comedy of the scene, someone had been unable to resist telling General Mälzer later. At least we assumed this when Sam Derry, in a warning letter to Furman and me a few days later, quoted a note the British Minister had just received from his German counterpart in the Vatican, Baron Ernst von Weizsäcker. The head of the Swiss Legation, it said, had been warned for the last time about giving material assistance to

British fugitives. If he continued, the German Command would be obliged to take action. In any case, the Baron went on, it was unnecessary for the Swiss to give this aid when Allied personnel in Rome were clearly so amply provided for through more direct channels. It was well known, he said, that British and American officers dined regularly at Rome's most expensive restaurants.

Fortunately, the SS had missed a minor detour by Dennis Rendell and me a week before, and I had seen no reason to burden Sam Derry with it. Leaving our friends after a good lunch at the Casino delle Rose, Dennis and I had walked down the west side of Via Veneto. The street was quiet. At the news kiosk, we instinctively stopped to look over at the German sentries on duty before the entrance to the SS headquarters hotel, the Excelsior. With no more forethought than Dennis murmuring a rhetorical 'Shall we have a drink?', we crossed the avenue, marched between the two sentries, up the steps, through the entrance door and into the reception lobby. A bell-boy directed us to the largest, tallest hotel lounge I had ever seen and, crossing the black and white floor tiles past giant baroque sideboards, we veered right again into a cosier grouping of corner tables and a long brass-railed bar. The bartender poured our two cognacs; we swallowed, paid and retraced our steps past the sentries to the sunshine of Via Veneto.

Going back on my resolution to stay away from the Casino delle Rose, between jobs I slipped in there alone for an early lunch. When I was leaving, Emilio, the head waiter, told me that a party of senior German officers was expected for a late lunch at two, with a special guest, Max Schmeling, the ex-World Heavyweight Boxing Champion. He was on a morale-raising tour.

This was too good to miss, I decided outside in the park. At a quarter to two I re-entered the Casino and sat on a stool at the American bar. Eddie winked and poured me a brandy. I waited. The restaurant had emptied.

At exactly two o'clock four German officers arrived with a tall, thick-set man in civilian clothes. I recognized the familiar features of the German champion. They stopped three feet away and ordered a drink.

Schmeling, who was facing me, appeared jovial and smiling as they chatted quietly in German. I had never thought of him as a Nazi; his 1930 World Championship pre-dated Hitler's rise. In fact he seemed somewhat ill-at-ease with his uniformed hosts.

One officer kept glancing over at me, the only other person at the bar. Should I offer them a drink? Or ask for an autograph? If my pocket's weren't stuffed with sensitive papers, I would have, but the gag didn't warrant the risk. As I got up to leave, I controlled a strong urge to butt in and shake his hand. I walked on.

It emerged later that one propaganda aim of Schmeling's visit went unrealized: the Pope did not grant him a private audience.

Inevitably the Ardeatine Caves massacre had intensified Rome's smouldering hatred of the occupying Germans. Just as vehemently, most Romans reacted with disgust and resentment against the Communist radicals, the GAP, who had perpetrated the pointless plot against the Germans. Thousands of citizens had a friend or relation who was incarcerated in Regina Coeli. Days elapsed before they could discover who had been lucky enough to remain alive in jail. At least five of those executed, Sam Derry established, had been imprisoned for helping escaped POWs.

However brutal, the German act of intimidation was effective. The numerous organized political undergrounds, even the Communists, would think twice next time. But any support the Germans had still enjoyed from residual Fascist elements throughout the city was evaporating; only the hard core of extremist Fascist police, the *Banda Koch*, still kept in step with their German counterparts.

25

GESTAPO HEAT

Republican Fascist Police raided our other oasis, the Hostaria dell'Orso, during the lunch hour. However, earlier at Fascist Police Headquarters, an employee, a friend of the owner, Signor Prantera, spotted the order being issued for the raid. Slipping out to a public telephone, he alerted Prantera. From noon Felix the bartender and Minelli the head waiter stood watch on the two approaches. Minutes before the raid they shooed away Rendell, Wilson and Dukate with the two Pestalozza girls, and just behind them Gil Smith and John Furman. In consequence the police check revealed only legitimate Italian patrons and a few Germans.

Meanwhile, in other parts of Rome our organization was taking some bad hits as we moved into Easter Week. A recent series of night raids by German SS squads had captured some of our escapers and their Italian hosts. We were puzzled. Under Gestapo interrogation, one or more of the captured Italians had been forced to talk. This had led to further arrests. Our security structure was springing leaks. So far my group had been untouched, but John Furman had just lost one young Italian helper rather mysteriously.

To Sam Derry the pattern of these arrests pointed to a worrisome conclusion. A month earlier the Gestapo had picked up one of the Monsignor's key organizers from the earliest days, 'Don' Pasquale Perfetti, the 'priest' – actually he was not an ordained priest at all – whom we had met at the Hotel Vulcania during our first days in Rome. While John and I had seen nothing of him since, apparently he had continued to operate widely for other groups connected with the Monsignor. To Perfetti it had been a business.

A week or so after his arrest reports leaked out that he was being tortured in Via Tasso. The Gestapo broke his resistance. His life would be spared, they fooled him, if he told everything he knew. This he had proceeded to do and several recent raids could only be laid to his break-down. Attesting to this grave development, others had recognized him twice on the streets accompanied by Germans, presumably leading them to buildings where Allied escapers and Jewish refugees were hidden.

With the tide running against us, we impatiently looked for signs of an Allied offensive in the south. Yet recent overcast days had inhibited Allied air interdiction of German supply columns and heavy rainstorms in the mountainous regions south of the *Campagna Romana* were impeding ground operations. It was as well for our morale that we did not realize the extent to which rain, melting snow and swollen rivers were turning the low-lying stretches around the Gustav Line and Cassino into quagmires, adding strength to the German defences and misery to the Allied forces.

On the continuing stalemate the BBC communicated little, but newly escaped POWs who, until their recent capture, had been on the peri-meter of Anzio, and whom our organization had tucked away in homes in the city, were convinced that a major Allied offensive was imminent. It was anybody's guess whether this would come as a flanking breakout in strength from Anzio or, farther south, a direct onslaught to penetrate the Gustav Line or, as Field Marshal Albert Kesselring apparently anticipated, a fresh amphibious landing on the Tyrrhenian coast north of Rome, most likely at Civitavecchia.

The patience of all the underground Resistance groups and political factions in Rome was being sorely tested. The past bitter months, with their long hours of curfew and constant vigilance, increasing food short-age and rocketing prices, had left their mark on our network of Italian friends. Fully aware of stepped-up police surveillance and conscious of increasing Gestapo raids and arrests, many of them had become under-standably reluctant to house our men. It took all our optimism to main-tain their spirits and keep their support. For new escapers turning up in Rome, mostly recently captured Americans, finding 'permanent' billets required persuasion.

Apart from the 200-odd escapers hidden in the city, some 2000 were still holding on precariously in the nearby provinces. Conditions were becoming treacherous for them too, as the Germans scoured village after village rounding up Italian males for forced labour. Yet few now tried to come to Rome; news had filtered through to them that Rome was dis-tinctly unhealthy. They were right. Immediately after the Ardeatine Caves massacre, Field Marshal Kesselring, as a precaution against a possible major insurrection led by extreme Resistance groups, notably the two Communist organizations, had allocated to Rome substantial police reinforcements, in the form of SS units and *Feldgendarmerie*. Now the German Command in Rome was employing this added police capacity to intensify daily *rastrellamenti* in the commercial areas of the city where daytime pedestrian traffic was heavy, sealing off entire blocks with truckloads of police who rounded up all able-bodied males under sixty and drove them off to work on German defences.

As Furman and I made our respective rounds during Easter Week distributing the April 'pay', the gaily-coloured banners fluttering in the sunshine outside every church did little to ease our concern. While reassuring each *padrona* that the Allied advance must start any time now, we warned each escaper to stay indoors.

In central Rome the stepped-up *rastrellamenti* had created a visible change. Streets were now deserted except for women, children and old men. While this gave us less cover, at least the trams and trolley buses had more seats.

Hopes of a calm Good Friday vanished when I arrived at Mrs M's. Father Borg grabbed me. 'Quick, the Monsignor wants you and John to meet him in front of St Peter's at 11.30. Something bad's happened.'

Since John was not expected till later, I co-opted a young Maltese fellow there called Gonzi. We took off quickly across the city. Whatever was up, it must be serious. Otherwise, why hadn't the Monsignor pulled Father Borg into action, instead of sending him to find me? Gonzi I did not know well, but John had spoken highly of him. He had guts.

St Peter's Square was all sunlight. The Holy Day had drawn big crowds, but we quickly located the Monsignor near the steps of St Peter's. He was upset. 'It's Paolino's place, the College. The SS raided it at seven this morning. I've had his basement full of young Jews all week and I put four British lads in there the other night too.' He turned to a small girl standing a few feet off. 'This is Paolino's daughter. She came to me right after it happened this morning. The Germans took Paolino and five Jews.'

Apparently, when Paolino had heard the pounding on the college's main door, before opening up to the Germans he had sounded the secret alarm bell to the basement. The four Britons had jumped from their bunks and squeezed into the one small hiding place which Paolino had allotted to them.

'The Germans didn't find your lads, but they're still jammed in that hole. You'll have to get them out and take them away.'

'Is the college still being watched?' I asked the girl.

'I don't know,' she replied in Italian, 'but I saw no Germans when I left.'

'Don't worry, Monsignor. Okay, Gonzi?'

My partner nodded. It could be a trap. Quickly we left with the girl. If we could extricate the Britons safely, Gonzi knew where two could be housed. I knew of one vacancy and felt that, at a pinch, Father Meunier at the French Seminary would take the other, at least for one night.

For Gonzi and myself to enter the college would be foolhardy, since the place might still be under surveillance, and our arrest would only make matters worse. I interrogated the little girl as we walked. Yes, she knew how to open the door of the concealed hiding place, and she had a sister aged 10. Despite her tender years, she seemed calm and clear-headed, so I gave her instructions. Gonzi and I would wait a hundred yards down the side-street from the door of the college, while she and her sister released the Britons inside. She would instruct two of them to follow her out of the college, a distance behind her. Two minutes later, her sister would lead the other two out.

As she disappeared into the college, Gonzi and I strolled back and forth keeping a lookout. If there were any interested onlookers, they were not in view. Soon the girl re-emerged, followed shortly by two poorly dressed, furtive-looking civilians. Gonzi went off with them and disappeared. I lit another cigarette. An even smaller girl appeared, looking around uneasily, followed by her two heavy-set men. I crossed over.

'Just keep calm and walk beside me,' I told them as I smiled a big *grazie* to the little girl. I headed for the nearest busy thoroughfare, Corso Vittorio Emanuele. My two charges were shaking visibly, not so much from nerves as from their five hours doubled up in the cramped hideout. Only when we reached the cover of pedestrians did I glance back. No one was following.

At a flat behind Via Cavour an Italian priest and his married brother, who already kept two escapers, agreed in the circumstances to take one, an Irish Artillery sergeant, off my hands.

Much relieved, I boarded a tram with the other, a bluff Cockney. At the door of the French Seminary Father Meunier raised both hands in gentle protest. For the limited number of refugees still with him he had a special hiding-place, but more he could not handle. I could not blame him. He had helped us out of many tight corners.

'Well, we're both hungry,' I said, as I led my Cockney friend across the cobbled old square, wondering where to take him.

'I should say, sir, I've 'ad nothin' since yesterday.'

The Orso was nearby. With the lunch hour over, and no German uni-forms, the head waiter, Minelli, soon fed us two steaks, after which I parked him across town with an accommodating family near Mrs M's. On a hunch I stopped by at Mrs M's. As I had hoped, John Furman was there and I briefed him on the raid on Paolino's college.

'Looks like Don Pasquale's trail,' he said. 'I'm afraid they've made Gino talk.' Gino, a bright young Italian, had been assisting John for weeks before the Gestapo arrested him. He had known Don Pasquale and had gone often to Paolino's college to pick up escapers.

'Does Gino know about Mrs M here?' I asked him.

'No, thank God!'

'Look, John, you'd better go easy yourself.' John nodded and I left for the Vatican. Ten minutes with the Monsignor sufficed to report where the men were now located.

'And tell John to be careful,' said the Monsignor, as I made to leave. We both knew that John, if caught again and identified as a Jew, would be in great peril.

★   ★   ★

Back in Flora's comfortable flat on the Viale Liege that night I felt despondent over our recent misfortunes. The rot started by Don Pasquale was deepening; several escapers and their Italian hosts arrested, then John's friend Gino, now Paolino. Gone too was Paolino's handy 'transit camp'. From our extensive use of his college, Paolino knew many of us. Could he withstand the brutality of interrogation? He might, but who could be sure of staying silent under the Gestapo's beating, head-bashing and red-hot needles?

Sensing my mood, Flora asked me what was up.

'Oh, nothing,' I replied and shrugged it off. The less Flora knew the better. She too was at risk. Various underground groups regularly used her flat as a meeting place. But two weeks ago Flora had been tipped off that her place was under suspicion. Her journalist friends stopped coming around. Only one particular writer called Guido, an old friend who had been resident here for months, stayed on – and myself.

At dinner with them two nights after the warning, Flora asked me if I knew a 'Maggiore Mander'. When I nodded, she asked if he was safe.

'How do you mean?' I asked her.

'Guido and I have been worried. Mander stayed here. Sandro Cottich brought him after the Gestapo raided that flat. He seemed all right, a bit arrogant, but we began to suspect he was German.'

'Why?'

'He had such a huge appetite for potatoes. Only a German could eat

152

potatoes like that.' To test him further, for breakfast she had served him boiled red beets. When he ate these too, she became scared. Guido had found an excuse for him to move out, but she was still nervous about it.

'Relax!' I said laughing. 'Mander's English all the way.'

In any case, because of the new warning, Guido decided that both he and I should leave the flat, at least for a while. To this I naturally agreed.

The following morning as we departed Flora was standing by the open door. Guido went out a few paces ahead of me. I was thanking Flora and saying goodbye when she leaned over quickly and whispered in my ear in Italian 'You come back tonight!' Surprised, I nodded quickly and followed Guido to the hallway and out.

Before the seven o'clock curfew I was walking toward her building on Viale Liege. If she wanted me back, I was delighted. Her flat, even my small basement bedroom, was comfortable and, in spite of this concern about being raided, it was no more insecure than any other home I knew. Could Flora have any silly amorous notions? No, ridiculous! For one thing, I was only 25; she was probably in her mid-thirties. But she was amusing and attractive, and an excellent cook. Moreover, there would still be the amusing little midget, Theo, whom she kept around as a handyman. On account of his odd-shaped head and long nose I called him 'Puck'.

Immediately before the front entrance a wrought-iron railing marked off the property line, inside which a grass lawn ran to the edge of the building. When level with this I heard a voice and stopped. Now a loud hiss and a muffled 'Guglielmo' came from inside the railing. Back against the wall of the building crouched Flora and Puck waving their arms. Were they warning me to go away? I peered again. No, they were signalling me to come into the yard. By now I was accustomed to the Italian hand-sign to 'come'; exactly like the British sign to 'go away'. Quietly I opened an iron gate and stole across the grass to where they stood. With a sign to keep quiet, Flora grabbed my hand and led me down the steps and through the basement door. Inside in the dark she led me past another door, closed it and turned on the light. We were in the familiar basement bedroom of her flat. I looked at her for an explanation. But she was amused. In fact, she was stifling a laugh when she reached up to my ear.

'Guido came back.'

'God, no!' I exclaimed. Flora nodded emphatically, still laughing, and pointed a finger upwards to indicate that in the flat above us at that moment was Guido, with whom I had departed that morning with the understanding that we would both stay away for a while. We had both returned. And it was right on the curfew hour. At my embarrassment, Flora laughed all the more. 'He decided to come back one more night to finish some writing he'd left behind,' she explained, 'but don't worry, you'll just have to stay down here all night. I'll bring dinner down.'

She left and I could soon hear the faint sound of her voice on the floor above. I was uncomfortable. It was one thing to be playing hide-and-seek with the German SS, but quite another to be hiding from friends, and in a situation now savouring of questionable motives.

Later Flora reappeared with a supper tray, wine and a knitting bag. She settled in a chair and began to knit. 'Oh, don't worry,' she said. 'He won't miss me. He's too busy writing in his room.'

I asked her about Guido. She laughed. 'We're old friends. Years ago ... in Milan, but now ... nothing. Too busy writing. He's just living here until things straighten out. It suits me.'

It was agreed I should remain in my room in the morning until Guido left. When I suggested I find another home on the morrow, she became emphatic that Guido would not return again; I should stay here.

The morning procedure went according to plan and, when somewhat timidly I returned the following evening at curfew time, I had the relief of being signalled by Puck to enter by the front door.

After dinner I suggested that we listen to the nine o'clock broadcast from Radio Rome. Flora led Puck and me to the radio in her bedroom where, with a glass of cognac, we were soon chuckling over the two infamous Axis voices of Sally and George. Each night their American-sounding voices chipped away in English at the morale of Allied forces in the south, identifying specific units in the line and with undeniable humour forecasting their fate. Their sing-song fade-out, 'Look out, boys, there's danger ahead!' was becoming famous. Flora knew almost enough English to follow it. Little Puck did not understand a word, but laughed anyway.

Two weeks later her literary friends still showed no signs of returning, but I asked no questions. I was careful each evening as I approached the building. The recent succession of arrests kept John and I constantly on the alert.

No such concern influenced the Chevalier household on Easter Sunday. Mrs M had specially asked me to come by in the afternoon.

Before some unanticipated 'jobs' popped up on Easter morning, I had also promised Signora Esmé Almagia to come for tea at her villa on the other side of town. Inside Mrs M's the scene was frightening. Risks or no, she had determined to celebrate the great message of the Resurrection. Fifty guests, half of whom were escapers, packed her living-room. The chatter was loud. Nothing bad could happen at Easter, she laughed. And the sandwiches were delicious.

Running behind schedule, I slipped out and walked the short distance to Piazza Salerno. I needed some little Easter gift to bring to the Almagias'. At the tram stop, I ran over to a florist. The only cut flowers left were long-stemmed 'Birds of Paradise'; not quite what I had in mind but I was late. With this armful I hopped on a tram as it pulled away. It was fairly busy. The quick wrapping of my purchase only covered the three-foot-long stems, not the colourful heads. As my flowers attracted looks from the other passengers, I tried to minimize their visibility by lowering the long package down the side of my leg to the floor. The next tram from Porta Pia along the Corso d'Italia was crowded, and I kicked myself for having acquired such an eye-catching load. The final tram on its circuitous descent to Piazza Flaminio was positively jam-packed, forcing me to hold the entire yard-long bundle of colour horizontally above the sea of heads, thereby blowing every precaution to stay inconspicuous.

At the villa on Via Stanislao Mancini, Butler Giuseppe opened the door and I joined Signora Almagia, Nancy Savelli, Fane-Hervey and the Lucidis for this special Easter tea, replete with gaily wrapped favours for all. My gift-wrapping was topped by a brilliant miniature of a kilted soldier. Blonde, pretty and American, Nancy was recounting how, at the Opera with me a week before, she had felt uncomfortable sitting between a German officer and a fake Italian. By the time I left, the Birds of Paradise stood on top of a grand piano in the circular hall.

Drawn by Gordon Horner at PG 21 – Chieti. From *For You the War is Over*, by Gordon Horner, London, Falcon Press, 1948. Reprinted with the kind permission of the author.

26

NO MONOCLE

At the eastern end of Piazza San Pietro on the Saturday after Easter something familiar about the gait of a man crossing the piazza caught my attention. My interest quickened as I changed course to see his face. Yes, by golly, it was the thoroughly detested Italian Camp adjutant, Capitano Croce, from our old prison camp at Chieti. A woman accompanied him. In civilian clothes he seemed different; his pointed beard and large monocle were gone.

This was one man whom any of 1200 British and American officers at Chieti would have enjoyed the chance to get back at. His suave, almost sinister, manner, combined with a singular ability for mean retaliation and generally making our existence more edgy at Chieti, had earned him the enmity of all the prisoners whom he had ruled with such relish. An ardent Fascist, he was alleged to have been a member of the Italian secret police and been officially posted to our camp in Chieti in that capacity.

What was he doing now? Was he still active in the secret police, or was he

also *incognito*, waiting on the turn of events? Certainly he was dangerous, and common sense warned me to let him go, but I had a compelling
desire to confront this man whom I had never expected to see again.
Perhaps I might be the only one of the old Chieti crowd ever to have
this opportunity. I couldn't miss it. Any outward show of real animosity
would of course be foolhardy, but at least I could shock him and let him
see that one of his old victims was at large.

In case he raised an alarm and I had to run for it, the wide pillars of
the colonnade towards which he and his companion were heading
seemed the logical place to encounter him. I made a brisk detour and
stopped between two pillars ahead of them. By now, just the idea of
meeting him on level – well, almost level – terms instead of under his
pompous command was stimulating. In these few minutes I had appointed myself the proxy for 1200 officer POWs from Chieti. The lady was
on his far side as they appeared around the pillar. When he came dead
in front of me, I leaned forward, close to his face.

'Good afternoon, Captain Croce!' I said in clear English. He stopped
short and swung around, startled.

'Who ... who are you?' he stammered. He was frightened and I was
happy to see it.

'I'm an acquaintance from the bad old days at Chieti,' I replied. The
lady, on a signal from him, walked on.

'What rank had you?'

'Lieutenant.' There was a pause, as he tried to place me.

'I'm afraid I do not remember. But how do you come to be...?'

Suddenly a hand grasped my arm. I swung around expecting to see a
policeman at my elbow, only to find Prince Carraciolo, a close colleague
of the Monsignor, standing there smiling.

'Bill! Look, these two fellows who've just arrived...' he began in
Italian, before I stopped him with a quick '*Zitta!*' and heaved him back
a few feet.

'Scram!' I hissed at him. With a look of shock, he turned on his heel
and disappeared behind a column. When I turned again to Croce his
face was a mask. He had composed himself.

'How did you get away?'

'It's sufficient for you to know I got away.'

'Did many get away?'

'Enough!'

'What happened to Colonel Marshall?' Croce was feeling for his
English and speaking slowly. All the time he glanced nervously from
side to side.

'God knows!' In fact I knew nothing of the Senior British Officer at Chieti; presumably he was now somewhere in Germany with the main body from our old camp.

'Were you not afraid to come up and speak to me like this? How do you know what my feelings are now?' Croce was more assured now; that old supercilious look was back. I felt my resentment rising, but the appearance of Italian policemen some yards away kept me calm. After all, my simple mission was accomplished.

'Knowing you as an officer and a gentleman, I knew I could trust you,' I lied. 'Couldn't let an old acquaintance go by without saying hello.'

Two Italian police with their rifles slung on their shoulders passed directly behind him. I watched closely, ready to bolt if he made a sign to them. For a few tense seconds of awkward silence I felt sure he was going to, but he didn't. His blank expression gave no clue to his thought, but he seemed ill-at-ease.

'I .. ah .. weesh you a good ... future,' he said in a dull tone, then turned abruptly and walked off toward his companion. I chose the opposite direction and moved away fast.

On the way back to Flora's I thought about Croce. In this no man's land of Italian politics convictions had long since vanished in the present fog of distrust, confusion and treachery. With forebodings of the future, one-time dedicated Fascists were running for cover; personal survival was all that mattered now. Maybe Croce too was lying low.

*   *   *

Adding to the contrast in types who were lying low was one Englishman who should have kept himself completely out of sight. The tall, dashing RAF Flight Lieutenant Garrad-Cole, since I had first ferried him from the Swiss Legation to the Lucidis' flat three months before, had successfully changed his appearance and his way of living. After 'Garry' had been obliged, along with the others, to leave the French Seminary, Monsignor O'Flaherty had placed him in the care of a charming and attractive Italian countess and then proceeded to make good his old prison-camp promise that, if Garry ever escaped to Rome, he would make him the best-dressed man in town. The eager assistance of the Countess soon had this accomplished and the tailor had done his job well. Too well perhaps, because Garry's height, girth and fair features made him conspicuous. Thus, as he rode by tram with his Countess one afternoon in early April, his smart coat and black Homburg hat evoked

Threadneedle Street in London rather than the Corso d'Italia. This triggered the curiosity of two short Fascist policemen in the tram. When Garry noticed their growing interest, he left the lady and alighted from the tram in busy Piazza Flaminio. The two policemen followed. From his earlier stay with the Lucidis, who lived three blocks to the north, he knew the area well and stepped out smartly toward the north-west corner of the Piazza. At the corner the two policemen, anxious not to lose him, ran up on either side of him and demanded to see his identity card. This Garry produced. After examining his card, one policeman asked him a question. Garry's Italian was fair but, as soon as he was obliged to speak, the policemen realized he was a foreigner and abruptly ordered him to accompany them to Police Headquarters. As they led him northward, Garry, incensed at this drastic turn of events, was frantic for a way out. His powerful six foot four towered above his captors, who seemed elated over their prize.

He was growing desperate. Then he saw that the next cross-street ahead was Via Scialoia. Around the corner lay the entrance to No. 18, the Lucidis', on the top floor. He swung back his arms with great force, sending both his escorts sprawling on the pavement, and raced ahead. In seconds revolvers fired and bullets whined past him as he gained the corner. Sprinting the 50 yards to No. 18, he dived inside and, ignoring the elevator, scaled the three flights of stairs to the Lucidis' door. He banged on it, gasping for breath. Adrienne opened it quickly.

'*Mon Dieu*, it's you! We heard the shots. Come! Quickly! To the roof.' Renzo was there now and led the breathless Garry up the short flight on to the flat roof. Near them stood a metal ash-bin, empty. Garry jumped inside. Renzo slammed the lid down on him and raced back down to his flat. From the landing he could hear no sign of commotion.

Down in the street the two enraged Fascist policemen, on reaching the corner, found their quarry gone. They raced for the first and only entrance on the block, No. 18, where stood another policeman, one of the Metropolitan force. They asked him if he had seen a man in a black coat and black hat enter the building.

'*Un' Americano!*' they sputtered. The *Metropolitano*, who had in fact seen Garry flash past him upstairs, feigned alarm, denied that anyone had entered, pulled his revolver and made to join in the chase. The bewildered Fascists could not know that their new ally was a good friend of the Lucidis, knew something of Renzo's activities with Allied escapers and currently used Renzo's basement cellar as his home. His timely appearance and quick thinking had thrown Garry's pursuers off the scent.

But all was not over. Police cars and reinforcements arrived and cordoned off the street outside No. 18. From windows all around people who had heard the shots leaned out and showered down a discordant mixture of questions, jeers and derisive encouragement to the Italian police.

Upstairs in No. 18, still unaware of the clever intervention of their policeman friend, the Lucidis waited tensely, fully expecting the police to search the entire building. And they had another reason to worry, for sitting in their living-room just then was an uninvited guest, the American 3rd Rangers officer, Bill Newnan, who had 'just dropped in for tea'.

With no sign of a search, Adrienne went up to the roof to fetch Garry. Quaking from shock and cramp, he emerged from his container and followed Adrienne down to the flat.

Renzo handed him a large brandy, led him to his tall son Gerald's wardrobe and told him to change fast into Gerald's sports clothes. His 11-year-old son Maurice, sent down to the street to eavesdrop innocently on the police, returned saying the police were looking for a tall American with a dark coat and a black hat.

Still fearing a search, Adrienne decided to remove Bill Newnan. Since he also was rather tall, this could be delicate, but his clothes were light and he wore glasses.

'Bill, I'll take your arm downstairs. When we get outside just smile at me as if you loved me!' Adrienne was in good form and surprisingly calm.

Down in the street, blissfully arm in arm as planned, they successfully passed the close scrutiny of six policemen at the corner. A few streets away Bill Newnan insisted on continuing alone, and Adrienne returned to the flat.

When the curfew was only an hour off, with the police still guarding the street, the Lucidis decided Maurice should escort Garry out, but he, now dressed in tweed jacket and grey trousers, objected that it was too dangerous for the boy. However, they insisted. Maurice would take his hand and chatter steadily to him in Italian as they walked slowly past the police. Garry would simply smile and keep quiet. Far from being nervous, young Maurice seemed delighted.

They departed and passed the police without a hitch. A safe distance way, Garry continued alone to the nearby home of some friends of the Countess and to a future of less sartorial panache.

27

CAUGHT

Dukate had something on his mind when I met him for lunch on 15 April. He looked uncharacteristically serious. After several moves from one home to another in recent weeks, he had accepted a strange invitation on the recommendation of what he described as a reliable friend, and for five days had been living with two men, half Italian, half Greek, who were employed by the German SS.

'It's a rum set up,' conceded Duke, 'but what could be safer? While they're working with the SS, I can't see their apartment being raided.'

'I'm sure you know what you're doing,' I said, feeling not sure at all.

'They're a wild pair, too. One of them has a nephew, about 16, who looks after the apartment. They booze it up every night, and they have their broads around. Not for me, thank you.'

'So?'

'These two guys are making a proposition,' he went on. 'They want to get a group together, about ten or eleven, organize a move to a village on the coast near Civitavecchia – they say they can get all the necessary German passes – charter a motor boat or launch up there and head south by sea to our lines – Anzio most probably – under cover of darkness.'

'Duke, please!'

Duke knew it had a strong odour, but thought it worth considering. It would cost 150,000 lire, 70,000 put up by them, 80,000 by Duke's friends, of whom they could take eight. Even if they were serious, this would be a tough undertaking. As to their motives, Duke assumed that they realized that, when the Allies arrived, their record would make it rough for them. If they pulled off the sea rescue it could wipe the slate clean. If, more subtly, they hoped to become a German plant behind our lines after winning Allied confidence through their bravery – and Duke doubted they were shrewd enough – our Intelligence chaps could take care of them. It was unlikely to be a straightforward ambush plan to hand the Germans eight Allied escapers and pocket 80,000 lire. Did Duke trust them? No, but they were serious about the deal.

'Why not come there with me tonight? Plenty of room. See for yourself.'

'OK. What have you told them about me?'

'Not a thing. You'll just be another guy I know.'

The idea appealed to me strongly. For months we had drawn blanks on plans to get men from the Rome area through to the Allied lines. Instead of being an escape line, Rome had become an escape terminus. While the reasons for this were beyond our control, it had nevertheless been frustrating, especially as Gestapo security tightened around us.

After letting Flora know that I would probably be away overnight, I met Duke again. At half-past six that evening he was leading me down some steps into a busy little basement trattoria on a quiet street two kilometres north off Via Flaminia.

'I meet them here every night,' Duke explained, as he looked through the haze of cigarette smoke. Someone waved and we filed over to a small table where two men insisted we join them. They were a contrast. Giorgio was of slight build, and his sallow complexion emphasized a thin black moustache and sharp dark eyes. Dino was broad, powerful-looking and blond. The customers who packed the small place were mostly working people, probably from the neighbourhood. During our black-market supper vino flowed freely.

With the lengthening days, the German Command had recently put back the curfew to half-past eight. Just at that hour, almost at dark, the four of us entered a substantial residential building 200 yards from the trattoria and climbed to a flat on the third floor. Inside, four rooms opened off a long hallway which ended in a large living-room. The flat had basic furnishings, tables, chairs and beds. It was untidy. Curtains were drawn. Low-hanging naked bulbs cast a cold yellow light. Their glare made it hard for a moment to observe the features of two cheaply attractive girls, to whom I was casually introduced across half-empty wine bottles standing on a stained, ash-strewn table. Giorgio's alert-looking nephew was respectful and friendly as he brought glasses from the kitchen. Dino's jacket landed on a chair as his arm grabbed a dark-haired girl from behind, across the low neck of her tight-fitting satin dress, pulling her off balance, while with his other hand he picked up a guitar from the sideboard.

'I'll show you our room,' said Duke, leading me to a room at the end of the corridor. 'That's yours.' He pointed to one of two low camp beds strewn with oddments of his clothes.

'The dark girl out there is new tonight. He had a different one last night, but they fought like hell and he sent her home. The redhead's been here often with Giorgio.'

Back in the living-room, the little redhead faced me with a flirtatious smile and a profile of tight emerald sweater which moved perceptibly as I almost failed to grasp the glass of wine she held out to me. No evening to be careless with drinks. At least I had a purpose in coming.

In the midst of chatter, wine and Neapolitan melodies on Dino's guitar, Duke signalled me into an adjoining room. Giorgio followed us and became business-like as he outlined his plan. With the German SS permits he could obtain, the scheme was assured of success, he insisted. His proposal was consistent with what Duke had told me. As I stood silent for a few moments, hesitating to ask questions which might reflect my distrust, Giorgio needled us jokingly with his limited English. 'Why you wait? Where is dees Engleesh-American *coraggio*?' I quickly assured him his idea was excellent. Duke and I would talk to one or two friends and let him know as soon as possible.

At the Vatican the next afternoon, in a written report to Sam Derry outlining the plan, I asked him what he thought and particularly whether the money to finance it would be available. The Monsignor echoed my own doubts as to these strange characters, but felt sure that money would be no problem.

'Here's a new identity card for you, Bill. It's very special.' At his request I had brought him passport photos a week before. 'I got them only for you and John, because of what you're doing. Don't tell the others you have them.'

I examined it with surprise. It was an authentic Vatican State document and signed by a ranking official of the German Legation. After having been Guglielmo del Monte for the last three months, I had now been re-christened William O'Flynn, Irish citizen, employed in the Vatican Library. Discretion stopped me from asking how he had obtained it. It seemed too good to be a forgery. This card could save our skins, especially if accosted by Italian Fascist police. In one of the *ras-trellamenti*, which we had escaped so far in spite of their growing frequency, it would be invaluable.

Sam's reply when I returned the next day was what I had anticipated. The cash would be forthcoming, and I should explore the plan in detail, particularly to the point of feeling reasonably sure that our Italo-Greek sponsors were in good faith.

Duke had undertaken to sound out Rendell, Wilson and Smith on the plan. The time was ripe, as they were all becoming concerned about our deteriorating position following the recent spate of German arrests. They were split up in different billets now. Most of their watering-places were virtually denied to them, except for emergencies: the Orso, the Lucidis', Mrs M's, another favourite restaurant of the Pestalozzas, Ascenzio's, where some pointed questions from Fascist customers had recently scared the proprietor into pleading with Galeazzo to keep the group away.

To one fairly safe meeting-place still available they had asked via Renzo Lucidi that John and I should come to review the situation at five o'clock in the evening of the very day I had received Sam's provisional go-ahead on the sea evacuation plan. Rompoldi's bar on Piazza di Spagna I had never visited. The English password to be admitted by Signor Rompoldi, who sat near the entrance, was 'How about three good drinks?' born out of a characteristic remark by Pat Wilson when first introduced to the place by Renzo.

On entering the bar I walked over to an elderly man doing the books at the cash-desk.

'How about three good drinks?' I said quietly. His head jerked up. After studying me he broke into a smile, left his booth and led me through a long old-fashioned bar to a room in the rear where the others were already settled with drinks. With them were Renzo Lucidi and Dedy della Campana. At the meeting my pitch was that, in view of the encroachments of the Gestapo and the SS, augmented by the Fascist *Banda Koch*, everyone should remain indoors and just hope that the Allied offensive would get going soon. With Duke, I explained the rather smelly proposition for sea evacuation. Each one declared himself an eager starter if we said it was 'on'.

When the others left Duke and I remained, discussing the Civita-vecchia plan. Until it was time to return to Flora's, I was content to sit with him having a drink.

'Hell, Bill, come up again tonight. Let's see if we can nail them down on this deal.' I was not keen, particularly as I had no way to let Flora know, but finally agreed. The sooner I reached a conclusion on these fellows and a decision on the plan the better.

After the tram ride north on Via Flaminia, we headed for the same trattoria. It was even more crowded tonight. From a rear table Giorgio shouted and waved to us. He shook hands vigorously. 'I been to a party all afternoon,' he explained gaily in loud English. He was half-drunk.

Giorgio ordered steaks with fried eggs on top. As we waited, Giorgio talked on, half in Italian, half in English. I told him to quieten down, but he just laughed. As the steaks arrived he broke into the strains of 'It's a Long Way to Tipperary'. The joint was noisy, but this was too much.

'Engleesh, you are Engleesh?' asked a short, shabbily dressed man, who suddenly appeared at the table. Giorgio sobered up instantly. In Italian he asked the stranger what he meant; how could he be so stupid? We often talked a little English among ourselves, he said with a gesture, for the hell of it. The little man gave a cursory nod and disappeared in the crowd of customers.

'Duke, I don't like this. Let's eat up and get out!' I felt uncomfortable.

'*Vede ché pauro!*' exclaimed Giorgio jeeringly, striking my arm. I shrugged at his allegation of fear. If only I could drag Duke away and make for some other house, instead of this doubtful flat nearby, but the rigid curfew was only seven minutes away. The nearest haven, the Lucidis', was a mile and a half south. I contented myself with asking for the bill and persuading the others to get moving.

Outside in the semi-dark as we headed for the flat Giorgio spotted a girl standing in a doorway. He went across to speak to her. Quickly the girl made it clear he should push off.

Down the quiet street near their building Giorgio again broke into 'Tipperary'. I hustled them inside and up the three flights of stone steps.

Inside the flat Dino sat strumming his guitar. The same two girls from two nights before were serving some food and the young nephew was filling wine glasses. Frustrated and somewhat annoyed, I wondered if I could expect to have any sane, responsible discussion with the Greeks about the evacuation plan. On our first encounter Giorgio had impressed me as confident and capable – I could understand Duke's enthusiasm – but, in the light of tonight's exhibition, my doubts were growing fast.

Bang! Bang! Bang! The loud noise came from the front door. The room fell silent. Dino and Giorgio exchanged apprehensive glances. A quick sign from Giorgio sent his nephew hastening down the long hallway. Bang! Bang! Bang! Louder now. The nephew shouted from the door. Giorgio, deadly serious, rushed out of the room. Duke sallied out after him, but returned in a flash.

'Germans! Germans!' he said, pointing back over his shoulder. Gruff voices barked in the corridor. I looked quickly around the room. It had no possible escape exit, and no place to hide. The windows? Three storeys up and no balconies, they were useless.

Three steel-helmeted German SS burst into the room with raised machine pistols. Hand grenades with long wooden handles bristled from their belts. They edged around, waving their weapons. A stern Sergeant-Major ordered us all back against one wall.

Behind the Sergeant-Major came a tall, hard-faced woman with short, unkempt grey hair, followed by Giorgio arguing fiercely with her. While his men stood taut and ready for any trouble, the Sergeant-Major quickly frisked us for arms. On Dino he found a revolver, which he passed to one of his men. Quickly he searched the room, behind the curtains, under the settee.

One faint hope remained for me, my new Vatican identity card signed by the German diplomat. Challenged when alone, I should have felt confident. Now, as the Sergeant-Major turned back to us, I doubted whether it would carry any weight in this weird and compromising group. The two girls standing beyond Duke looked scared. Dino on my right was grim. At the entrance to the room the steely-eyed female still screamed at Giorgio, who was waving his arms.

'*Carta d'Identità!*' demanded the Sergeant-Major. He took the two girls' documents first, and after a quick examination gave them back. Next Duke handed over his Italian identity card. It was good, but didn't seem to convince the German, who regarded Duke with suspicion.

'*Sono Italiano,*' volunteered Duke, '*ma sono stato molto tempo in America.*' Duke was serious, offering his standard plea about really being Italian, but having spent a long time in America before the war. Ignoring Duke's patter and holding on to his card, the Sergeant-Major moved up to me. With a look which I hoped indicated innocent bewilderment, I handed him my Vatican card. He looked at it, opened it, read it through, then half-turned away and re-examined it carefully. For fear of conflicting with whatever story Giorgio was telling the mysterious woman, I kept silent. If the Germans asked me, I would explain that I didn't know these people, that I had just met them and come up here at their invitation because of the curfew. But the German was hurrying. He looked at me again without speaking, kept my card and moved on to Dino on my right.

Dino pulled out a handful of papers. The Sergeant-Major took them over to the light on the table. While he examined them closely, Dino talked fast in Italian, insisting that he was directly associated with the very SS unit to which the Sergeant-Major belonged. But the German was taking no chances.

With the irate woman at his heels, Giorgio stormed up to the

Sergeant-Major and, gesticulating angrily, pointed out that he too was employed by the local SS.

'This woman is crazy!' raged Giorgio in Italian. 'You're all wasting your time here.'

The Sergeant-Major, unimpressed, waved him aside. Giorgio lost his temper.

'Shut up!' barked the German in Italian. 'I and my men here are the SS police, and nobody else!' Two soldiers swung their machine pistols threateningly on Giorgio, who, realizing the futility of further protest, backed down.

The Sergeant-Major led the woman out of the room. Giorgio and Dino followed them. The Sergeant-Major came back and signalled Duke and me out into the hallway. Brusquely he stood us together facing the wall. One of his men shouldered his machine pistol, stepped forward with handcuffs and clamped them around Duke's left wrist and my right. The soldiers spun us toward the open door and pushed us downstairs. Halfway down I glanced back. The muzzle of one automatic was a yard from our backs. Dino, Giorgio and the two girls were following under guard a flight behind us.

Duke and I did not speak. Our thoughts were identical. From the moment the raid began, I had felt no nerves, only a tense alertness. Now, as we descended the stairs, I sensed that Duke too was ready to grab any possible chance. Under this heavy guard our position seemed hopeless but, in the darkness of the street below, unless other Germans were on guard, would there be a fleeting moment, even manacled together, to make a mad dash?

At the bottom of the stairs a gun prodded us forward to the street door. Through my handcuff I felt Duke stiffen. We were poised as we stepped out into the dark, but there on the pavement another guard was pointing his gun straight at us.

At the curb stood a black limousine, the rear door open. Another push from behind propelled me into the back seat, tugging Duke after me. A German sat in front behind the wheel. As the door slammed on us, I glimpsed the outline of Dino, Giorgio and the girls being bundled into a larger car in front. We settled back in the seat. This was it. We had had it. Suddenly I froze. My wallet! With horror I remembered that, besides some 8000 lire, it contained written messages, addresses, receipts, even a couple of photographs – clues enough to lead directly to a dozen escapers and our friends.

'God, my wallet!' I whispered to Duke. 'It's loaded!'

'I've got some choice items too,' he muttered back.

As the car in front rode off, the rear doors of our car opened and two hefty Germans swung themselves inside and sat squarely on our knees. The Sergeant-Major climbed into the front seat. The doors slammed and the car took off with a jerk which threw the two bulky Germans back against us.

I was scared about the evidence I carried. If we didn't get rid of the papers somehow, the SS would descend on a dozen more flats tonight. Around the broad back of my German burden, I peered in the dark at the car windows on both sides. They were closed. Almost wishfully my eyes fixed again on the window on my side as I feverishly tried to think of a solution. The car screeched around a corner, and the two Germans leaned forward. The headlights of a passing truck showed up something I could hardly believe. I focused more closely on the window on my side. At the top it was actually open half an inch. I tugged on the handcuffs and leaned cautiously over to Duke.

'My window!' I whispered. Our free hands moved carefully but quickly into our pockets. The car was speeding now. The Germans, eyes ahead, lunged back and forth on our knees. My hand gripped the wallet in my inside pocket. Although the 8000 lire it contained could be useful, this was no time for fumbling to extract it. As the car took another corner, my German strained forward to keep his balance. With my eyes fixed on his head, I pulled out my wallet, moved it along the seat, up the side of the window until my fingers felt the narrow opening, then jerked it out. I prayed that some thoroughly dishonest person would pick it up and, in order to keep the money, would not hand it over to police. In Rome right now the prayer had a strong chance of being answered.

Duke tugged on the handcuffs. We leaned close.

'I can't get it out with my free hand,' he breathed. Something incriminating in his left hip pocket was out of reach. As he pulled his manacled hand over and, without moving his body, twisted it into his seat pocket, the sharp tight-gripping handcuff bit into my wrist. I gritted my teeth. Finally his hand came out. The tyres squealed around another corner. My free left hand crossed behind the German and, in the dark, grasped the papers clutched in Duke's fist. In seconds they were jettisoned from the car.

'I still have 10,000 lire,' Duke muttered.

'Mine's gone ... give me some.' It would look strange to have nothing at all in my pocket. Cautiously he passed me five 1000 lire notes. My German still leaned forward, watching the road ahead. We were speeding across a bridge over the Tiber.

I felt something in my left inside pocket. Curling my free left hand into it, I pulled out a large fold of paper. A passing headlight showed the masthead *Avanti*, the Communist underground newspaper. 'Read it as a matter of interest,' a friend had said yesterday as he handed it to me. The car slowed down and turned into a narrow lane. Quickly this last embarrassment followed the same path and disappeared through the merciful opening.

Seconds later the car stopped in front of a large, dimly lit doorway. An SS man opened the car door and we stumbled out. With machine pistols trained on us, the SS marched us through the entrance into a wide, semi-circular well, around which rose six high gates of thick iron bars. In one of these two men in dark blue uniforms turned a huge key and the gate creaked open. Through this our SS escort pushed us and marched us down a long, stone-paved floor, walled on both sides by a line of closed wooden doors, each of which had set in it a small barred opening. Above were two higher floors, along the front of which ran high-railed metal balconies.

'Can't be Via Tasso,' I muttered to Duke.

'Right, must be Regina Coeli.'

Halfway down this long floor a German guard barked. From his hand motions we understood he wanted us against the wall. Dutifully we moved over and stood with our backs to the wall. At this the German growled, stomped over and, grabbing Duke by the shoulder, spun us around to face the whitewashed wall.

I pulled out a half-empty pack of Seraglios. We had scarcely lit the cigarettes when a fierce snarl made us look around. The same gruff German, obviously angry, pointed at the wall above our heads. In the semi-darkness we could not see what he meant. He roared and pointed again. As we spotted a notice saying *Vietato Fumare*, we smothered a smirk and extinguished our cigarettes.

'Nice guy!' murmured Duke as, for the first time in many months, we reverted to the old prison-camp habit of slipping the stubs back in our pocket.

'Look, Duke, d'you think you've any chance of persuading them that you're an innocent Italian?'

'For about ten seconds!'

'OK then, let's work out our stories. I've just got a damned good identity card saying I'm an Irishman working in the Vatican Library. It's probably hopeless, but I'm going to make a fuss. Nothing to lose. Now, if you're interrogated, say that until this afternoon you'd never set eyes on me before. I'm going to say that I was on my way back to the Vatican after a day off when I ran into you quite by chance in a bar on

Piazza Flaminio. You were pretty high and, since you seemed like a nice chap and spoke English well, I offered to help you home. Hence my presence in the flat. Naturally I knew none of the other people there. It was getting near curfew time, so your friends insisted on my spending the night and returning to the Vatican tomorrow morning. All right?'

'Got it.'

A German came up and removed our handcuffs. Taking Duke by the arm, he led him into a lighted office. I followed and stood outside, near the door. Duke was questioned. I could hear his replies, in Italian. He proclaimed he was Italian and once again explained that he had spent many years in America studying before the war, but in 1940 when things began to look black for his 'Mother Country' he had hastened back here.

When he came out I went in. A German Sergeant-Major seated at the table asked me my name, nationality, occupation and address. Another German went through my pockets. When he found my cash, he counted it and then to my surprise handed it back to me. I was about to begin my Irish protest when I was summarily ushered out again and left standing beside Duke. Presumably this office was only concerned with basic documentation; the Sergeant-Major was not interested in stories.

From down the hall, three men in plain clothes approached us.

'Ah, you are English,' said the tallest.

'Listen!' I began, before Duke could start his standard patter again. 'I'm not English. I'm Irish, my home is in Dublin and I'm an employee of the Vatican. If I don't turn up for work tomorrow morning, there'll be some awkward questions to answer, both for me and for you. This is all quite ridiculous! Why I've been arrested, I don't know.' Two shorter civilians, who looked Italian, were expressionless as they turned to the tall one, who sounded German.

'You are Irish?' he asked, grinning at my show of irritation. 'Ah no, you are an English officer. No? In fact you are Scotch!'

'Where in heaven's name did you get that idea?' I protested with as much anger as I could muster. This fellow's English was good, well-pronounced. Had he worked this out from my speech? Possibly. More likely, Giorgio, who knew I was Scots, had said too much back at the flat. 'Look, let's not be stupid. I'm Irish. If you don't believe me, get in touch with the Vatican Secretariat or somebody and find out for yourselves, but please do something quickly.'

'That is all right. Do not worry.' His derisive grin had gone. He turned his attention to Duke.

'Well? English, eh?'

'*Io sono Italiano!*' began Duke emphatically, waving his hands excitedly. '*Sono state molto tempo in America, ma son Italiano!*' The tall civilian laughed, cutting short Duke's compelling tones and manual gestures. I bit my lip. The German with his two Italian aides moved away.

'Did they search you in there?' I asked Duke quietly.

'They sure did. But I had nothing left but cash and they handed it back to me.'

'Me too. Thank God for that window in the car. Can you imagine if ... phew!'

'Yea, it's kinda hard to realize what's happened. Bill, boy, in case you didn't notice, you're now back in the bag!'

A German appeared from the office and directed us up a zig-zag iron stairway to the third and top tier of cells, thence along a metal balcony which ran around the entire inside well. There had to be some 200 cells in this *Terzo Braccio*, the third wing of Regina Coeli. The German stopped at Cell 321, unlocked it and motioned me inside. As the heavy timber door closed on me, I winked to Duke who was headed for another cell.

One small electric bulb high on the wall above the door cast a dim half-light across the stillness of the cell. Three bodies lay on the floor, on dirty straw-filled palliasses. Three apathetic unshaven faces gazed up at me. I nodded to them. One, youthful-looking, sat up and smiled, the second, also young, leaned around on his elbow, while the third, an older man, from his prone position down the side of the cell muttered a feeble '*Buona sera*'.

The cell was about fifteen feet long and seven feet across. The palliasses of the three men already covered most of the floor. The youth in the corner pointed to a spare palliasse, stained and dirty, rolled up in the corner by the door. Resignedly I rolled it out across the remaining floor space and gingerly laid an equally filthy-looking blanket across it.

'*Cos'é successo?*' inquired the youth. What had happened?

'I was arrested tonight with some other people,' I explained simply in Italian. 'I don't know why. Certainly, as far as I'm concerned, the whole thing's a complete mistake. I hope they'll call me for interrogation or something very soon, because I just have to get back to work tomorrow.' All three smiled.

'Interrogation?' yawned the youth. 'Oh, there's plenty of time for that. You'll be lucky if they come for you within a couple of weeks.'

Each of them had apparently waited for weeks after being arrested before anything happened. The youth had been here for four months

171

and the older man for two months. The third remarked dolefully that this cell had been his home uninterruptedly for six solid months.

The youth asked me if I was hungry and offered me a small piece of bread.

'*Grazie, no,*' I assured him, adding unfairly without thinking, 'I had a big steak two hours ago.'

'You're lucky,' observed the youth, laughing. 'You may find it a little difficult to adjust to the diet here. It's somewhat plainer and lighter.'

I asked them what they did for a toilet. They pointed to a bucket in a corner.

All seemed about to go to sleep. I sat on the palliasse and removed my jacket. Breaking a few stitches in five places in the lining, I pushed through each small opening one of the 1000 lire notes and with one finger flattened them out inside the lining. The Germans had handed this money back, but they might change their minds. With nothing further to do except wait, I lay back on the hard palliasse in my clothes. A jumble of thoughts tumbled through my head. This had all happened so quickly. Who had given us away? When would the Monsignor, Sam or John find out? But my disjointed thinking was interrupted. Despite appearances of sleep, the other three were not yet settled for the night.

'We have a nightly sport,' began the cheerful youth in Italian from his palliasse in the corner. 'This palace of ours is a friendly place. We have hundreds of visitors every night. You see those two ventilating grilles up in the wall there, on each side above the door? Don't be surprised at what happens after we turn out the light.' He rose as he spoke, moved across the cell in a crumpled shirt, switched out the miserable light and, stepping over the others, returned to his palliasse. Two minutes of silence went by. The youth moved again and switched on the light. Looking up at the ventilators, my eyes widened. Down the wall on each side of the door moved scores of little black specks. Others were pouring out of the ventilators after them. My apparently sleepy cell-mates sprang to life from the floor. Emitting muffled war whoops and holding out before them broad sheets of old newspaper, they rushed the wall. In a frenzy of excitement, they 'blotted' the entire surface as high as they could reach, inflicting mass death on hundreds of Regina Coeli's unquenchable army of bugs.

'Do they stop now?' I asked in Italian, as the others, their nightly attack over, picked their steps back to their flat straw mattresses.

'Oh no! When the light goes out now, they'll pour in all night.'

'And where do they go?'

'Over you ... and me. But don't worry, you don't even feel them!'

172

Hmm! Folding my jacket as a pillow, I pulled the coarse blanket around me on the palliasse. A cool draught of air came from a large opening protected by stout vertical iron bars, recessed high in the wall farthest from the cell door.

The light out, silence settled in the cell. I was wide awake. Flora would be really worried. Tomorrow she would ask John Furman, or maybe Sandro Cottich. Word would flash around soon enough. Mrs M ... Renzo and Adrienne ... old Miss May ... they'd all be concerned. Monsignor O'Flaherty and Sam Derry would be worrying about what evidence I had on me when caught. It would be harder on the organization now, with 'Whitebows' in hiding and, thanks to the perfidy of Don Pasquale, John Furman vulnerable at every move.

Who had informed the Germans tonight? Was it that curious man at the trattoria, when Giorgio was talking in English? Unlikely. The gaunt woman who had come with the SS, what had she to do with it? She made the accusations, against Giorgio and Dino too. It appeared prearranged; I was just unlucky enough to be there. What had Duke said about Dino throwing a girl out the other night? She must have known Duke was American. Maybe this was her mother ... or her 'Madame'?

Unless they called me soon for questioning, tonight or tomorrow morning, the Irish identity plea wouldn't hold water. I'd stick to William O'Flynn anyway, just in case. Would they suspect my connection with the organization? They already knew much about it. Would they pump me after exploding the William O'Flynn story, in the hope of adding to their case against the Vatican? Well, the good old rule – name, rank and number, then shut up. Would they take me to Via Tasso? Would they ...? To avoid this unpleasant thought I turned involuntarily on the straw. The old man across the floor was breathing heavily. The whole jail was surprisingly silent, except for the remote clink of boots on the metal paving down below. I yawned into my jacket pillow. What a wonderful soft bed at Flora's these last few ...

A wild scream pierced the silence, and died in a wavering wail of agony. It was followed by another, higher, more chilling. From somewhere down below, it seemed. In the cell, somebody stirred.

'*Cos'e?*' I asked quietly. All three were awake.

'Every night we hear this,' murmured the youth in Italian. 'Comes from the Interrogation Cell on the ground floor. They do their beating-up mostly at night.' The victim screamed again.

'How do they do it?'

'Usually they tie their victim, naked, to a metal bedstead, stretched out, face down. They just beat him with heavy sticks until he talks.

Most nights we just hear moaning, the odd cry. But tonight it sounds like a different technique. If the beating doesn't work, then they take him to Via Tasso. More imagination there.'

'Interesting! *Buona notte.*'

Jailed

28

TERZO BRACCIO

'I'll ask my cousin,' whispered young Michelin on the fourth morning, as I dried my face on my handkerchief. I liked this young fellow and, because of his straightforward manner, I had decided to take him partly into my confidence. Four months earlier he had been arrested with his sister and cousin when the SS raided their home. Why they had been raided he did not volunteer. At their trial two weeks ago his cousin, who was now acting as prison doctor in a hospital made out of two adjoining cells on the ground floor, and his sister had been sentenced to several years' imprisonment. The Tribunal had not convicted Michelin because of 'lack of proof', but he saw no sign of being released. In prison Michelin had developed a skin infection, and each morning his cousin, the doctor, visited the cell to treat him.

While sticking to the William O'Flynn identity, I had told him of my anxiety to send word to an Irish friend in the Vatican. He suggested that, if his cousin could smuggle out a note inside a bundle of laundry, a relative outside would no doubt take care of its delivery. On a scrap of paper I wrote a note to Monsignor O'Flaherty. I had been arrested and had told the SS who I was – William O'Flynn. I hoped they would realize their mistake quickly and release me. Another fellow called Dukate, suspected of being an American, had been brought with me to Regina Coeli.

When the 'doctor' arrived, Michelin slipped him the note and whispered some instructions. If it reached the Monsignor, at least he would know what name I was using.

The doctor gave Michelin the sad news that his sister, along with other convicted women, was to be shipped that afternoon to a concentration camp in Germany. Before long the cell door opened again, and his sister, a bright-eyed, attractive girl, was ushered into our cell by a German guard, who remained outside. She had half an hour to say goodbye to her brother.

If Michelin was a courageous young man for his years, his sister was no less so. Despite the prospect of being carried off to slave labour, she was in high spirits and discounted the gravity of her plight.

'Think of the fun we'll have fouling up all the jobs they give us,' she laughed. In this small cell they could have no privacy, and only when the German guard returned to take her away did their composure crack.

Since that first night the unsavoury prospect of interrogation had become my first concern. I was conditioning myself. If nothing happened within the first seven days, I would demand a hearing and register my Irish protest once more.

Another worry was hunger. The first two days had been tolerable; now I felt it keenly. The diet was choice: four deliveries each day. These, like all the other service chores in the gaol, were carried out by *scoppini*, orderlies who were Italian civil prisoners in the other wings. Under the gruff, frequently brutal, direction of the German police on duty, these *scoppini* dragged giant tureens around each floor three times a day. When the guard unlocked the cell door, each inmate pushed a tin bowl outside to receive his ration. At nine in the morning and in the evening at five o'clock it was weak, bitter ersatz coffee; at noon a thin watery soup containing a suggestion of potato, the dirty end stalks of vegetables and a few bits of macaroni. The fourth delivery was by far the most important. At eleven each morning the *sportello*, the cell door's small barred window generally kept closed by a bolt on the outside, opened long enough for a *scoppino* to push through one five-ounce bread roll for each prisoner. This had to sustain us for twenty-four hours. Twice a week a two-ounce morsel of dubious meat would come with the soup. Even the early months at Chieti, when half the camp had come down with jaundice through malnutrition, had been bountiful by comparison. I wondered how my cell-mates had survived this near-starvation for months.

In the light of this gnawing awareness of real hunger, there was some psychological value in the crudity of our furnishings. Things took longer. Each morning the palliasses were rolled and shaped with the dirty old blankets into a two-seater 'sofa' and two single 'chairs'. These were positioned so as to leave the longest walking distance diagonally across the cell – seven paces up and seven back.

The two facilities had to be taken in turns also: the latrine bucket in the corner, removed twice a day by the *scoppini*, and an old metal basin in which, with water from a large metal jug, we washed without soap.

These functions contributed at least an hour of conscious, and at first self-conscious, activity to the passive life of the cell.

Razors were forbidden. Once a week, the others said, a German guard decided whose beard looked heaviest and let him out to visit a barber-shop cell on the ground floor. There two barbers, themselves prisoners in this wing, worked each day on these chins.

Even if young Michelin doubted my Irish-Vatican story, he at least considered me a bona fide prisoner here and warned me to lookout for German 'plants'. These informers, he explained, could be legitimate fellow-prisoners who, if confronted with damning evidence against them, might be persuaded to squeal on careless cell talk in return for offered leniency at their trials. Thus, while the atmosphere was friendly, no one voiced any true hint as to why he had been arrested, and each groaned about the injustice of it all. The older man failed to see why he had been put in prison just because of a silly argument with some Germans over a couple of pigs. The Germans, he complained, were actually accusing him of dealings with Allied escaped prisoners. Ridiculous idea!

Still uncomfortably fresh in the minds of all was the recent massacre of 335 Italians at the Ardeatine Caves. This cell had contributed one victim, a young man who had spent two months here and against whom the Germans appeared to have little evidence. His cell-mates had liked him. They doubted whether he had committed any offence, but nevertheless he had been called out when the fatal second list had come around. From the time the news got back of the horrible fate of their recent companion and the others, they had been living in fear of further incidents in the city, with similar retaliation exacted by the Germans.

'May Day's coming up,' observed the old man. 'I hope these damned Communists don't go crazy again.'

Michelin's cousin, the doctor, was proving useful. He found out Duke's cell number and brought me change for a 1000 lire note. On 23 April I bribed a *scoppino* to deliver a note to Duke, as a result of which we both succeeded, when the afternoon clean-up took place, in obtaining our respective guard's permission to visit the latrine at the end of the floor at the same time. Nothing had happened to Duke yet either.

'As and when they ask me,' he said, 'I'm just going to declare myself an American POW. No point in kidding around.'

'Right, but I'm sticking to Ireland for the moment. Tomorrow's the seventh day. If they haven't come for me, I want to see them. It's hopeless, but I might as well have a bash at it. Remember, Duke, if they ask you, you never set eyes on me before that night. Found any cigarettes?'

'No, I'm out, but one of these *scoppino* guys is doing a real cagey black market in them here. He doesn't trust me yet, but I'll let you know.'

'Come on, we'd better get back. How's your appetite?'

'Meet you at the Orso for lunch tomorrow!' he laughed, as we separated.

All next day, whenever the *sportello* was open, I shouted at every German guard who passed, requesting an interview with the Sergeant-Major in charge. They ignored me. Then, to my surprise in the early afternoon, the cell door was unlocked. A German guard standing in the opening called 'William O'Flynn'. He motioned me to collect my belongings and follow him. The others helped me gather my few things. They thought my moment for interrogation had come. Frankly so did I.

'*Saluti! Auguri!*' followed me as I left the cell.

In the ground floor office the heavy-set senior Sergeant-Major regarded me from behind his desk. Another of the same rank, a tall, lean one who spoke English, stood to my left. They asked me a few simple questions about my name and identity. To my surprise, when I had answered these, they appeared to be finished and signalled me toward a waiting German guard outside.

'Wait a minute!' I said. 'I've been trying to see you for a whole week now. I explained quite emphatically to your people when I was brought here last week that this was all a mistake, that they should check for themselves, but in any case to get me out of here as soon as possible. I'm still here!' The English-speaking Sergeant-Major was listening intently. My employers, I went on, were bound to be wondering what had happened to me, but naturally would never guess I was inside Regina Coeli. The lean Sergeant-Major translated in German for his senior, who seemed impressed by my indignation.

'You gentlemen *must* let me know as soon as possible when I may return to the Vatican to my work.'

Both men now looked apologetic. The stout one spoke quietly in German to his interpreter.

'We are only the guards,' explained the tall one in English. 'We are only responsible for running the prison. All papers concerning you are in the hands of our Headquarters. Only they have the authority.'

'Well, get in touch with them,' I said, taking courage from their attitude. 'But hurry up! tell them to check it with the Secretariat of the Vatican, or with the Irish Free State Minister for that matter, but don't let this thing drag on any longer!' The fat Sergeant-Major shrugged his shoulders, but said nothing.

A German soldier led me from the office, but not back to the third floor. Instead, he stopped beside the first cell door on the ground floor beyond the iron stairway, opened it, motioned me inside and locked the door. Why this change, I wondered. Duke, as far as I knew, was still upstairs. One point did occur to me. This cell was right across from the interrogation chamber.

29

SCOTTISH CHEQUES UNCHECKED

An unexpected bank transaction was about to jolt my family on a cold, blustery day on the Firth of Clyde in south-west Scotland. As they went about their affairs they were conscious, as they had been now for six months, of an overshadowing worry as to my whereabouts and uncertainty as to whether I was still alive. Only one short, less-than-reassuring communication back in November had broken the pall of silence since September, 1943, and that had originated no doubt from the War Office's monitoring of Vatican Radio's transmission of serial numbers.

The *Gourock Times*, a weekly newspaper published by my family, still appeared every Friday morning. Gourock, a normally tranquil town of 10,000 souls, many of whom commuted daily the twenty-six miles to Glasgow, spent much of its life oscillating between gale-borne downpours from the Atlantic Ocean on the west to bright sunlight, revealing the glory of mountains and lochs to the north. The River Clyde, from its source north of Glasgow, wound westward through the world's most renowned shipbuilding yards, begotten in Britain's Industrial Revolution, until it expanded into a two-mile-wide estuary. Here, on its south bank, Gourock was a hinge around which the Firth wheeled southward to flow into the Irish Sea.

Three miles south from the hinge of Gourock a 'boom', a gigantic steel-chain underwater curtain, stretched from the Cloch Lighthouse north across the Clyde to Dunoon in Argyll. A carefully monitored 'gate' in mid-channel opened for ships to pass. Thus, the immense anchorage of the Clyde Basin was virtually fool-proof against German U-boats. As the shortest route from North America, the Clyde off Gourock had become the principal disembarkation point in Britain for US and Canadian troops and war matériel being amassed in anticipation of the Allied invasion of Europe.

One morning, in the Gourock branch of the National Bank of Scotland, the Accountant while sorting the incoming mail stopped when he came to a clutch of odd-looking papers which had arrived from a bank in England as cheques to be honoured. Quickly he left his stool and took them to the Manager, Roderick Smith.

Within minutes bowler-hatted 'Roddy' Smith was off to the printing and publishing office of J. & R. Simpson where he showed these rudely drawn cheques to my startled father. They bore dates from late December until mid-March. Absolutely no doubt, Mr Smith stated, that the signature on each was William's. He knew; I had worked for him for over two years. The cheques mentioned no place of origin, and the only bank clearing stamp was of a Lloyd's Bank branch near London.

The emotional relief must have been considerable as first my brother James and sister Mary at work in Gourock and my mother, by phone, welcomed this unexpected evidence that, at least until the middle of March, the missing and youngest member of the family was alive somewhere. In a day or so the next youngest, George, would receive the word at his Royal Corps of Signals training camp.

My oldest brother Bob, an Army Intelligence Corps officer attached by coincidence to Port Security at Gourock at that time, while equally elated, was professionally perplexed as to how those cheques had somehow found a hole in the country's security – from some enemy country to a London bank. Little could anyone know that Sir D'Arcy Osborne's resourceful butler, John May, rather than continuing as the banker for the mounting total of cheques cashed for us, had availed himself, perhaps a shade naughtily, of the Minister's diplomatic 'pouch' to transmit all the cheques to his wife near London, for clearing through her local bank, before any bureaucratic questions might arise.

30

GROUND FLOOR 'SPECIAL'

In my new ground-floor cell, three men, with casual nods from folded palliasse seats close to the floor, acknowledged my arrival. The cell layout was the same, but, on this lower level, high outer walls cut off much of the daylight. The friendly spirit of upstairs was absent here; these men were maintaining a reserve. My involuntary incursion upon them seemed to leave them defensive. Although they were obviously curious, the tentative questions they asked me were too discreet. Two of them either suspected me of being a 'plant' or were trying tactfully to hint that care in conversation was highly recommended.

The routine here was about the same. When we settled on the floor that night, however, I stayed awake for hours, keyed up. I fully expected the guards to call me out for interrogation, but nothing happened and finally I dozed off.

As the days crept by, the atmosphere improved slightly. My companions were an unusual trio. One, a youth of 20, tall, thin and nervous, was trying hard to maintain a cheery exterior. Why he had been arrested he did not even hint. With five others, he had been taken by the Germans in a village not far from Rome. His trial was due soon, his Italian lawyer had told him. Allied escaped prisoners, I felt, had something to do with his presence here.

The second, and by many years the oldest in the cell, was a paunchy pleasant type, about fifty. Bald, apart from a few tufts about his ears and neck, he had a jowly, round face, long bulbous nose and a wide mouth which, when he laughed, as he did frequently, revealed gaps where teeth had once been. His head sank between rounded shoulders. As his splay feet carried him on his daily constitutional diagonally back and forth across the cell, with hands thrust deep in his pockets, he presented a picture of dejection, offset, however, by a keen wit and a philosophical attitude. He came from a little village in the Alban Hills, near the Pope's summer palace at Castel Gandolfo, south-east of Rome. After three months here, he expected any day to be called before a German Tribunal. This was not his first sojourn in Regina Coeli. Fifteen years before, he told me, on account of anti-Fascist sentiments which he had continued to express too boldly to please the ruling régime, he had spent several months in this same prison, followed by a year's confinement in a concentration camp. This time it had been German police who had arrested him on suspicion of sabotaging freight trains near his home. They were of course entirely mistaken, he insisted.

The last creature in the cell, a sullen young Neapolitan, brooded in the far corner most of the day. Months of semi-starvation had left their mark – a sickly pallor and a distended stomach. Though his story did not arouse my sympathy, the ironic circumstances of his arrest did. A Sergeant-Major of Signals in the Italian Army, since the Badoglio surrender he had worked in a German Headquarters in Rome as a radio telegraphist. Cut off from his wife and two children in Naples, he had often spent his spare time with an old army pal who, unknown to him, was one of a daring band who operated powerful radio transmitters and passed intelligence continuously to the Allies in the south. One of the group, a former Captain, had been arrested and during interrogation had fallen for Gestapo offers that, if he disclosed the whereabouts of the rest of his group, his own life would be spared. Days later, at a café meeting in the city, the SS had grabbed the lot. Later our cellmate was pulled in on suspicion. Their trial was due soon and the espionage charges were expected to carry the death sentence.

In view of his admitted Fascist background and recent service with the Germans, I suspected that the other two in the cell were afraid of him. Now in a tight corner, he might turn informer. In fact I had had a few awkward moments myself during the second afternoon when, after I explained my Irish nationality and employment in the Vatican, he asked me if I knew this person and that, individuals he had known years ago when an electrician inside the Vatican. My work in the Vatican libraries had kept me isolated, I replied, and, apart from one or two other Irish friends and priests, I had little social intercourse with the rest of the State.

Most nights groans and screams came from the Interrogation Room directly opposite. The chilling thud as a heavy *bastone* beat down on flesh accompanied the relentless verbal blitzing of successive interrogators far into the night.

Located so close to the Wing's office, to the Interrogation Room, and housing a clandestine radio suspect, an accused train saboteur and a mysterious young man awaiting trial, and now me, our ground-floor cell was clearly 'special'.

With each interminable day the tedium grew. No joy either was the constant awareness of hunger. The one daily bread roll was our main sustenance. Like the others, I had learned to eat only a quarter of it at each of four intervals spread across the day – with mastication to rival a cud-chewing ruminant. Yet hunger, real as it was, did not bother me now because my whole being was preoccupied with the scary prospect of interrogation. Fear I would not admit to myself. Constantly, in mental rehearsals of what I imagined would happen, I drilled myself that, if the inquisitors started the rough treatment, I would answer any and all questions by simply quoting my name (real name), rank and serial number and claiming the status of a prisoner of war. Yet deep down I knew I was afraid. My concern was not so much for the actual physical pain I might have to endure as it was for the possibility that I might crack and be forced to divulge some piece of information that could imperil the organization or any of its members.Hence the constant mental drills. When these thoughts became unnerving during the nightly beatings across the hall, I reminded myself that, when our captors had dragged Duke and me in, they had not found a scrap of incriminating evidence, thank God; I might get away with polite stonewalling unless, from an outside source, they suspected my connection with something of greater significance. Diplomatic circles in the Vatican had long known that the possibility of Hitler ordering General Wolff's Waffen SS in Italy to invade the Vatican and abduct Pope Pius XII to Liechtenstein or Germany was very real. For months the Gestapo and the SS Command in Rome had been accumulating evidence of activities which would be construed as breaches of Vatican neutrality. One vivid example was Monsignor O'Flaherty's organization.

Inside the cell conversation was difficult. The Neapolitan contributed nothing but gloom, and, while the other two were growing more friendly to me, I felt they still suspected that I might be a 'plant'.

Duke was still up on the third tier. On the odd occasion when he passed on his way to the barber's shop, he would stop for a few seconds if my *sportello* was open. No more was possible, because any loitering outside a cell quickly attracted the boot of the nearest guard. Duke's dark and heavy growth won him a trip to the barber about every fourth day, it seemed. I was lucky to make it once in ten days.

Twice a week personal food packages were permitted from family or friends on the outside. In the afternoons when, after thorough German examination, the packages were distributed to their addressees, they created a temporary flurry of anticipation. Two in my cell had relatives in the area and received packages fairly often. Despite their meagre contents, mostly cold cooked spaghetti, inadequate even to satisfy their own hunger, they insisted in sharing everything. Knowing how they too would be hungry again an hour later, I admired their generosity. Equally important were the newspaper wrappings in which the food arrived. These we read avidly, trying to glean some facts from their slanted reports. Occasionally a note hidden inside a loaf of bread gave us real information.

To the transparent relief of the entire gaol, May Day came and went without any Communist violence in the city.

When silence had fallen on the wing at about nine o'clock the following evening, angry shouts echoed down from an upper level. Through a small peep-hole which some painstaking earlier occupant of this cell had laboriously bored in the closed *sportello*, I could partially see what was happening. Three *scoppini* had failed to return to their cells in the civil wing at the correct time. They now felt the full weight of the Sergeant-Major's heavy boot and landed in a heap at the bottom of the metal stairs. As they struggled to their feet just outside my cell, two German guards booted them into sprinting up to the far end of the 150-yard concrete floor of the gaol. There more guards' boots propelled them into running back past our cell to the other end. By now other guards were posting themselves at 20-yard intervals up and down each side. One well-aimed boot after another spurred the hapless youths to run the gauntlet faster. Unremittingly for the next hour vicious kicks rewarded any faltering or slackening of pace. Finally, when the victims staggered from complete exhaustion, the Germans congregated and laughed as they administered a last volley of kicks and blows and hounded them back, bruised and bleeding, to their own wing.

I felt angry and sickened. I had never really hated the Germans until now, even when the going had been rough back in Libya. Enemy symbols I had long detested – the uniform, the black and white cross on a bomber's fuselage or on the side of a tank. But from my limited exposures to Germans, in Tobruk after it fell and in Sulmona and Rome during the last seven months, to me the simple truth was obvious that, while some basic character elements were in contrast, the average German was just as unwittingly drawn into this gigantic struggle as the average Briton or American. As a member of the Wehrmacht his motivations were comparable: national duty, the compulsion of discipline.

His emotions were no different either: learning to rough it and to overcome fear under fire, a fear springing from a question deep in his mind for which he could find no articulate answer, as to why he was obliged to destroy himself or others. But everybody like him was in it; it must be right.

However, the SS storm troopers assigned to this gaol duty appeared to be a different brand of German. The English-speaking Sergeant-Major epitomized the type – a sadistic bully. At my first meeting with him I had thought he was reasonable. Now I had witnessed enough to hate his guts.

The monotony was relieved slightly by the arrival of old paperback books inside one of the food parcels. Among them were P.G. Wodehouse's *Piccadilly Jim* and Rudyard Kipling's *Kim*, both in Italian. Though my vocabulary was hardly up to the task, I tackled them eagerly. They were a diversion. Hunger, inactivity, the nightly screams and the waiting were beginning to tell on me. Twice in the middle of a long quiet afternoon (which seemed to be the worst time), while one of the others paced the cell, I had felt the walls begin to close in, felt an urge to hit the wall with my fists, even my head, until I gripped myself and shook it off. It worried me.

Thus at that time each day, I took to bunching up my folded palliasse directly underneath the cross-barred opening, a glassless window high in the end concrete wall. Standing on it and looking up gave a view of a patch of sky. Flights of swallows swooped and circled in the sunlight outside. I let my thoughts soar with the swallows. Inevitably these led to faraway Scotland. My mother and father, through their quiet faith, would be interceding for me every day. My own faith I had taken for granted. I had rarely presumed to seek God's help, or express gratitude, in a personal way. Yet in Sulmona, when almost miraculously the searching Germans missed our hideout and Anna Carugno had said, 'The Lord heard me,' I had stopped to think.

Leaving the swallows, I would step down and return the folded palliasse to my assigned floor space near the cell door. I felt easier. Sitting low on the flattened straw bundle, I fell into a kind of reverie, formulating silent prayers, prayers of reflection, of supplication asking God's help. Daily, as these thoughts became more articulate, my tension and fears began to subside.

Old 'Baldy', the accused train wrecker from the Alban Hills, was an asset. Each evening after the bitter coffee at five o'clock, he slouched up and down the cell for more than an hour singing one tuneful Italian ditty after another. I was more grateful to Baldy than he could guess; at this dreary period of the day his light-hearted performance eased the claustrophobic pressure of these walls.

The second week of May brought the trial of our despondent Neapolitan friend and the gang of twelve with whom he had been accidentally mixed up. At noon on the third day of the Tribunal, he returned in high spirits. All had been sentenced to imprisonment in Germany.

In the afternoon, however, the Tribunal recalled them and sentenced them to death. He slipped into despair. Like the others, he had the opportunity to address a plea for mercy to Field Marshal Kesselring. I banged on the closed *sportello* and pleaded paper and envelope. Finally the Sergeant-Major brought these. The Neapolitan would not write a formal plea. We composed it for him and forced him to write it. After that he sank back and would not be roused. If our cell had been gloomy before, it was doubly so now. Each of us tried to console him, but he ignored us. As the days passed, his ghostly colour and slumped body, motionless for hours on end, engendered about him an aura of death. Only his breathing proved he was alive.

If nothing else, this atmosphere allowed me to speculate. Three weeks had passed since I sent my note to Monsignor O'Flaherty. I had half-expected that by now they would have found a way to smuggle a reply to me. If my note had not arrived, he and Derry would not realize that I was still using the identity of William O'Flynn. They might not even know I was here. Somehow I had to find a way to 'mail' another note, if possible through a channel that could bring back a reply. If the Monsignor could reply, he could send money too. But how to send word?

On 9 May a British sergeant appeared at my *sportello*. During my first week upstairs he had occupied the cell opposite mine and I had talked to him several times. As a result of being caught in a Rome flat with Italians who had assembled a sizeable arsenal of weapons, he had been subjected to many nights of rigorous interrogation by the Gestapo at Via Tasso, without, however, being tortured. He had claimed his status as a former POW. Frequently now he was permitted to visit the prison hospital.

When I explained my anxiety to get a note delivered outside, he said he could fix it. Michelin and his doctor cousin had been moved out, but another long-term prisoner posing as a doctor was now running the hospital cells. This 'doctor' was allowed a weekly visit by his wife. She apparently 'took care of things like this'.

On 10 May a note from me written on a crumpled scrap of paper was on its way to Monsignor O'Flaherty, giving him the latest on Duke and myself and asking him to give the bearer of the note 10,000 lire for me. If by any chance I was no longer here when the money arrived, I added, it would go to prearranged friends.

Actually my first note *had* reached the Monsignor. Moreover, my protests to the German Sergeant-Major about the 'mistake' of my arrest had made an impression. German SS Headquarters had phoned the Irish Minister to the Vatican, Dr Kiernan, and asked him if he knew of a Vatican employee called William O'Flynn. Yes, he did, said Dr Kiernan, but after a quick check, had to reply that the real William O'Flynn, a priest, was there in person in the Vatican! Sam Derry heard of this about the same time he received my first note. Anxious now to warn me that my alias was exposed, he was afraid to make a move for fear of further compromising me.

Immediately following our arrest, my slim hope that the Vatican card along with my protests might persuade the SS to release me instantly was long gone. That had not worked, but I had seen no reason since then to change my identity. In fact I felt there was some point to keeping my real name away from the prison rolls as long as possible. So many of John Furman's group of escapers and Italian helpers had been arrested that, from interrogation of the Italians, John's name was well-known to the SS, and he correctly suspected they were out to get him. Since I had known some of his group, it was highly likely that my real name had been spilled too. It was as well left out of the record.

In the meantime my Irish name was foiling salvage attempts by some brave outside friends. My caring hostess Flora had apparently been distressed over my capture, so much so that, through the introduction of a friend, she had boldly approached a high-ranking Fascist police officer who was a deputy Commandant of Regina Coeli and pleaded with him to intervene to obtain my release. While she was to be admired for her courage and good intent, the move was quite unrealistic. Desperately striving to persuade the Fascist, she insisted that I was a nephew of the wife of the ex-King of England and that his co-operation would be richly rewarded.

In the calm of Mrs Almagia's luxurious villa a tall blond German in sergeant's uniform of the *Feldgendarmerie* listened intently. As the English widow 'confessed' to him that a steady traffic of American and British officers had been coming through her front door for months, a smile broadened on the face of Sergeant David Yorck, more correctly Sergeant the Count David Yorck von Wartenburg. He waited for her point.

Graf Yorck had been walking a fine line. He was German, but he loathed the Nazi régime. Back in Silesia, Yorck's American wife and two young children were living in fear of internment. His uncle, General Yorck, was plotting with other high-ranking Germans who saw that Germany would not win. Their imminent attempt to kill Hitler would fail, and General Yorck would be executed. Unlike his uncle, David Yorck had studiously avoided rank in the Wehrmacht, doing just enough to protect his family. As a modest Sergeant in the German military police, he had found himself stationed near Rome. In his prewar travels as a Berlin banker he had cultivated influential personal ties in Britain and the US. Among his friends in Italy was the Signora Esmé Simpson Almagia. Often Signora Almagia had told John Furman and me at teatime that her old German friend had been there for lunch.

'I know how he feels,' she had said, 'but for his own sake I don't tell him anything about you.'

Similarly, for her sake, Sergeant Yorck had not divulged that, on every opportune occasion at other *Feldgendarmerie* locations further north in Italy, he had helped recaptured Allied ex-POWs to 'disappear'.

Perhaps it was that this lady's maiden name was Simpson – I was her long-lost cousin, she always said on the phone – or maybe her inability to help her own venturesome son 'Gigi' Savelli, since he had fled south to join the Allies. Whatever it was, she was aroused over my capture. When she asked Yorck if he could help, he undertook to trace me and if possible to get me out of gaol. To cover his tracks in the event that he succeeded, he would use a false name himself. Ingeniously, to give me a sign, she handed him the kilted toy soldier which had topped the wrapping of her Easter gift to me.

Days later, armed with credible documents authorizing him to remove a William Simpson for interrogation, Sergeant Yorck entered Regina Coeli. In the office he searched the prison rolls, but no such name appeared. He scanned them again and noted the cells, about twelve in all, in which the rolls indicated some Britisher was located. He visited each one, called my name and carefully displayed the toy soldier. No one responded. Puzzled and balked, he left the prison and reported the impasse to Signora Almagia.

Back at the Vatican, the fortunes of the organization had sunk perilously low. John Furman and Renzo Lucidi had taken over my list of billeted escapers. The chain of arrests following the original betrayal by the bogus priest Pasquale Perfetti had continued unbroken with disastrous results. Half of John's list of protégés and their hosts had been put in gaol; a few John had been able to warn in time to flee. He himself was a marked man and, had it not been for the urgent need of the organization, many of whose key helpers were now in gaol or 'grounded',

John would have wisely gone into hiding. Instead, he dyed his red hair black, cut off his moustache, switched clothes and kept answering the Monsignor's emergency calls.

Quick-witted Renzo Lucidi was now invaluable. The more the hard-pressed Monsignor threw at him, the better he liked it. Besides his heavy load within the city, part of which he passed over to Adrienne, he was becoming the trouble-shooter on urgent calls far beyond Rome. Thus, when in mid-May word reached the Monsignor from a point thirty miles north of Rome that groups of escaped Russian prisoners-of-war receiving shelter from Italian peasants desperately needed funds, Lucidi was quickly heading north, armed with money and instructions from Sam Derry.

When some 400 Russians were first located further north, Monsignor O'Flaherty had arranged for a Russian priest in Rome, Father Dorotheo Bezchctnoff, to look out for them with financing from Sam Derry. The accepted rationale for their presence was that, following their capture by German units on the Russian Front, the *Wehrmacht* had mustered them into labour formations and brought them to Italy.

Soon Renzo, after skilfully bluffing his way through police traffic blocks, returned to Rome and handed over to an astonished Monsignor a thick pile of receipted forms bearing incomprehensible names and strange hieroglyphics. Sam Derry had wanted names, ranks and numbers, so Renzo, thorough as ever, had obtained them.

Almost inevitably the sword finally fell on Mrs M's. Just enough warning of the impending raid, however, was flashed by an informer within Fascist Police Headquarters to allow her to evacuate the three escapers she had taken back after their window-rope escape from the home of butcher Giovanni. When the detachment of SS arrived minutes later, no traces remained in her flat of the many months of escaper traffic, and the innocent appearance of Mrs M and her large family of girls in this modest flat convinced the raiders that their lead must have been wrong.

However, this near-disaster was too much for her strained nerves. The next day she evacuated her family with a few hastily gathered belongings to the country. Where they were at this point nobody in the organization knew.

On the plus side, little Paolino, the college caretaker, was released from gaol and returned home, but not before the Gestapo had indulged in a little original sadism. Under rough interrogation, Paolino had pleaded convincingly that he was just the caretaker of the religious college and only did what he was told. No, he didn't recall who had dumped these five Jewish refugees in his college; in fact, he thought he had been out at the time. Soon his interrogators decided he was probably an innocent tool.

'All right, little man,' his chief inquisitor had said, 'if you won't talk to us, we'll make sure you don't talk at all!' Then, grabbing the helpless Paolino's tongue and lower lip, he forced them between the levers of a giant paper stapler from his desk and clipped them together! But at least Paolino was alive and free.

31

ALLIES ON THE MOVE

'Gustav Line Repels Allied Attacks.' 'Valiant Axis Forces Counter-Attack.' The bold headlines of the garlic-impregnated newspaper wrappings from my cell-mates' food packages on 16 May confirmed that our offensive in the south had begun. Since the opening Allied attack across the Rapido River five days before, rumours had flashed around the gaol. Now here it was in Rome's *Il Messaggero*. Masking of the truth was inevitable, but these stale reports gave us at least a minimum estimate of the Allied advance.

In the gaol spirits soared. Tin mugs, the 'bush telegraph' for communicating from cell to cell, were working overtime. When a faint knocking signal came through the thick wall, one of us placed the open end of a tin mug against a known spot on the wall and flattened his ear against the bottom. Through this 'receiver' he could hear the voice from the adjoining cell talking through the wall. In turn, we would knock on the opposite wall and pass the message on. In this way news tit-bits, often highly seasoned with rumour, circulated quickly throughout the wing.

The Germans were fiercely defending every inch of ground, but, when the Gustav Line began to crumble, following the hard-fought capture of Cassino on 20 May, the entire Allied offensive was poised to break loose from the long winter stalemate.

Hope, however faint, began to emerge. Was it possible that we might still be here in prison when our Forces arrived? As a thought it was encouraging; as a practical possibility it was remote. When the Anzio landing had started, John Furman and the others had been rushed north. Thus, as soon as this offensive began to threaten Rome, the German Command would likewise evacuate all British and Americans inside Regina Coeli, even if they had to leave behind the political prisoners. Whatever the prison records showed, Irish or otherwise, they would probably rope me in.

On the evening of 13 May, the SS Guards had mustered 400 prisoners on the ground floor. They were all Jews – old men, young boys and women of all ages, clutching their scant little bundles. Through the *sportello* I had spotted with sadness an acquaintance, the helpful Jew who on our first arrival had taken me to Via Sicilia for the shopping expedition. When the laborious check-off was completed, they were herded off to destinations and fates unknown.

For weeks four British parachutists still in uniform had occupied a cell diagonally across from me. On two rare trips to the barber I had sneaked a few words with them through their *sportello*, but never for long enough to find out much about them. The senior of the four, a Captain, did volunteer that, after their capture back in November, they had all been sentenced to death. On the very morning they were due to go before a firing squad, four British Red Cross food parcels had arrived at the gaol for them from the Swiss Legation. This act on the part of the Swiss apparently prompted the SS to recognize them as prisoners-of-war instead of enemy agents. However, the threat of their unaltered death sentence still hung over them. On the morning of the 21st, when I looked out to give them the usual wave from my *sportello*, no one was there to wave back. Duke, when he stopped at my *sportello* for a moment, was equally convinced that we too would be carted off at any time. Still no message or money had reached me from Monsignor O'Flaherty. Whether my second letter of two weeks ago had reached him or not, I could not know, but the British Sergeant, my go-between with the 'doctor', had been confident of its early delivery.

★   ★   ★

At Fascist Headquarters, the fanatical half-Italian, half-German Chief of the Special Police unit, Colonel Koch, had no delusions about his future. For months now he had outdone the German Gestapo in sadistic excesses at his headquarters on Via Principe Amadeo. Behind him and his *Banda Koch* lay a bloody trail of torture and death. If he dared to remain in Rome until the Allies arrived, his own fate was sealed. Any day now he would have to withdraw north with the Germans. But he had a mother. Such was the widespread hatred of his name in Rome that he was afraid even his mother would suffer if left unprotected. He also had a particular adversary, one who so many times had slipped through his grasping fingers. Ironically, Koch now realized that this individual was the only one who could help him, the only one whose word he could trust.

Thus, the indefatigable Monsignor O'Flaherty was shocked to receive a written message delivered by an emissary from Koch. It offered a deal. If the Monsignor would guarantee safe conduct for Koch's mother to Naples when the Allies arrived, Koch would undertake to leave behind, when the Germans withdrew, all the British and American captives in Regina Coeli. The Monsignor's reply was quick. He would accept, but first Koch must show his good faith by having two prisoners released immediately, one William Simpson, the other Armstrong, both British.

Koch moved fast. The Monsignor waited; if these two, whom he considered to be in grave danger, were set free, it would be one load off his mind. Armstrong's plight was precarious. He had been captured many months before in enemy territory as a British secret agent and, from information which had trickled out, the Monsignor felt he was doomed to be shot.

Back in Regina Coeli, news had not yet reached us of the Allied break-out from the Anzio beachhead on 23 May, following the Allied breaching of the German second line of defence, the Adolf Hitler Line. But our captors could not shut out the racket of bombing planes.

Nevertheless, it was quiet on the afternoon of 24 May, an unusual time for someone to be opening the *sportello* on our cell door. I looked up from the last laborious pages of *Kim*. A face peered through the bars.

'O'Flynn?' I got up and walked to the door. What was this? Interrogation now? If so, why didn't the door open?

'You are O'Flynn?' asked the quiet, almost friendly voice in English. A second man looked over his shoulder. Both wore uniform different from the German guards. I nodded.

'You are not English?' The German was almost smiling.

'No!'

'British?'

'No! I'm Irish.'

'Your name is not Simpson?' His look seemed to apologize for asking the question.

'No, my name is William O'Flynn,' I replied emphatically, hoping to hide my surprise at the last question. The spokesman looked at the other, looked back at me, shrugged his shoulders and moved off.

What caused this, I wondered. They were new faces. Neither of the Sergeant-Majors was with them. A trick, maybe, to have me admit my name was not O'Flynn? I was still sticking to it. As I had planned from the start, only if the going got really rough under interrogation would I declare my correct name, rank and number, and demand status as a prisoner-of-war.

As I sat down, the others in the cell, including the morose Neapolitan, were looking up curiously.

I stared at the pages without reading and tried to understand the strange visit. The attitude of these two Germans had been so different. But it could have been a trick, I kept telling myself and, after weeks of waiting without daring to relax, I was sticking to my resolve.

When Koch's representatives reported back to him that they had searched the records of Regina Coeli without finding anyone by the name of Simpson or Armstrong, the once-fearless Police Chief was agitated. He dispatched his emissary again to St Peter's.

Near an open door of the basilica, ready to dive for cover, Monsignor O'Flaherty met the emissary. Since no one in the gaol answered to these names, would the Monsignor please suggest the name of another prisoner? Colonel Koch was most anxious to prove his good faith.

The Monsignor gave another name, but he was worried. This unexpected last-minute chance to save us, particularly Armstrong who was so close to execution, had cheered the Monsignor. Now his hopes fell.

Possibly Armstrong was also using another name, but it was unlikely since the Monsignor had learned through the Swiss that he was there in Regina Coeli.

Two developments within our cell struck a contrast. Old 'Baldy' was taken off to be tried. When he returned a day later, joy was written all over him. The German Tribunal had failed to prove the charges against him and had found him not guilty. He was so surprised he could hardly believe it himself.

The happy atmosphere over this faded instantly the next morning when the cell door creaked open again and the stout German Sergeant-Major signalled to our little Neapolitan to collect his belongings and follow him. We chilled. While helping him wrap his few things, we talked lightly about his bad luck in being 'transferred to a concentration camp'. But our condemned man seemed to sense that his last hours were approaching. As he lifted a moist hand in a poignant gesture of farewell, I hoped he felt our compassion for him. Even if he had been trying to 'squeal' on us for weeks, he was a lonely human going to his execution, condemned for reasons he had probably never understood.

Near a main highway north of Rome three days later he and others were put before a firing squad and shot. The bodies were left where they fell. Later, one was to be identified as Armstrong.

On the evening of 30 May a fundamental change developed within the prison, as a new heartening sound reached us, the distant but unmistakable rumble of gunfire. My *sportello* was still open after 'coffee' distribution when an unexpectedly clumsy squad of a new Military Police arrived. They were quite unlike the disciplined German SS Guards, who just then began to parade in front of the Guards' office. Only when the newly arrived squad dispersed to various points throughout the three floors of the prison did it become clear that a change of guard was in progress. Like lightning, word flashed through tin mugs from cell to cell that the new arrivals were Austrian.

The Germans marched off. Excitement grew among the prisoners as the import of the change became clear. The more valued German SS troops were being whisked away out of reach of the advancing Allies, and the duty of guarding the prison left to their Austrian counterparts.

The Austrians recognized their predicament; they would be left behind. Their morale was low. Only a sturdy little Sergeant-Major seemed aggressive and efficient as he strutted around giving orders.

Quick to sense the more lax attitude of the new guards, the prisoners wasted no time in trying them 'for size'. Before long most of the *sportellos* had been opened by the guards, and they stayed open. Some of the guards were even talking to prisoners.

One major relief swept through me. If the German SS Guards were being withdrawn, almost certainly the Gestapo must be packing up too. My six-week-old dread of interrogation vanished.

A new hum of voices ran throughout the prison the next day. Walking around freely were a few long-term prisoners who, even under the Germans, had for some reason enjoyed latitude of movement. The Austrians wondered at the large number of inmates who expressed the necessity of being allowed out of their cells to report to the hospital.

'Hey, things are lookin' up!' Duke wore a broad grin as he looked through the bars of the *sportello*. 'D'you think there's a chance we might even be left behind here?'

'Good thought, but I doubt it. I'm surprised they haven't called us out already.'

'Yeah, it doesn't add up.' Duke felt sure too that we would still be sent north.

From far away came the faint booming of an artillery barrage.

'How long d'you think before these guns get up here?' I asked him.

'A week maybe? According to these newspapers, never! We're retreating every day!'

I had tried to visualize how we might be transported from here. The first part had to be by road. This led me on a visit to the barber to beg for one razor blade. First it would slash a man-size hole in the tarpaulin of an army truck. Second, quick removal of my untrimmed moustache would change my appearance. I was therefore elated when the barber stopped at my *sportello* that afternoon and slipped me a blade.

On the night of 1 June 'Doctor' Solinas from the hospital stopped at my open *sportello*. Whatever his motive, I welcomed the chance to talk to him.

A parachutist Captain in the Italian Army, he said, he had headed a band of partisans until arrested on a visit to Rome. After two months in Via Tasso, he was given the death sentence, later commuted to life imprisonment. No doctor, he had professed enough medical knowledge to have the Germans keep him here running the hospital. He helped the prisoners in any way he could. In particular he had kept many female prisoners from being deported to concentration camps. On them, he explained, he had performed certain minor 'cutting jobs', enough to categorize them unfit to travel whenever a move threatened.

Fresh speculation started when, on the afternoon of 2 June, the Austrian guards came around the cells calling out names from long lists. On the ground floor, they assembled two hundred male prisoners, all young.

On some pretext I persuaded an Austrian to let me out to go to the hospital. Grabbing my jacket, I slipped along to within feet of the clumsily assembled crowd. At the door of the hospital stood Duke.

'They figure they're being taken for forced labour on new defences up north,' said Duke.

'This might be an easy group to escape from,' I muttered, as the half-hearted Austrians took a roll-call of the listed names under the alert eye of the Sergeant-Major. From the hospital door I watched for a chance to slip across into the crowd, but guards stood every few feet. When all were checked off and recounted, the Austrians marched them away.

'Doctor' Solinas pulled Duke and me into the small ante-room of the hospital.

'Are you two interested in escaping from here?' he asked in whispered Italian. Duke and I nodded emphatically.

'*Va bene*; there might be a chance tonight if you want to take it. You know the tall thin *scoppino*, the one who gets black-market cigarettes?' We nodded again.

'He's got a plan, and he's told me he's willing to take three or four of you along. Two of the Austrians are co-operating with me already, and I've fixed it that the side door here on the ground floor will be left unlocked at nine o'clock tonight. The *scoppino* plans to slip out then and creep in the shadow across the courtyard and around two other buildings to the outside wall. It's about seven metres high. There's an outhouse at one point, and its roof is only two and a half metres from the top of the wall. Somehow he's arranging for a rope ladder to be in position there after dark.' The *scoppino*'s fiancée, Solinas went on, lived in a tenement only 200 yards from that point and, though it would be long after the curfew hour, he planned to make a dash for her flat and hide there.

'Sounds good,' I murmured. 'What d'you think, Duke?'

'Sure.' We still felt something bad could happen if we stayed where we were.

Solinas sent word to the British sergeant on the third tier and to John Sperni, an Anglo-Italian civilian the sergeant knew who had worked with Monsignor O'Flaherty's organization until arrested some months ago. Only three days back, Sperni's trial had ended. By ingratiating himself to the Tribunal, he had been lucky enough to be sentenced only to three years' imprisonment. The British Sergeant's interrogations had stopped weeks ago; it looked as if the local SS had not had time to bring him to trial. But both were afraid of what might happen to them at the last minute.

When they joined us in the ante-room, we explained the proposition. The main danger lay in being spotted by the Italian Metropolitan Police who patrolled the grounds day and night. In the dark, they might easily shoot off their carbines at any sound or moving shape, but the risk had to be taken. If a guard was bold enough to stop us without shooting, we could probably bribe him.

'How much money do we have?' I asked. Together we had 7000 lire.

'I have 5000 lire,' said the British sergeant after a pause.

'You do?' I remembered him saying he had no cash when he had arranged to have my letter to Monsignor O'Flaherty smuggled out.

'Yes,' he went on slowly, 'I got it sent in from friends outside a few days ago.' He wore a guilty expression. So that's why I hadn't heard from Monsignor O'Flaherty. The money in response to my letter had stopped at the Sergeant. More importantly, a letter may have come with the money. If he admitted to 5000 lire, he probably had all 10,000 lire. He could easily have let me know. But I let it pass.

In any case, 12,000 lire in all was not an impressive sum, and the idea of bribing in these circumstances was about as sensible as 'putting salt on a hen's tail' to catch it. Equally impractical, we wrote six notes on scrap paper, 'The bearer of this note has assisted me to escape from Regina Coeli', and signed them with our names and ranks. No doubt any of these policemen, concerned about their future, would value these – if we could ever get close enough to explain before they shot us.

The tall young *scoppino* arrived, confident of success. Sperni and the sergeant, however, backed down. The sergeant offered me the 5000 lire, but I told him gruffly to keep it. Success depended on us not being seen at all. If we were challenged, then the only hope lay in responding quickly with '*Inglese!*' or '*Americani!*' and trusting to the psychological shock of this.

'All right, we two will go with you,' I told the *scoppino* in Italian. 'What time?'

'Nine-thirty – here.'

'Right!'

Since Solinas warned that the Austrian Sergeant-Major inspected the hospital, for the last time, at about half-past six each night, we dispersed to our cells. To return later should be no problem.

My two cell-mates sensed something was in the air. For security's sake I side-stepped their questions, but finally told them my true identity. They laughed, and in turn admitted why they had been arrested. 'Baldy', if only half of what he said was true, had engineered the destruction of much German rolling-stock on the railway line near the Alban Hills. The younger man had been caught hiding Allied escapers in the country. Baldy admitted that for a long time they had suspected me of being a plant in their cell, a German informer.

At seven o'clock, with a little persuasion, an Austrian guard opened my cell and I went to the hospital. Duke was already there with Solinas.

'I'm going to lock you in and leave,' whispered Solinas. 'See you later.'

Behind the locked door of the dimly-lit ante-room, Duke and I sat on the one hospital bed to wait out the two and a half hours. The tension grew. We both knew only too well what could happen. We were relying completely on this *scoppino*. We would have to follow him over prison barriers we did not know. The odds on reaching the wall without being seen were heavily against us, and the jittery Italian sentries would hardly wait to ask questions. But the stakes were worth it, to be in Rome when our troops arrived in a few days, instead of on a last-minute trek to Germany.

Slowly the minutes ticked away, nine-fifteen, nine-twenty. We were taut. 'Could use a martini about now,' muttered Duke, clearing his throat.

At twenty-five past nine, as we paced up and down the small room, each with nerves on edge but trying to appear calm to the other, hurried footsteps entered the front hospital cell. A key turned in the lock and Solinas burst in with a look of panic. Behind him came our *scoppino* escaper.

'The Major upstairs, you know, the red-headed one who walks around,' sputtered Solinas in Italian, 'I've just come from him. He's heard of your plan to escape and begs you to drop it!'

'Drop it? What do you mean? Why?'

'It might wreck his plans for everybody. He's kept it quiet, but he and his friends have a plan all set for half past ten tonight, a mass plan to free everybody in the whole wing!'

'*What?*' I couldn't believe my ears.

'Yes, yes, really!' Solinas was frantic.

Duke and I looked at each other, dazed. This was the last thing we had expected. The *scoppino* stood nervously watching our reaction. He too was keyed up. At this last minute, before zero hour, to be asked to abandon our plan was too much, and in this high-pitched state we were loath to give way. The principle of not jeopardizing any plan intended to free a larger number was all too clear to us, but it was hard to avoid feeling that the Italian Major's plan, whatever it was, might be built more on wishful thinking than on firm resolve.

'Oh hell, this sounds like a lot of hot air!' Duke grunted to me in English. 'What if we call it off and then this big-deal plan fizzles?'

'I know. We'll be right back where we started.' I turned to Solinas and quizzed him about the mass-escape plan. He was emphatic that everything was ready.

'They've found a way to open all the cell-doors within five minutes.'

'How?'

'With the handle end of a big spoon!' I gave Solinas a jaundiced look, but he insisted it was true.

'We've no choice, Duke. We have to give way.'

With undisguised contempt, we shrugged our shoulders in surrender. Solinas sighed with relief and shot out of the hospital to inform the Major in his cell upstairs that the crisis had passed.

The *scoppino*, Duke and I stood there in a state of shock. Moral compulsion had obliged us to quit, but our tense nerves could not adjust. Grudgingly we came out to the hospital door. Shaken by the anticlimax, we followed our equally frustrated *scoppino* accomplice across to a cell opposite. Inside sat several other *scoppini*. One waved a bottle of Marsala wine. A drink! With unsteady hands, we grabbed the tin mugs they passed and gulped the wine.

What we feared then happened. Up on the third tier, word of the intended mass break had leaked to a number of cells. Two of the planners who knew the spoon-handle trick had been impatient; already small groups of excited prisoners were running around on the metal platform above. The commotion brought the Austrian Sergeant-Major from his office. Quickly sensing something was amiss, he immediately called out his entire force of guards, who soon chased the wanderers back to their cells and locked them up.

While we squatted swallowing wine the cell door opened. There stood the Sergeant-Major, stern and silent, with two guards. Meekly we rose and dispersed to our cells. On the way Solinas whispered to me that the Austrian had telephoned outside for emergency reinforcements. I swore, vilely and loud! A foul-up like this was exactly what Duke and I had feared.

With the surprise element lost, the Italian Major called off the plan. Between rage at this and nervous uncoiling from the evening's emotional build-up, I tossed around on my palliasse all night. Sleep was impossible. The only slight solace was the rising crescendo of gunfire which seemed to be drawing ever closer.

From dawn, my face was glued to the *sportello*. The barber walked by. I waved him over.

'What gives now?' I asked in Italian.

'Last night was a wash-out, but don't worry, it's laid on for nine o'clock this morning.' His smile was confident.

At a quarter to nine the tall, red-haired Italian Major on whose plea Duke and I had aborted our escape last night descended the metal stairs with two younger accomplices and walked up to the Austrian Sergeant-Major, who stood in the centre of the floor keeping his own personal watch on everything, twenty yards from my *sportello*. The ensuing conversation was inaudible, but it was clear from the Major's facial expression that he was confronting the worried Austrian with an ultimatum. Everything, he was saying, was ready for a break-out; within a few minutes all the cell-doors would be open, and there was just no point at all in the Sergeant-Major and his guards, most of whom were already demoralized, trying to resist. Already excited voices were shouting on the upper balcony. When the conscientious Austrian realized he no longer possessed the means to command he dropped his shoulders and, turning on his heel with a pained look of defeat, walked slowly back to his office. For a moment I felt sorry for him. If only in his place could have stood his bullying German predecessor.

With his aides around him, the Italian Major took command. Already on the upper floors two prisoners moved along rapidly opening cell-doors. However, the sudden prospect of freedom was too potent; in a frenzy of near-hysteria the prisoners were rushing around upstairs, shouting and screaming.,

The Italian Major knew that, without careful control, the plan could be compromised. 'Get back into your cells!' he bawled. 'Until then nobody moves.' Surprisingly, quiet fell on the upper tiers and the prisoners returned to their cells.

In a loud voice the Major explained the plan. Each floor when instructed would file down, form up on the ground floor and await directions. Rome was packed with Germans. The prisoners would move out in small groups.

As hundreds started to pour downstairs, the Major crossed to my *sportello*, from which I had not moved now for three hours. I was as excited as a dog about to leave its kennel.

'You are an English officer?' he asked in Italian.

'Yes.'

'Do you know where the other English and American prisoners are located?'

'I'll find them!'

'Right. Muster them at the far end of the hallway there. The women will go out first. Your men will go out next. After you're gone, I'll handle this crazy bunch myself!' His voice was clear and unhurried. The permanent Italian warders on duty outside our wing at the main exit were, he added, all privy to the plan.

One of his aides stepped forward and, with a snap from a spoon handle, opened my cell door. I thanked the Major for offering us this preferential sequence, then quickly found Duke and the British Sergeant and sent them circulating. Within five minutes, sixteen American and British prisoners had gathered behind a long column of excited women who were already filing out. The Major had asked us to ensure no Italians were among our number, to prevent any of the civil prisoners from other wings slipping out with us.

As the last of the women disappeared, our group moved through the tall iron gates into the central hall.

32

FREEDOM

'D'you all know a safe place to go when you get outside?' I asked, looking them over. Several familiar faces were here. They all quickly affirmed that they could look after themselves.

'Don't go to Mrs M's. Don't go to the Lucidis'. Anything may have happened to them, and we don't know how long it'll be before our lads get here.' They nodded again.

Only one was completely lost, a young American GI. He was still in American uniform: a short leather jacket, leather boots, khaki shirt and trousers. Early this morning I had seen him arrive in the wing, and later watched him led upstairs to a cell. He looked confused.

'OK. You stick close to me,' I told him.

After re-checking the number, the Italian Major signalled us on.

'Thank you again, Major, and good luck with the others.' I shook his hand warmly and joined the others moving off. As we passed through the remaining gates, the regular Italian warders beamed at us happily. I could hardly believe it. We were actually walking out of this bug-ridden hole of starvation and fear to freedom. Freedom! But we were not yet off the premises.

As we pushed through the last door out into the cobbled lane, the sunlight made me blink. Immediately we broke formation and spread out as we walked up the gradient leading to the main street running alongside the Tiber.

While we had assembled inside, the tall young *scoppino* who had initiated our escape plan the night before had slipped into our group, camouflaged in a raincoat. Although he was a civil prisoner, I had turned a blind eye. We had only gone a few yards when shouts arose from behind us. A Metropolitan policeman, one of several watching the exodus in which they too were co-operating, had recognized the *scoppino* and tried to grab him. The *scoppino* ran for it. The policeman, raising his carbine, started in pursuit. On an instant reflex, I and others blocked his way and, before he could obtain a clear field of fire, the *scoppino* was out of sight.

What would I do with my new charge? His American uniform was unmistakable. I'd have to get him off the streets. I remembered a house not far away behind St Peter's and started to head for it, but at the second corner we drew up short. Twenty yards from us stood two open trucks, each packed with German Military Police, sitting erect, fully armed, and presumably ready to respond to emergency calls within the city. We quickly turned about and retraced our steps to the river. Only two hundred yards from these German riot trucks Regina Coeli was disgorging its political prisoners.

At the tram stop on the Ponte Mazzini, Duke stood among waiting civilians.

'We made it!' he exclaimed gleefully in English.

'It's unbelievable. Where are you heading?'

'I dunno yet. I just want to breathe!'

'I'd better make for Signora Almagia's and get your countryman here organized. You could hardly say he's disguised.'

'No, and these folks here are catching on. I'll move off. See you later.' Eyes were turning in our direction. A few faces were quietly smiling. My companion's whole appearance with his horn-rimmed glasses left little doubt about his nationality. 'Let's walk on,' I whispered and led him off by the arm. 'We'll walk the whole way if necessary.'

We headed north on the Lungotevere past Castel Sant' Angelo. It felt good to walk, to throw off the confinement of that cell. I felt exceedingly happy. I didn't care about my friend's American uniform. Neither apparently did the German Army, hundreds of whom lay in our path, resting under trees which lined the road, tired and exhausted. We picked our way through them, stepping over legs and heads. A *carrozza* trotted by. I hailed it and we drove on toward Via Stanislao Mancini.

The American explained that he had been taken prisoner near Velletri in heavy fighting, brought to a camp outside Rome and early this morning transferred to this gaol. He had been a bookie in New York.

A hundred yards short of the door of Signora Almagia's villa I stopped the *carrozza*. While all was probably well inside, there was no point in walking into trouble. With a certain satisfaction I pulled out a 500 lire note from the lining of my jacket and gave it to the driver. When I indicated I wanted no change, he was at first suspicious, then he beamed happily at receiving ten times the fare. This outcome to the last seven nightmarish weeks was intoxicating and beyond my wildest hopes.

'Now you stand back over there,' I told the New York bookie, as we reached the villa. 'When the door opens, if you see me run, then you run too, and good luck! But I don't think we'll have to.'

I knocked on the door and it opened. Old Giuseppe, the butler, started back. Shedding his dignity, he spun around and ran into the lobby hollering, '*Signora! Signora! Ecco Bill! Bill, Signora!*' I waved to the GI and we both followed him inside.

Dressing-gown flying, Signora Almagia came rushing down the staircase with arms outstretched. 'Bill! Bill!' The normally imperturbable matron threw her arms around me and we jumped up and down.

'And look!' she said, pointing to a table in the corner of the hall. In a tall vase drooped the withered but recognizable remains of long-stemmed Birds of Paradise. 'I just refused to throw them out so long as there was still a chance.' Through her laughter, she wiped a tear. 'Two months they've been there.'

'Oh, I forgot; meet our new American friend,' I said, turning to the confused GI. When I explained, Giuseppe led him off to a hot bath and fresh clothes.

It was a fair assumption that I myself had not left behind all the livestock of Regina Coeli, but they had only been bugs. They were harmless. In any case, there was no time for a bath now.

'What about the Lucidis?'

'They're fine. In fact, some of your friends are probably there now.'

'Well, I just have to run around and see them. Hello, Nancy!' Nancy Savelli joined us and, after more greetings, explained that Fane-Hervey was out somewhere with Gigi, her husband, who had recently returned via parachute from the south.

Giuseppe handed me a cup of coffee.

'Aren't you hungry?' asked Nancy.

'I'm starving! But there isn't time right now.'

'Promise to come back for lunch. Others will be here.'

'Certainly.'

In the supreme joy of the bright sunlight I knew neither weakness nor hunger. I almost ran the 400 yards to 18 Via Scialoia. Free! No more mental strain, uncertainty, starvation, bug-hunts, done with the seven paces up and seven paces down, no longer the maddening crush of those four walls. Thank God! My legs felt shaky, as the lift carried me to the third floor.

Just as I stepped off, the Lucidis' door opened and Renzo appeared.

'Renzo!'

'Bill! *Accidenti!*' He jumped on me with a howl, then dragged me inside. The living-room went wild, as Adrienne, Pat Wilson, Dennis Rendell, Joe Pollak and, I was relieved to see, John Furman crowded around. After the last 18 hours, my glands had no adrenalin left to pump. The joy on their faces cracked me. When they heard that Duke was free too, and for that matter all the prisoners from the Terzo Braccio, they were ecstatic. Everybody cheered.

Somebody handed me a brandy and the music on the radio stopped. 'This is Radio London. We interrupt the programme to give you a special news bulletin just received. Allied troops are at the gates of Rome.'

'How are all the others, John?' I asked, moving to one side with John Furman.

'We haven't fared too badly. The Monsignor and Sam are in great shape. The Monsignor had a chance to get you out a week ago, but nobody could find you.'

In fact, at that moment, Sam Derry, from his vantage point over-looking the Vatican wall, was relaying by short-wave transmitter a steady flow of information to forward elements of our advancing troops.

Furman filled me in quickly. The whereabouts of Mrs M and her family were still unknown. Plain-clothes Gestapo had tried again a few weeks ago to capture Monsignor O'Flaherty near the steps of St Peter's but watchful Palatine Guards had foiled them.

'What about Flora?' I asked.

'Oh, she's fine. Saw her the other day. You got the girl quite upset, you know ... but more of that later. Bill, I must run to the Vatican and tell the Monsignor you're free.'

Rumour had it that some sort of military accommodation had been brokered by the Vatican and the diplomats of both camps. For two days endless German columns had been retreating through Rome. Opinion was that the German Tenth Army, now completely on the run to avoid being ensnared by British 8th Army advances northward to the east of Rome, would not fight a rearguard action in the city. However, Germans were suspected of plans to blow up the many Tiber bridges at the last minute, and several Italian Resistance groups in touch with advancing Allied formations had been charged with the task of trying to prevent this.

An hour later, back at the Almagias', an unusual group assembled for lunch. The New York bookie from Regina Coeli, now dressed in civilian clothes, was easing his confusion over a second sherry.

'Bill,' whispered Signora Almagia, drawing me aside, 'the tall man who's just come in with Fane-Hervey is the German who used to come here for lunch. He tried to get you out of Regina Coeli, but couldn't find you. His name's Yorck. He's decided to become Fane-Hervey's personal prisoner.'

Nancy handed me a sherry, as I greeted Fane-Hervey. The tall, fair-haired gentleman beside him was well-groomed in a dark suit. In this last day of Rome's nine months of oppression, Count David Yorck had decided this was the moment to join the Allies without dangerous repercussion on his family in Germany.

For the little New Yorker standing beside me, meeting 'Mr Yorck' appeared to be traumatic. It was confusing enough, following his capture on the battlefield two days ago, to have spent last night in a prison enclosure outside Rome, to have been transferred to a huge gaol in Rome this morning only to leave it two hours later with British and American fellow-prisoners, and be led through a German-packed city to this friendly English-speaking villa. Having only just convinced himself that he was free again, he was now dumbfounded to meet this David Yorck who, he said, was the dead image of a German Sergeant who had spoken to him in friendly English the previous day in the prison near Rome. I quickly guessed what had happened and reassured him he was with friends.

At the Lucidis' in the afternoon I had a shower, slumped on a bed, but sleep would not come. The exhilaration was too intense.

33

GERMAN RETREAT

In the early evening down on Via Flaminia the conglomeration of retreating German traffic moving north was strange. Clusters of German soldiers clung to each tank which rumbled by. Armoured personnel carriers were overloaded. Interspersed with army vehicles, civilian cars – commandeered by foot-weary soldiers from garages and lock-ups throughout the city – bumped along, some running without tyres on buckled metal rims, and all packed tight with soldiers escaping north. Hundreds more, unshaven, bedraggled and dispirited, lacking transport and devoid of any semblance of formation, trekked on wearily, dropping here a pack, there a rifle, as they passed.

This was the glorious Wehrmacht! A vast contrast, I reflected, to the fatal final days in Tobruk two Junes ago. Poor fellows, they couldn't help themselves, but, as one vivid recollection after another of incidents over the past two years came flooding back, I tingled with satisfaction at this passing cavalcade of a defeated army – in full flight, yet unable to run.

We stood there, Adrienne, her son Gerald, and the attractive Vittoria who had helped me and our organization many times, on the edge of the vibrating pavement, fascinated like the scores of civilians lining both edges of this main route north, or like others cautiously gazing from windows above. The passing troops seemed unconscious of our existence. Faces were expressionless. To many of them during leaves in the past nine months, Rome had been a Mecca, a city of which they retained glowing memories. Now it was a place to leave quickly; it spelled defeat, this first European capital to be lost to the Axis.

To most Romans the passing drama signified the opposite. After the many months of waiting, of cold, hungry, fearful waiting, during which their faith in ultimate delivery had at times run low, the growing

clamour of approaching battle had lifted their hopes into happy anticipation of freedom.

On the other hand, there were undoubtedly many to whom the arrival
of Allied armour would bring the inevitable day of reckoning. The old
Fascist elements, and the foolhardy new who, emboldened by the
display of incoming German military strength following Italy's surrender nine months ago, had flocked to the flimsy flag of a post-Armistice
Republican-Fascist government, directed at a safe distance from Salò in
Lombardy, were, if not already in flight before the rout started, quaking
that night with apprehension. Too many evil deeds, too many vile atro-
cities had been committed, brother against brother, for pardon and for-
giveness to be expected on the morrow. Their heyday, their temporary
gain, they had enjoyed. Now the old comfort of fawning German assurances for the future had left them. The fiery propaganda of Radio Roma,
the lying but flattering daily headlines of the prostituted *Il Messaggero*,
which right up to this morning had still proclaimed the invincibility of
German strength in the south, tonight must be sounding treacherously
hollow.

As we walked toward Piazza Flaminio, without talking, contemplation
of the immediate future sped our individual thoughts along divergent
paths.

For Adrienne, to witness this retreating German Army was in itself
rewarding for her unceasing efforts throughout the war year. It was the
consummation of years of hoping, striving, in a country of enemies; the
liberation, not only of Rome in a few hours, but of her own spirit, stifled
for so long.

To Vittoria, younger, highly intelligent, politically conscious for her
years, it signified a new beginning. To her idealistic mind, this passing
torrent of Nazism was carrying with it the last remaining stagnancy of
Fascist ideology and corruption. Any minute now her *Partito d'Azione*,
no longer just a hunted clandestine force with much underground
achievement to its credit, would come forth as a legitimate influence in
the land and begin to practise its socialistic but avowedly democratic
principles, in the difficult days of *risorgimento*, of reconstruction. Did she
fully appreciate the dangers ahead for her torn country, when the many
underground political parties which, until now, had worked in harmony
against the common foe, would each emerge with equal conviction, each
flying its own banner of a colour ranging from Communist scarlet to
Savoian green? But Vittoria was an optimist.

Gerald, as he walked on our flank, was in his normal quiet, almost
sullen, mood. A thinker for his modest eighteen years, he, like thousands

of other young people in Rome, had had the misfortune of living his formative years in this atmosphere of uncertainty, fear, insincerity and treachery. His university education had been totally interrupted for nine months. He had also known the inside of Via Tasso. Always reminded by his mother of his French blood, this evening he was pondering the decision he had made to join the Free French ranks of General Charles de Gaulle.

Piazza Flaminio was different tonight. In the centre, by the tram lines the kiosk which had many times served me espresso while I waited for Renzo or John Furman was closed. In front stood two 88 mm anti-tank guns, manned by solemn German crews. As streams of trucks, tanks, armoured troop carriers and pathetically incongruous civilian cars passed through the square these guns stood covering their retreat.

Strangely, in the last hour the roar of battle to the south had died and, apart from the occasional distant rattle of a machine-gun, the fighting seemed to have stopped. Perhaps this ancient city, for whose survival the Pope had appealed so fervently last March, was to be spared after all. Although these heavy guns in front of us, and no doubt others like them at every key point throughout the city, were ready to blast anything which tried to stand in the way of the retreating columns, it was becoming clear that the advancing Allied columns, even while meeting only minimal opposition from retreating German forces on the run, had called a deliberate halt just south of the city.

As Bishop of Rome, the Pope no doubt hoped to prevent widespread bloodshed within the city. In many of the Vatican's difficult political dilemmas since Nazi forces occupied Rome, its ultimate guiding principle, as it agonized between the growing evidence of religious and racial persecution in Nazi Germany (where the Pope had been Papal Nuncio for many years) and its absolute opposition to Communism and the Soviet Union, appeared to be its basic priority to save souls before lives. But for Rome the Pope's appeal had been broad. To avoid irreparable destruction the Allies were giving the Wehrmacht time to clear out north before the chase resumed.

At nine o'clock the traffic fell off sharply. The gun crews sprang into action. In minutes the guns were on their wheels. A last dilapidated truck loaded with expressionless soldiers drove into Via Flaminia. The tractors and guns swung across the tram lines and rumbled after it.

When the noise of their tracks died away the silence over the city was complete.

34

CHEERS IN THE NIGHT

Fatigued after thirty-six hours without sleep, I returned with the others to 18 Via Scialoia and after a light snack – all my shrunken stomach requested – crawled into a bed. It might be morning before our troops would enter the city.

Only twenty-four hours ago Duke and I, fearful of last-minute deportation, were bracing for a jail-break. Tonight the scene was a peaceful bedroom in the security of the Lucidis' home, with Rome outside a virtual No Man's Land.

On this, the eve of liberation, how many tortured minds were reliving the nightmare of the past nine months? Faces and incidents crowded in on me. Hundreds here in Rome had earned our gratitude and respect; to thousands of *contadini* in the surrounding countryside, in fact throughout Italy, we were equally indebted. Something would have to be done. It would be a big problem, but must not be put aside.

I remembered the teasing of Monsignor O'Flaherty: '*Quando vengono questi benedetti Inglese?*' From tomorrow on this great man, who had sacrificed so much for us would be able to hit a golf ball farther than the length of the carpet in his room.

I was falling asleep when Renzo barged into the room. 'Bill, wake up! We need your help.' I sat up, half-dazed. Behind him came his old policeman friend Giovanni who had once put Garrad-Cole's pursuers off the scent. 'I know you're exhausted, Bill, but none of the others is around. We'll need petrol for these cars tomorrow. Giovanni here says there's a large stock in that police barracks across the river. If we wait till the morning, it'll be too late. If you come with us – a British officer – we can grab a supply and set it aside.' I could not refuse.

Outside a rising three-quarter moon barely cut the dark. The streets were deserted. In the eerie silence, nothing moved. Rome for the moment was the eye of the hurricane. From the end of Via Scialoia we carried on across Ponte Nenni. A short walk along Viale Giulio Cesare brought us to the police court enclave. At the gate a small crowd clamoured for entry, bent on looting. Behind the locked gate one Italian officer with two soldiers pleaded with the crowd. Giovanni, in his Metropolitan Police uniform, pushed to the front and beckoned to the police officer.

'*Silenci, tutti,*' the officer shouted, standing on a box above the crowd. '*Qui c'e un ufficiale Inglese!*' Immediately the crowd fell back, awed that an English officer had arrived.

'Renzo, I'll take care of this,' I said, pushing forward. 'Go on inside and look around, but hurry.'

The Italian officer saluted me from his platform. Renzo ran toward some buildings inside. I spoke to the Italian officer. In a moment he was repeating my orders to the crowd. They must prevent disorder, go home quietly, and certainly remove nothing from the compound. The officer was only doing his duty; they must obey him.

Renzo and Giovanni reappeared. They had hidden away some gallons. 'OK. Home now?'

No, Giovanni was pleading, his Police Headquarters was only a short distance away. There they could commandeer a car for our immediate use if I went with them. Too tired to argue, I agreed.

'How much farther?' I asked wearily, after ten minutes' walk.

'The garage is just over here,' Giovanni apologized. 'We'll get a car first, then drive up the hill to the Headquarters.'

At a large garage, when Giovanni explained my presence to an officer, the response was electric. Immediately an old square-bodied car, complete with chauffeur, was rolled out for us.

When we entered the headquarters office a dozen officers snapped to attention. Already their Fascist lapel badges had disappeared. Renzo and Giovanni talked fast. The senior officers looked in my direction. Renzo pocketed a Beretta revolver and handed one to me. I let them talk on. Renzo was enjoying himself, and Giovanni was clearly impressing his superiors.

To a shower of salutes we re-entered the car and drove down the hill again. Renzo and I sat in the rear, while Giovanni stood on the running-board directing the chauffeur in the dark. Outside the car, all was silent until a loud bang jerked the car to a halt. The rear tyre had blown.

'Come on, let's walk,' I said, becoming exasperated by this adventure in No Man's Land. But they would not hear of it. To the grating of gears, we started again and bumped along noisily.

214

Near the turn into Viale Giulio Cesare, Giovanni on the lurching running-board couldn't contain himself.

'*Inglese! Ecco un ufficiale Inglese,*' he shouted. Two men stepped forward and began clapping their hands. In seconds others began applauding. The demonstration spread; as our crippled vehicle bumped along at 10 mph, from each successive corner rose a crescendo of cheering.

We abandoned the car in the police compound and walked on. At the bridge armed Italian partisans had mounted guard. Back at the Lucidis' flat, this was not a night for sleep. I woke with Adrienne shaking me, but this time not to whisper fearfully that Gestapo men were taking Renzo away. 'There's noise outside ... from Via Flaminia,' she said excitedly. 'Come on, we're going down.' It was still dark.

On Via Scialoia, in the faint moonlight of 4 June's early hours, people poured out of buildings and scurried toward Via Flaminia, whence came the rumble of heavy trucks. As we started to run, a dark monster shot up sparks from the roadway. '*Tedeschi! Tedeschi!*' a timorous creature shouted, causing a moment's panic. Some dived for cover; others laughed. But, as more of these tanks lumbered past the mouth of Via Scialoia, there could be no doubt. Still hardly believing, we ran to Piazza del Popolo. Into the immense circular piazza poured column after column of tanks, guns, trucks and jeeps. Barely illuminated by the first struggling light of dawn, hundreds of cheering Romans converged from all points.

Adrienne ran over and planted a large kiss on the dusty cheek of the nearest American, an unwilling Captain dangling a leg from his jeep.

'Can I help you?' I asked the officer at the head of the nearest column, as he studied a map with his flashlight.

'No!' ...... Of course.

'Have a Camel,' yelled Nancy Savelli, appearing out of the crowd, laughing and brandishing a symbolic fresh pack of cigarettes. We hugged, spun around, her blonde hair flying and her legs kicking behind her. 'Wheeeee,' she shrieked, then fled to the next jeep, the next tank, waving, cheering. Everybody, everybody was cheering.

'Aye, Monsignor.' My voice was swallowed up. 'They're here!'

EPILOGUE

Two days after Rome's liberation on 4 June, 1944, from Allied bases all over Britain 'Operation Overlord' sprang the mightiest invasion force in history to land in Normandy, thus opening a major western front against the Third Reich. Already on Hitler's eastern front, Soviet counter-offensives were forcing the entire German line to pull back, from the Gulf of Finland to the Crimea.

In the Pacific theatre American naval air and ground forces had turned the tide against the Japanese.

The remaining Axis partner, Republican Fascist Italy, was of no more military significance than its puppet leader, Mussolini, sitting powerless in Salò in Lombardy.

Ultimate Allied victory was in sight, even if much struggle and sacrifice still lay ahead.

★ ★ ★

Almost two years after Allied armour had rolled into Rome, on Friday, 24 May, 1946, the audience in the Teatro Adrianno, the largest indoor theatre in Rome, hushed as the British High Commissioner in Italy, Sir Noel Charles, began to speak. All the seven hundred guests who filled the theatre had sheltered Allied escapers during the nine months of Nazi rule.

Arc-lights for newsreel cameras illuminated the wide stage supporting three tiers of British, American, South African and French diplomats, Allied military brass and a select core of very special Italians. In good Italian, the Commissioner expressed the British Government's gratitude to every guest present. In aiding hundreds of Allied fugitives here in Rome, and keeping them free from enemy re-capture, they had voluntarily undertaken grave risks – the dangers of imprisonment, torture, confiscation, and of forfeiting life itself. These risks they had assumed without thought of recognition or reward.

Beneath the centre microphone, a red light confirmed that his voice was issuing simultaneously from radios throughout Italy.

As Sir Noel finished amid applause from every corner of the vast auditorium, the American Chargé d'Affaires, seated in front of me on the dais, rose to the microphone. His supplementing words of commendation were warmly received and, in the ensuing applause, the theatre lights went up. Guests came on stage by name to receive an engraved Certificate of Merit from the hand of the diplomats, or from American Admiral Ellery Stone, or British Brigadier Alban Low, Rome Area Commander, or South Africa's General Théron. To expedite the process, fifty officers of the Allied Screening Commission, manning draped tables set up in each pre-planned seating section of the theatre, expanded the chain of presentations.

The ceremony was over. The theatre had cleared. At a reception in the spacious backstage area, with a bar and waiters serving champagne, public figures and modest artisans mixed together.

The hundred special guests now chattering at the reception were those who had been most deeply involved, those who had undertaken the greatest risks time and again, during these long interminable months of Gestapo terror. Judging by the ascending decibels of champagne *chiacchiera*, they were enjoying the occasion. Yet the atmosphere fell short of gaiety; rather it reflected an intensity of emotion as experiences, still too starkly recalled, drew this diverse group into a unique common bond. They were recounting shared crises and perilous moments which, while never enunciated as such, had generated within each of them a self-esteem of knowing they had voluntarily performed brave acts on behalf of total strangers in need, acts which had aroused within them qualities of boldness and quantities of courage which might never otherwise have been tapped.

Reticent and dignified, Sir D'Arcy Osborne, the British Minister to the Holy See, understood. When those delicate months in the Vatican had ended in June, 1944, it was he who had persuaded General Sir Harold Alexander, the Supreme Allied Commander of the Italian campaign, to devise some way of acknowledging the debt owed to so many gallant Italians.

The Very Reverend Monsignor Hugh O'Flaherty, CBE, indefatigable in his brilliant leadership of underground help to Allied escapers throughout the Nazi Occupation, had felt awkward when decorated in

1945 by the British Government. Before long the US Government would award him its Medal of Freedom (with Silver Palm).

Prince Filipo Doria Pamphilj, the long-standing opponent of Fascism who had supported Monsignor O'Flaherty was now Rome's dedicated and respected Mayor.

Along with the Commissioners and Generals, these notables departed. For the others, this was a party. I knew them all well; so well that it hurt, because within a week I would be back in Scotland released from the Army.

Quickly after the liberation of Rome, General Sir Henry ('Jumbo') Maitland Wilson, Supreme Commander of Allied Forces in the Mediterranean Theatre, had authorized the formation of the Allied Screening Commission to undertake the project of recognizing and reimbursing all who had assisted Allied escapers in Italy. Initially, in collaboration with my underground colleague John Furman, I had been fortunate enough to help create, staff, train and, for the most of this time, to command the unit, based in Rome. Already 65,000 Italian family claims had been 'screened' and settled from cities to mountain tops all over Italy. Another 10,000 or so, mostly from locations in Northern Italy, liberated only in May, 1945, remained to be completed.

This concentrated work had been gratifying. Through the distribution of forms to every *Commune* in liberated Italy, these thousands of invited claims reached the *Commissione Alleate di Screening*. Arriving from MI9 in the War Office in London and the MIS-X in the Pentagon in Washington, the 'Restricted' transcripts of information sought from all repatriated escapers and ex-prisoners-of-war about help received in enemy territory, sorted by escaper name and Italian locality, became an important 'screen' through which all claims passed. With this cross-reference, investigating officers evaluated the evidence submitted, largely consisting of 'chits' and letters left by escapers with their Italian hosts. False claims were rare.

In hundreds of subsequent formal ceremonies on village greens and town squares Italian-speaking officers of the Screening Commission addressed assembled 'helpers' expressing Allied gratitude, and presented one by one the official embossed Certificate of Merit bearing the recipient's name, along with a package of calculated cash reimbursement.

Recently an impressively-staged ceremony in Milan had been a success. I had addressed a special encomium to the extraordinarily courageous and brilliant Giuseppe Bacciagaluppi whose escape line had ferried 1800 POWs from Milan to Switzerland. Now, it was Rome, the largest and the grandest.

In the noisy backstage reception, old friends were being kind: Renzo Lucidi, my intrepid colleague of many tense escapades, his effervescent French wife Adrienne, happy in this shining group with her brave young sons who had foiled the Gestapo; the gracious English widow, Mrs Almagia, whose magnificent villa had often been our haven; 'Whitebows' Robert, the Maltese teaching Brother, gently flattering the ladies; calm, smiling Maltese Mrs Chevalier whose fearless, untiring work as 'Mrs M' had earned her a George Medal, and the lovely Flora Volpini, recalling with champagne clarity the fonder moments of past refuge in her flat.

Tied to their new staff duties at MI9 in London, Sam Derry and John Furman could not come.

When only a few effervescents remained with Screening Commission hosts, something drew me back into the theatre. From the centre of the wide stage, the empty rows fading back into the dim silent auditorium were strangely alive to me, and, as the exhaustion of relief settled after weeks of planning, I slumped on a reversed wooden chair, chin on my hands, gazing out over the sea of departed faces.

The speeches, which I had tentatively drafted for the diplomats, had been well delivered. Yet I had felt the urge to talk to these people myself, to let them know in a more intimate way that hundreds of other ex-prisoners, the men they had saved, scattered across the globe now, all felt as I did. For what they had done for us, whether in a barn or a palace, we loved them.

Alone with my ghost audience, I was soaring back to moments of fear, of excitement, of comedy and pathos, of fatal coincidence and improbable luck.

The phenomenon which had culminated in this formal assembly today and in the hundreds of smaller ceremonies across the country had grown from individual acts of simple courage in unlikely places, of sacrifice prompted less by national conscience than by the warmth of a stranger. In all areas of Italy, separated by distance and culture, a common factor had emerged. Italians, whether artisans or farmers or aristocrats, took in unknown quantities, speaking another language, and stuck their necks out for them. Going far beyond charity, they had soon become emboldened and tenacious champions of these fugitives, ex-enemies, stranded at their door or exposed in their fields.

Yet the very extent of this countrywide reaction beseeched a broader motivation. The Italian heart was aching to retrieve a modicum of national esteem, and the attitude of Italians everywhere was undergoing complex change. The conscripted soldier's eyes had been opened to a world more diverse than the one bounded by the horizon of the fields which his family had worked for generations to glean a meagre, almost serf-like, living. When he had dropped his carbine and found his way home, he would not pliantly resume the old life.

Ranging up through higher strata of education, of political and social sophistication, the town artisan, the city merchant, the widening band of middle class, sought to participate in creating a saner future.

Everywhere citizens, disoriented like their country, waited to reach out to the prospect of a free democratic philosophy.

While thus groping in late 1943 for a sense of purpose, for direction in their society which, with a broken compass, had lost its bearings, thousands of Italians kept running by coincidence into thousands of liberated Allied prisoners of war, most of whom also lacked a compass. And these fugitives were flesh and blood representatives of the very democracies with whose cultures the Italians had always felt more in harmony. Through this partly subconscious but common polarity, a circuit closed between them.

Why then had Italy, which fought with honour alongside the Western democracies in World War I, incurred such derisive criticism in World War II?

In the peaceful thirties, Mussolini's vainglorious adventures to recreate an empire in Africa had stimulated no more native militancy among the populace than did his commitment in 1941 to enter partnership with Nazi Germany – at a moment when Germany's blitz through the Low Countries and France made Hitler look like a winning bet. The Italian heart wasn't in it. The resulting view of the Italian military establishment had been less than flattering. Even more than the Allies, their German war partners despised it.

Thus conditioned, tens of thousands of Allied troops captured by Rommel in Libya and westward across North Africa, when steered to Italian prison camps regarded their Italian guards with little respect. Only as large numbers, through liberation at the time of the Italian Armistice or by escape, came in personal contact with individual Italians, with their families and with instantly developing support groups, did they sense the abeyant nobility of these freshly motivated people.

Thousands of American, British and South African escapers found that the Italian – from the remotest village to the crowded city – was not only a good-humoured generous friend with compassion but, as the circumstances became mortally threatening, an increasingly courageous and ingenious protagonist.

In a NOTE endorsing an official Report dated 17 October, 1944, on the work of the 'British Organisation in Rome' (Public Record Office Files WO204/1012), Sir D'Arcy Osborne, the British Minister to the Holy See, observed:

'It is inevitable that, on account of their nature and purpose, neither the Report nor the despatch can more than very superficially convey the dramatic background and detail of the work of the many helpers and agents outside the Vatican City, in Rome and in various districts of Italy, without whose courage, charity and self-sacrifice the Organisation within the Vatican City could have achieved little. Among these loyal, gallant and resourceful collaborators some of the ex-prisoners of war themselves, notably Lieutenants Simpson and Furman, take a leading place.

'I take this opportunity to record my admiration for, and gratitude to the numberless Italians, mostly of the poorest peasant class in the country districts, who displayed boundless generosity and kindness to our men over a long and trying period; it must be remembered that, in so doing, not only did they refuse the financial rewards for the denunciation of British prisoners of war which the Germans offered and which would have been a fortune to them, but they also showed magnificent abnegation and courage in sharing their few clothes and scanty food and, above all in risking their lives and the lives of their families and friends in disregarding the increasingly severe German injunctions against harbouring or helping British Prisoners. A number of them indeed were shot by the Germans. We owe a debt to the Italian people in this respect that should not be forgotten and cannot be repaid.'

Reinforcing this, Field Marshal Earl Alexander of Tunis, when leaving Italy to become Governor General of Canada in 1946, stated:

'Before leaving this Theatre, I would like to pay tribute to all those civilians who at one time or another voluntarily rendered, at considerable personal risk, very valuable assistance to Allied fugitive ex-prisoners of war and airmen, who were escaping from the enemy in German-occupied territory.

'The gallant efforts of these countless helpers resulted in the safe and early return of thousands of our men to their homeland and families, and in many cases soon afterwards to further service with the armed forces. I know I am speaking on their behalf when I say they would all wish, if it were practicable, to thank their helpers personally and endeavour in some way to repay the debts which they have incurred. It is however my intention that due recognition be awarded and all material debts be repaid to every individual civilian who rendered assistance of whatever nature to Allied escapers. I am glad to say that this immense task is already in hand. It will of course take months to finish, but I give my assurance that everything will be done to see that no one is forgotten.'

To the full extent to which formal recognition could acknowledge this debt, the Allied Screening Commission pursued this course. Before ending the task in September, 1947, it had validated over 75,000 family claims of assistance to Allied escapers, with the presentation of official Certificates and cash reimbursement.

Regretfully, the Allied Screening Commission's citations for specific awards to outstandingly deserving Italians were ultimately blocked at the British Foreign Office, lumped with larger numbers from other sources on behalf of Italian Resistance members. By late 1947, following the Peace Treaty with Italy, Foreign Office desks, on an admittedly difficult problem, erected arguments against processing the citations: awards of decorations to Italians would give offence to British families bereaved at Italian hands; some might be Communists; if some were awarded reaction by others could be counter-productive. And the War Office constituency at MI9 was gone – Colonel Sam Derry and Lieutenant-Colonel John Furman had been released and the Screening Commission dissolved.

The sole remaining advocate pressing for these awards was Sir Noel Charles, now British Ambassador to Italy. Even his final strenuous appeal directly to Foreign Secretary Ernest Bevin [FO372/4902] fell victim to the fuzz of a constrained Whitehall grown tired as the Empire slipped.

Otherwise, the huge job had been completed. An extensively researched paper, 'To Pay a "Debt of Honour" – the semi-secret operation of Britain's MI9 to recompense Italians aiding Allied escapers in World War II', by the Reverend Robert Graham, SJ, published in *La Civiltà Cattolica*, Rome, 19 May, 1990, summarized the Commission's significance, 'a story of disinterested humanity among ex-enemies, marked by generous and tragic sacrifices, reciprocated by massive and spontaneous gratitude.'

Finally a word of postscript on my favourite hero. Monsignor O'Flaherty became Chief Notary of the Congregation of the Holy Office. Despite the resulting demands on his time, he regularly visited in prison the man who had tried so hard to 'catch' him, SS Lieutenant Colonel Herbert Kappler, Commandant of Via Tasso, sentenced to life imprisonment by an Italian Tribunal. In 1959 he baptized Kappler into the Christian faith.

Scarcely a year later, after suffering a severe stroke, he had to give up his position in the Vatican. Following a period of pastoral service in the

Archdiocese of Southern California, he returned to his old home in Cahirciveen, County Kerry, where, after another stroke, he died in October, 1963.

With undiminished affection, I salute the many thousands throughout Italy who, with courage and style, helped us to survive to tell the story.

BIBLIOGRAPHY

Absalom, Roger, *A Strange Alliance*, (Leo S Olschki, Florence, 1991)

Bertoldi, Silvio, *I Tedeschi in Italia – album di una occupazione – 1943–1945*, (Rizzoli, 1994)

Chadwick, Owen, *Britain and the Vatican during the Second World War*, (Cambridge University Press, 1980)

Derry, Colonel Samuel I., DSO, MC, *Rome Escape Line*, (Harrap, London and W.W. Norton & Co., New York, 1960)

Foot, M.R.D. and Langley, J.M., *MI9 – Escape and Evasion – 1939–45*, (Little, Brown Co., Boston, 1980)

Furman, Lieutenant-Colonel John, MC, *Be Not Fearful*, (Anthony Blond, London, 1959)

Graham, Rev. Robert A., SJ, 'To Pay a "Debt of Honour" – the semi-secret operation of Britain's MI9 to recompense Italians aiding Allied escapers in World War II', *La Civiltà Cattolica*, Rome, 1990

Kurzman, Dan, *Race for Rome*, (Doubleday, New York, 1975)

Newnan, Lieutenant William L., US Rangers, *Escape in Italy*, (University of Michigan Press, Ann Arbor, Michigan, 1945)

Public Record Office, Kew, nr London – File WO204/1012: *Activities of the British Organisation in Rome for assisting Allied escaped prisoners of war*, 1944

Trevelyan, Raleigh, *Rome '44*, (Martin Secker & Warburg, London, 1981)

INDEX

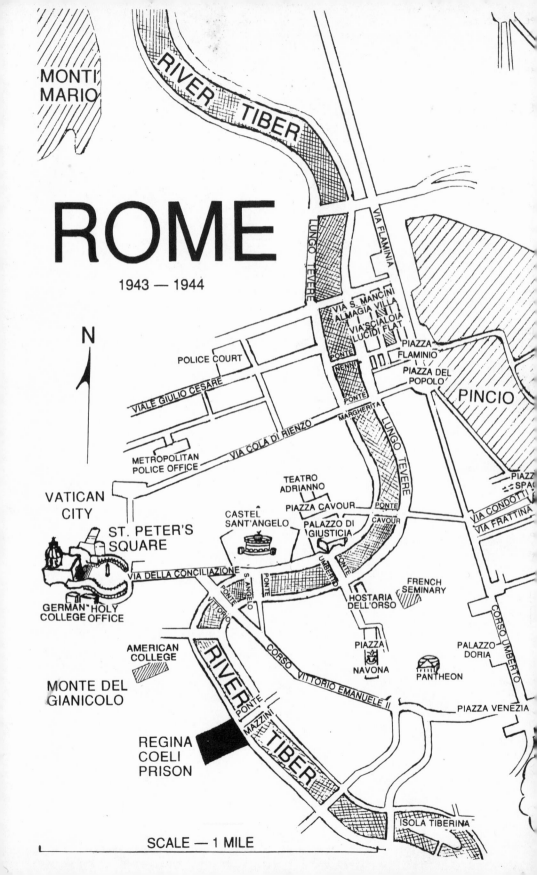